america's corner store

america's corner store

Walgreens' Prescription for Success

John U. Bacon

WILEY

John Wiley & Sons, Inc.

Published by John Wiley & Sons, Inc., Hoboken, New Jersey.

Published simultaneously in Canada.

For general information on our other products and services, or technical support, please contact our Customer Care Department within the United States at 800-762-2974, outside the United States at 317-572-3993 or fax 317-572-4002.

Wiley also publishes its books in a variety of electronic formats. Some content that appears in print may not be available in electronic books.

For more information about Wiley products, visit our web site at www.wiley.com.

Library of Congress Cataloging-in-Publication Data:

ISBN 0-471-42617-2

Printed in the United States of America.

10 9 8 7 6 5 4 3 2 1

contents

preface

Late one night, Sean Smith, an eight-year-old boy living in Wilmette, Illinois, called his mom to his room to tell her he had a sore throat.

"I think I need a prescription," he informed her, then opened wide.

"I don't know, honey," she said, gazing into his open mouth. "It depends on what kind of sore throat you have."

"What kind needs a prescription?" he asked.

"Well, strep throat is one kind that needs a prescription."

"Then that's the kind I have," he concluded, with complete confidence in his self-diagnosis.

"How do you know?" his mom asked.

"Whatever kind needs a prescription," he said, "is the kind I have."

It happens every time. Whenever Sean Smith gets sick, he informs his mom that he needs a prescription. No, Sean is not a junior lobbyist for the pharmaceutical industry. But he knows that when he needs a prescription, he gets to go to Walgreens. His mom acquiesces because she knows she can fill his prescription, pick up some chicken soup, and grab a knit hat, all in just a few minutes. And Sean, of course, knows Walgreens has one of the best selections of toys around, which is enough to make young Master Smith one of Walgreens' most loyal customers—despite the fact that the Smiths live three miles from Walgreens, but just across the street from an Osco-Jewel Pharmacy.

A lot of history went into that little transaction—more than a century's worth. It's easy to take such convenience and selection for granted now. But before Walgreens came along, pharmacies didn't have wide aisles, bright lighting, or economical store brands; they didn't provide self-service, allowing customers to roam the store freely without waiting for a clerk; and they certainly didn't have Intercom, a computer network connecting the pharmaceutical databases of all 4,000-plus Walgreens stores, making Walgreens the world's second-largest satellite user behind only the U.S. government itself.

Other stores, of course, pioneered customer-friendly innovations, too. However, unlike so many of Walgreens' long-time retailing peers—Kmart, Montgomery Ward, and A&P, for example—Walgreens is not only surviving, it is thriving.

Walgreens was born when Charles R. Walgreen Sr. used all his savings plus a loan from his father to buy his first store on the South Side of Chicago in 1901. Today Walgreens' 150,000 employees in 44 states run more than 4,000 stores—and will run more than 6,000 stores by 2010 (all in the United States). Walgreens sells more merchandise—$33 billion worth in 2002—than CVS.

Walgreens' 600,000-some shareholders have been rewarded many times over for their investment—over 125 times, in fact, over the past three decades, a performance that trails only that of Southwest Airlines and Wal-Mart.

Charles Sr., however, would be heartened to learn that the company he started over a century ago has succeeded by sticking to the basic values he established in his first store: Put the pharmacy first, even when it's not making the most profit; hire people on character and promote internally based on performance; treat your employees like family; and, most important, treat every customer "like a guest in your home," as he said.

From the beginning, Walgreens combined these basic values with a surprisingly bold sense of adventure that prompted the company to invent the milk shake, expand the lunch counter, introduce self-service, and launch an unprecedented expansion program it is riding to this day. Walgreens' chief executive officers have gambled the company's future more than once; and so far, their calculated risks have paid off enormously.

Walgreens' formula, if it can be called that, has survived depressions, recessions, boom times, and wars, while countless business trends—and the superficial, often unethical companies that trumpeted them—have come and gone, falling by the wayside, wave after wave. Walgreens prides itself even today on being a "boring company." But when you compare it to once-proud concerns like Kmart who've lost their way and to the Enrons of the world who've taken thousands of innocent employees and investors down with them, you gain a renewed appreciation for the Walgreens Way.

This book tells the story of how it started and why it has thrived.

JOHN U. BACON

Ann Arbor, Michigan
March 2004

acknowledgments

When I set out to research and write this book about America's greatest drugstore chain, I quickly realized I faced more obstacles than the average author might have. This is primarily a business book and secondly a historical work, subjects that I enjoy and understand. But it's also a biography of a pharmacy, something I knew little about. To put it bluntly, I didn't know my mortar from my pestle.

Enter Dr. Ara Paul, Dean Emeritus of the University of Michigan Pharmacy School. He was as patient teaching me about his favorite subject as he was educating thousands of students over his long career. Because he is also a trusted friend of three generations of Walgreens, two of whom graduated from Michigan's College of Pharmacy, Dean Paul also served as my ambassador to this very private but friendly family. Without his help, I don't think I would have had the opportunity to talk with either

Charles Jr. ("Chuck") or Charles III ("Cork"), both of whom were affable, insightful, and vital to the production of this book.

Although this is not an "authorized" history sponsored by the company, the people from Walgreens were gracious and helpful, particularly current CEO Dave Bernauer, retired CEO Dan Jorndt, archivist Donna Lindgren, divisional vice president of corporate communications Laurie Meyer, manager of media relations Michael Polzin, and former general counsel Bill Shank. (In classic Walgreens' style, they've asked me to list them in alphabetical order.)

I've done my best to report as objectively as possible on Walgreens, but I can't deny I admire the company very much—a view shared by virtually every reporter and researcher who has studied the company over its 103-year history. One of the company traits I admire most—its institutional aversion to publicity, even as less deserving companies do flips to grab the headline—made it difficult to find enough primary sources to create a comprehensive account of Walgreens' triumphs and tribulations. I had to rely more than I anticipated on three internal publications—Myrtle Walgreen's *Never a Dull Day*, Herman and Rick Kogan's *Pharmacist to the Nation*, and Marilyn Abbey's *Walgreens: Celebrating 100 Years*, for access to old interviews, company newsletters, and newspaper and magazine articles. Walgreen Company graciously provided permission to quote from all three books, as did James Collins from his groundbreaking best seller *Good to Great*.

Outside the company, the staffs of the American Institute for the History of Pharmacy in Madison, Wisconsin, the Chicago Historical Society, and the graduate and pharmacy libraries of the University of Michigan directed me to more good material than I thought existed on this subject. Financial advisor Brian Weisman patiently walked me through the LIFO-FIFO accounting systems and did it again when I decided to overhaul the section. Pete Uher, currently enrolled in the Michigan MBA program, was as efficient as he was tireless in finding all manner of information on the economic history of our nation, Walgreens, its competitors, and the retail industry itself by digging through countless books, articles, and Internet web sites and then helping me boil it all down to its essence.

I owe my greatest debt to Debra Englander, my editor at John Wiley & Sons, who not only conceived the idea for this book but also asked me to write it and provided exceptional guidance and patience throughout. Her assistant, Greg Friedman, handled endless issues, large and small, with grace and good humor. Production editor Mary Daniello, production manager Jamie Temple, and copyeditor Judy Cardanha all performed with consummate skill under serious deadline pressure, for which I am grateful. My agent, Carol Mann, is one of the best in the business and one of the most responsive, too; and she proved to be both throughout this process.

Most of all, though, I want to thank Walgreens itself. Not only is it a very good company, but for almost two years, it was, for me, very good company.

J. U. B.

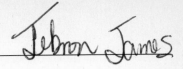

from humble beginnings

the apple and the tree

There was little about <u>Charles Walgreen</u>'s childhood that would have led you to believe he would become a success story, let alone a multimillionaire who would transform an entire industry. Walgreen never seemed cut out for the pharmacy business—and there was no shortage of pharmacy owners ready to tell him this. They might have been right. Charles never longed to become a pharmacist or a businessman (as confirmed by his checkered career bouncing around at least a half dozen stores in his twenties). But his fastidious attention to detail, coupled with his engaging personality, commitment to customer service, and surprising willingness to defy conventional wisdom on how to run his business, proved to be an unusually potent combination—a combination to which his son and his grandson have adhered, even as the industry did several flip-flops over the decades.

But the fact is Walgreen was a solid but uninspired student and a positively desultory employee. Another twist: Walgreen did not descend from a line of Walgreens but was the first Walgreen born, by name, a Walgreen. Because Swedes traditionally took the first name of their fathers for their last names (adding the familiar "son" as a suffix, as in Johannson), military units suffered endless confusion with so many people sharing the same surname. In the 1780s, Charles's great-great-great-grandfather, Sven Olofsson, adopted the surname "Wahlgren" during his military service, a family fact passed down over the generations. When Walgreen's father, Carl Magnus Olofsson, arrived in America, he decided—for reasons lost to us now—to change the family name to Walgreen. (The original name would resurface years later when Charles Walgreen decided to give his company's "Pure Norwegian Cod Liver Oil" the fictitious family moniker, "Olafsen's.")[1]

Carl Magnus Olofsson grew up in Bola, Morlunda, Sweden, in a solidly middle-class family. Nonetheless, Olofsson decided to leave home for the New World in 1859, changing his name to Carl Walgreen when he arrived. He started a family with Anna Louise Cronland, but after bearing two children, she died from complications in childbirth. In 1871 Walgreen married the former Ellen Olson, who grew up in a small town north of Stockholm. Although Olson's family lived comfortably there, her father, like Olofsson, decided the future lay in America. So he led his wife and nine children on an arduous four-week trip across the Atlantic to find out if he was right. Since the family never returned, we can safely conclude their father's belief in America's future was vindicated. Ellen raised Walgreen's first two children and two more of their own, including Charles, who was born on October 9, 1873.

Walgreen grew up on a farm near Rio, Illinois, 14 miles north of

Galesburg—in other words, in the middle of nowhere. But it made for a safe, contented childhood. When Charles first met his future wife, Myrtle Norton, as she recounted in her autobiography, *Never a Dull Day*, he told her that he had had "a happy home"; and all signs suggest it was true.

Walgreen's parents were typical Swedes—stoic, with an understated sweetness. They spoke Swedish at home—a language Charles spoke and wrote his entire life—"but never in anger," he said. His father was firm but fair, unquestionably the family patriarch. He might have admired his adopted country's democratic form of government, but he made no pretense of practicing it at home. What Carl said, went. Carl's authoritarian streak—hardly uncommon for the era—might explain why Charles so often bristled years later when taking orders as a store employee.

In the 1870s, the entire "educational system" of Rio, Illinois, consisted of a one-room schoolhouse. But for at least one year, it was lead by a special teacher named Maggie Phillips. Walgreen never forgot her. And as a result, Walgreens' employees never did either. Every day, Miss Phillips would write an inspirational quotation on the blackboard and have the students memorize the phrase.

Her methods worked. Some five decades later, during the Great Depression, Walgreen shared one of Miss Phillips's quotes with his thousands of employees through the company newsletter, *The Pepper Pod*.

True worth is in being, not seeming,
In doing each day that goes by
Some little good—not in dreaming
Of great things to do
By and by.[2]

It is safe to say that Walgreen, and the vast majority of his employees, took those words to heart. The company has been characterized by an almost religious devotion to substance over style, to this day.

Miss Phillips's tutelage aside, however, Walgreen's father believed his son would need a bigger, better school system to reach his full potential;

and he felt he found one 60 miles northeast in Dixon, Illinois. Walgreen's older half brother Edwin was attending classes there at the five-year-old Northern Illinois Normal School and told his father, "This was the place."

When the Walgreens moved there in 1887, Dixon still had muddy roads and wooden sidewalks, but its location on the Rock River guaranteed continued growth. Established in 1830 when John Dixon set up a ferry service there, the spot became known as "Fort Dixon" during the Black Hawk War of 1832, which started when Chief Black Hawk roused the local Potowotami and Winnebago tribes to take back the land. The war drew hundreds of Union troops, including a host of future famous Americans, among them Jefferson Davis and Abraham Lincoln—the presidents involved in the Civil War. The outnumbered and overpowered tribesmen stood little chance; and after just a few months of fighting, they were forced to surrender. "The Rock River was a beautiful country," Chief Black Hawk said. "I loved it and I fought for it. It is now yours. Keep it as we did."[3] (Chicagoans honored the warrior a century later when they named their NHL hockey team the Blackhawks.)

The Black Hawk War literally put the tiny settlement of Dixon on the map and, having introduced the soldiers from around the country to the area, served to spread the word about the area's appeal. Lincoln returned to Dixon's Nachusa Hotel, where he had boarded during the war, for business trips and campaign stops decades later. (A century later, another U.S. president, Ronald Reagan, grew up in Dixon, serving as a lifeguard on the Rock River and as a caddy for Charles Walgreen Sr. on the Dixon Country Club golf course, which Charles Sr. saved from bankruptcy in the 1930s by purchasing 100 memberships. Like Lincoln, Reagan returned as an honored guest while campaigning for president, staying at the Walgreen family's Hazelwood estate.)

Dixon looked pretty good to Carl Walgreen, so he sold his two farms in Rio to set up a real estate office in downtown Dixon in 1887, when Charles was 14. The community might not have been much by today's standards, but it must have been exhilarating to young Charles, moving from miniscule Rio to Dixon, a town with 5,000 people, electric lights, and even, in a few prosperous businesses and homes, telephones, "the lazy man's friend," in the words of the *Dixon Evening Telegraph.*

Dixon also had what Carl Walgreen most wanted: a good high school for his son, with a planned, new, state-of-the-art building. Charles did well in his studies, but it was sports, not school, that thrilled him. He played baseball and swam all summer, hunted in the nearby woods each fall, and skated on the frozen Rock River in winter.

Charles thrived on the freedom that came with growing up but chafed under the additional responsibilities. At age 16, at his parents' urging, he entered Dixon Business College but stayed only a year. "When I asked him how he liked business college," Myrtle Walgreen wrote in her autobiography, "he just shrugged."[4] In his early years, indifference marked Walgreen's reaction to work in almost any form.

Fortunately, "Accuracy was a kind of passion with him," Myrtle wrote, so Walgreen was able to find work as a bookkeeper for the I. B. Countryman General Store, Dixon's largest. He performed passably well, but once he recognized that his daily duties would hardly change before he died an old man, he quit again. "He didn't think it'd be too good to run a bookkeeping operation the rest of his life," Chuck recalled.[5]

(Walgreen might have ditched the bookkeeping job, but he remembered the lesson. If you don't give your employees a chance to advance, you'll lose them. Providing its employees opportunity for growth based on ability, not merely on longevity, has been a pillar of Walgreens' policy to the current day.)

Leaving the white-collar world for a job at the Henderson Shoe Factory in town, Charles Walgreen soon learned that manual labor also had its downsides, especially in 1889. As he toiled at one of the stitching machines one day, he caught his left middle finger in a sharp steel tool and watched the contraption chop the top joint off. A local doctor named D. H. Law treated the wound and told him he wasn't even to hold a book until it healed. But Charles was not about to put off his love of sports just because of a little finger injury. When Law caught him playing baseball with his buddies the very next day, he scolded the young man. He then asked Charles if he would like to work in a drugstore instead of the factory.[6]

"Charles did not care for the idea at all," Myrtle recalled, simply because he preferred playing baseball to any job you could name. But Dr. Law persisted, asking Charles every day he saw him playing outside if he wanted to reconsider his offer. Finally, albeit grudgingly, Charles agreed to take the job that Dr. Law had set up at the biggest of Mr. David Horton's five drugstores, which sold the "finest perfumes, pure drugs, medicines, toilet articles, shoulder braces, homeopathic remedies, cigars, soda water, and lamp goods," according to the ads in the local paper.

Not surprisingly, the work at Horton's didn't appeal much to Charles, but the princely sum of four bucks a week was certainly attractive. More important, however, unlike the factory, the drugstore offered the amiable young man lots of social contact. Although Charles was initially apprehensive about waiting on customers, he quickly discovered he had a knack for it, the one part of the job he actually enjoyed. (Genuinely friendly customer service has also been a Walgreens' hallmark from the start.)

Like all of Walgreen's jobs, however, this one would be short-lived, lasting only a year and a half. "One nasty winter day, [Mr. Horton] told me to get the snow and ice off the front sidewalk while he was out to lunch," Charles recalled about 10 years later. "I thought he ought to have a porter for such jobs when we were busy, but I really did intend to shovel the snow." After Walgreen's boss left for lunch, a friend stopped by to chat, which interested Walgreen far more than shoveling snow. The time flew by, and Mr. Horton returned to find the snow and ice still stuck to the sidewalk and his clerk inside with the shovel in his hand, chatting up his friend.

"I caught the look on his face," Walgreen said, "and remembered the ice fast enough to blurt out, 'I've quit!' Mr. Horton said I couldn't quit; I was fired!"[7]

Thus began the single greatest career in the pharmacy business.

sweet home chicago

Having been unceremoniously let go from a decent job by a decent man, another 18-year-old might have felt guilty or dejected, but Charles Walgreen took his untimely dismissal instead as a long-awaited invitation to see the world beyond Dixon, Illinois. He borrowed a $20 bill from his sister Clementine, who worked as a stenographer in the Dixon Circuit Clerk's office, then hopped on the Chicago and Northwestern railroad line for Chicago.

His timing could not have been better. When he arrived at the Northwestern station in the winter of 1893, the architects and organizers were working furiously to put the final touches on the World's Columbian Exposition just a few blocks away in Jackson Park, on the city's South Side, in time for the May opening.

The stakes were enormous, for both the city and the country. Chicago's 1893 fair followed Paris's incredibly impressive 1889 World's Fair—which introduced the Eiffel Tower, among other attractions—and had to redeem the United States for its embarrassing, half-baked displays in Paris. Chicago also had to wow its countrymen to prove that it was no longer a vulgar, Western outpost fit only for doomed cattle.

It is impossible to talk about the history of Walgreens without discussing the history of Chicago. The two have been intertwined since Chicago's eighty-sixth year and Walgreens' first. Their personalities are very similar. They share a hard-working, no-nonsense mindset, yet both are utterly unafraid of great challenges.

For the company's first 10 years or so, Walgreens was based almost entirely in Chicago, and the values of that city and its people have stamped the company, even as Walgreens has spread across the United States. In a real sense, Walgreens remains a Chicago company that happens to have outposts in 44 states in the country. As former chief executive officer (CEO) Dan Jorndt said in 1981, when Walgreens had a mere 150 stores in Chicagoland (compared to today's 350-plus), "We know Chicago better than anyone. This is our home, where it all started."[8]

Eastern capitals like Boston and New York were already major cities in the seventeenth century, and even "Western" enclaves like New Orleans or St. Louis were established outposts by the early nineteenth century. But Chicago didn't even exist on any map until well into the nineteenth century. What this utterly forgettable landscape did have, however, was a seemingly minor river running through it—and that made all the difference. Columbus left the Old World to find a passage to the Orient—and failed. Lewis and Clark left the East Coast to find an easy waterway to the Pacific Ocean—and failed. But when French missionary Jacques Marquette and his traveling partner, explorer Louis Joliet, set out on the last leg of their North American journey from the Great Lakes to find the Mississippi River in September 1673, they succeeded. The answer to their riddle was traveling the tiny Chicago River (*Chicago* being a bastardized version of an Indian word for skunkweed, or wild onion, which covered the river banks), followed by a short portage into the Des Plaines River, which runs into the Illinois before joining the Mississippi.

Marquette and Joliet's discovery went largely ignored for 157 years, however, because it was too impractical to exploit. That changed dramatically in 1830, when government planners working for the 12-year-old state of Illinois decided to dig a canal between the Chicago and Des Plaines rivers, ending the need for the troublesome portage, with two small towns—Ottawa and Chicago—planned for either end of the canal.

In August 1833, settlers signed papers at the rustic—some reporters called it rancid and wretched—Sauganah Hotel, incorporating the village of Chicago as a town, with a standing population of 150 people. Milwaukee, Wisconsin, and Michigan City, Indiana, had a big head start on the nascent hamlet; but after the pioneers finished cutting the canal between the Chicago and Des Plaines rivers, the clot in the waterway broke, allowing easy travel from the Atlantic Ocean to the Gulf of Mexico. There was now at least a reason to travel through this wasteland.

The town's rapid growth was driven by sheer utility, a place where grain, cattle, and immigrants came in and flour, meat, and migrants went out. But in Chicago's first decades, it still wasn't much to look at. An early historian reported the place suffered from "a most woe-begone appearance, even as a frontier town of the lowest classes."[9]

The townspeople built their homes, businesses, and even corduroy roads out of the acres of virgin forests that Michigan's lumber barons logged and shipped to Chicago daily. There seemed no end to the raw building materials the Great Lakes state could provide, but that would prove to be a shortsighted solution at best.

On October 7, 1871, George Francis Train, who was "a popular lecturer on moral themes," according to Donald Miller, gave a speech in a Chicago hall that went unrecorded, except for his final caveat: "This is the last public address that will be delivered within these walls! A terrible calamity is impending over the city of Chicago! More I cannot say; more I dare not utter."[10]

We will never know what Train knew or how he knew it; but 24 hours after delivering those fateful words, he would be proven right beyond anyone's imagination, perhaps including his own.

On October 8, 1871 (two years before Charles Walgreen was born), at about 9 P.M., Mrs. Patrick O'Leary's cow knocked over the infamous lamp in her barn on the West Side of the city, igniting some loose hay. By the next morning, over 300 people had been killed, and almost a third of the city's 300,000 people were suddenly homeless, comprising the greatest single disaster in the United States to that date. One witness said he thought he was witnessing "the burning of the world."[11]

The hyperbole was understandable. A modern reader looking at the photos of Chicago that week is reminded of Hiroshima or Dresden, with the landscape covered as far as the eye could see in rubble and smoldering coals, with just a few chimneys and bewildered onlookers left standing. As stunning as the event was, the recovery was even more incredible—and almost as fast—a testament to Chicago's character.

Instead of feeling defeated, "Chicagoans were convinced they had survived a biblical test," Miller wrote, "a terrible but purifying act that had cleared the way for a vast regeneration that would transform their ruined city into the master metropolis of America."[12] By the end of that horrible

week, the resilient Chicagoans had already built 5,000 temporary structures and started 200 permanent ones, which inspired *Chicago Tribune* editor Joseph Medill to write, "In the midst of a calamity without parallel in
the world's history, the people of this once beautiful city have resolved that
CHICAGO SHALL RISE AGAIN."[13]

And rise it did, perhaps like no other city in the world. In contrast to
Tokyo and Berlin, which lost much of their ancient charm during their
similarly massive rebuilding projects, Chicago had little of lasting value
to lose in the bargain. Chicago happily began to replace its seamier sides
in favor of stone buildings, planned streets, and an infrastructure built
to last.

This ability to adapt to sudden changes (which gerontologists tell us is
one of the most common traits of those who live to be 100 years old) plus
the capacity to surmount daunting obstacles and take on great challenges
with complete conviction have long been central to Chicago's identity—
and, not coincidentally, Walgreens', too. As recent chief executive officer
(CEO) Dan Jorndt wrote to his minions, "Don't be afraid to bite off more
than you can chew: You'll be amazed how big your mouth can get."[14] It's
no accident that Walgreens has drawn its trademark resilience, grit, and
understated confidence from the city that gave it birth.

In addition to possessing more than a little moxie, Chicago had all the
raw materials it needed to fuel a roaring renaissance after the Great Fire,
including Lake Michigan's endless supply of fresh water to the east,
Wisconsin's vast acres of lumber to the north, the Midwest's fertile fields
to the west and south, and the all-important shipping channels running
through it. By the time a young architect named Louis Sullivan took the
train from Philadelphia to Chicago in 1873, his new city was home to the
largest livestock, lumber, and grain markets in the world, with the biggest
rail system to distribute all of it around the country. As Sullivan noticed,
biggest was the most popular word in the Chicago lexicon. "I thought it all
magnificent and wild," Sullivan said of Chicago at the end of the nineteenth century. "A crude extravaganza; an intoxicating rawness."[15]

"No large city," Miller wrote, "not even Peter the Great's St. Petersburg, had grown so fast, and nowhere else could be found such a combination of wealth and squalor, beauty and ugliness, corruption and reform."[16]

Chicago's population skyrocketed from a mere 150 pioneers in 1833 to over a million people in 1890, vaulting it past Philadelphia as the second-biggest U.S. city. These people all had to live somewhere, of course; and with property values soaring, architects like Sullivan and company decided the only solution was to build higher.

To do so, however, Chicago's new generation of architects had to figure out ways to build on the region's notoriously squishy soil and to get people to the top floors comfortably. They solved the first problem by creating their own artificial bedrock—a new technique—and the second by soliciting the help of Elisha Graves Otis. Contrary to popular belief, Otis did not invent the elevator—it had already been around for some time when Chicago started building skyward. But he invented something just as important: the mechanism for halting an elevator in free fall, without which no architect would have dared to build higher. Because the new tall building transcended existing terminology, Chicagoans invented a new word for it: *skyscraper*. The ground floors of skyscrapers would soon become Walgreens' preferred location for most of its early corner stores.

Less than two decades after the Great Fire wiped out a third of Chicago, wrote Erik Larson in *The Devil in the White City*, "They had not merely restored it; they had turned it into the nation's leader in commerce, manufacturing, and architecture." But, he added, "all the city's wealth . . . had failed to shake the widespread perception that Chicago was a secondary city that preferred butchered hogs to Beethoven."[17]

Like most perceptions, this one existed for a reason: It was true. Even the soaring skyscrapers could not cover the coarse character of the frontier town still bustling on the ground below. Near the end of the nineteenth century, fully one-fifth of Chicago's population depended on the stockyards, either directly or indirectly, for economic survival. John B. Sherman's monolithic Union Stockyards alone employed 25,000 workers, who slaughtered some 14 million animals a year. (The horrific working conditions and revolting practices of the stockyards were unforgettably

recorded in Upton Sinclair's classic *The Jungle* in 1906. When Sinclair arrived in Chicago to begin his seven-week study of the stockyards, which he
called "rivers of death," he was first struck by the city's "elemental odor,
raw and crude; it was rich, almost rancid, sensual and strong."[18] While the
novel ultimately did little to forward Sinclair's socialist theories, it did
prompt President Theodore Roosevelt to create the Food and Drug
Administration [FDA], which, among other things, governs the conduct
of the pharmaceuticals to this day.)

The stockyards added immeasurably to the misery of Chicago—the
smell often wafted across the entire city—but they were far from the only
source of unpleasantness. The city burned so much coal that, during winter days, visibility extended just one block. The noise from trolleys, trains,
and carriages made leaving windows open during the stultifying summers
impossible. Even if the streets were silent, keeping your windows closed
would have probably been advisable anyway, just to protect your nose from
the pungent smells of open trash, horse manure, and fetid animal corpses
rotting on the streets and in the river. It is not surprising that in 1885 one-
tenth of the city—about 80,000 people then—died from an outbreak of
cholera and typhoid from fouled water. (You can appreciate why so many
residents sought succor from their local druggist, the most trusted man on
their block, then and now.)

And there was more. Larson wrote:

Anonymous death came early and often. Each of the thousand trains
that entered and left the city did so at grade level. You could step
from a curb and be killed by the Chicago Limited. Every day on average two people were destroyed at the city's rail crossings. Their in-
juries were grotesque. Pedestrians retrieved severed heads. There
were other hazards. Streetcars fell from drawbridges. Horses bolted
and dragged carriages into crowds. Fires took a dozen lives a day. In
describing the fire dead, the term the papers most liked to use was
"roasted." There was diphtheria, typhus, cholera, influenza. And
there was murder. [By the 1890s] the rate at which men and women

killed one another rose sharply throughout the nation but especially in Chicago, where police found themselves without the manpower or expertise to manage the volume. In the first six months of 1892 the city experienced nearly eight hundred violent deaths. Four a day. Most were prosaic, arising from robbery, argument or sexual jealousy. Men shot women, women shot men, and children shot one another by accident."[19]

French editor Octave Uzanne called it, "that Gordian city, so excessive, so satanic." Rudyard Kipling went one better. "Having seen it, I desire never to see it again," he said in 1890. "It is inhabited by savages."[20]

Chicago was desperate to change its reputation, both in the United States and overseas. The way to do so, it believed, was not by improving inch by inch, but by taking a gigantic leap forward. All agreed that topping Paris, with the world watching, would do the trick. But first, the city of smelly stockyards had to beat out both New York and Washington, D.C., for the bid for the Exposition. If Chicago could win Congress's eighth ballot, cast on February 24, 1890, it "would dispel at last the Eastern perception that Chicago was nothing more than a greedy, hog-slaughtering backwater; failure would bring humiliation from which the city would not soon recover; given how heartily its leading men had boasted that Chicago would prevail. It was this big talk, not the persistent southwesterly breeze, that had prompted New York editor Charles Anderson Dana to nickname Chicago 'the Windy City.'"[21]

When a *Tribune* employee posted the final results of the vote, the waiting crowd erupted in joy, literally dancing in the streets; and the city leaders got to work. "Make no little plans," the legendary architect Daniel Burnham wrote, in a statement that could serve as Walgreens' official motto. "They have no magic to stir men's blood."[22]

In little more than two years, Burnham's band of architects, builders, and organizers created a gorgeous square-mile park from swamp land and erected some 200 buildings on it. The biggest of them, the Manufacturers and Liberal Arts Building, was big enough to house the U.S. Capitol, the

Great Pyramid, Winchester Cathedral, Madison Square Garden, and St. Paul's Cathedral, all at the same time.

The structure that drew the most attention, however, was a colossal contraption created by a young man named George Ferris. The Ferris Wheel became the fair's emblem, "a machine so huge and terrifying," Larson wrote, "that it instantly eclipsed the tower of Alexander Eiffel that had so wounded America's pride."[23] Chicago's Fair also introduced Cracker Jack, Shredded Wheat, and the Pledge of Allegiance (which, as an aside, did not have the words "under God"; they were added in 1954). Of longer-lasting value to the city of Chicago, however, was the use of safe electricity and clean drinking water that the Exposition brought about.

As *Newsweek*'s Malcolm Jones said, the Chicago Exposition represented "America's chance to prove that, technologically and culturally, it could sit at the grown-ups' table. The fair's directors gambled everything. And they won, seducing the world with the architecture of Louis Sullivan and the technology of Edison."[24]

"There is in the life of any great city a moment when it reaches its maximum potential as a center of power and culture and becomes fully conscious of its special place in history," Miller wrote. "For Chicago that moment was 1893."[25]

The fair's guests included Susan B. Anthony, Archduke Ferdinand, Jane Addams, George Westinghouse, Clarence Darrow, Philip Armour, and Marshall Field. They were joined by 27.5 million others, almost half the entire U.S. population in 1890, including two people who were utterly unknown at the time but who would rank among the city's most prominent figures when the World's Fair returned to Chicago in 1933: Charles Walgreen Sr. and Myrtle Norton.

the state of the profession

Another visitor to the World's Columbian Exposition, a man who went by the name of Dr. Holmes, set up a pharmacy just a few blocks from the grand event—and not far from the drugstore where Walgreen started working. Dr. Holmes made national headlines two years later when police discovered he had murdered dozens of unsuspecting young women (and a few children) in his specially designed killing chambers located in the basement of his store. Erik Larson turned the horrifying story of Dr. Holmes into a 2002 best seller, *The Devil in the White City*.

While Dr. Holmes's criminal record isn't important for our purposes here, his well-documented dual careers in medicine and pharmacy go a long way toward demonstrating just how rudimentary those fields were when Charles Walgreen Sr. entered the pharmacy profession. Holmes also serves as the perfect foil to Walgreen, the duo representing the two faces of the field as practiced a hundred years ago.

To understand how Walgreens changed the way drugstores operate in our country forever—by providing uncommonly honest advice and efficient service; by finding new ways to educate customers; by insisting on raising the professional standards of the pharmacy profession and, especially, those of its own pharmacists; and by working in close cooperation with doctors instead of at odds with them—you have to understand the environment in which the chain was born, and grew.

Like medicine, pharmacy had a checkered past until the twentieth century, when both disciplines emerged from the shadows of superstition and charlatanism to the clear light of rigorous scientific research and objective professional standards.

People have been mixing concoctions and finding herbal remedies to cure what ails them since the beginning of time, but most historians credit Babylon with the birth of an organized apothecary.[26] The ancient Roman Galen (A.D. 131–201) "created a system of pathology and therapy that ruled western medicine for 1,500 years," according to Edward Kremers and George Urdang's authoritative *History of Pharmacy*, in explaining why his reputation endures to this day.[27]

The art of pharmacy remained a sketchy matter for centuries, especially as practiced by witch doctors, priest-kings, and alchemists; but bit by bit, societies saw the need for a more structured approach and acted accordingly. As the Dark Ages began to give way to the Renaissance, public pharmacies and universities started spreading across Europe, a movement capped by German Emperor Frederick II's proclamation, delivered about 1240, "that was to be the Magna Carta of the profession of pharmacy," Kremers and Urdang wrote. In it, Frederick established three tenets of pharmacy practice that remain pillars of the field to this day: (1) "the separation of the pharmaceutical profession from the medical profession" (Walgreens would forever rearrange this historically dicey relationship for the good of all health care practitioners after World War II); (2) "official supervision of pharmaceutical practice" (something for which Charles Walgreen Jr. successfully fought during his tenure at the company's helm); and (3) "obligation by oath to prepare drugs reliably, according to skilled art, and in a uniform, suitable quality." In other words, Frederick II sought to replace the sloppy, slapdash work of unregulated locals with the measured, consistent practice of a professional class of pharmacists.[28]

The Age of Enlightenment may have transformed mathematics, physics, and astronomy, among other sciences; but it was slow to improve medicine and pharmacy. Through Colonial times, anyone could call himself or herself a pharmacist and practice pharmacy in any manner he or she saw fit. In much the same way that blacksmiths often doubled as dentists in preindustrial days, printers often doubled as pharmacists. As odd as it might seem today, their extra downtown floor space lent itself to selling sundries, and printers had the ability to advertise their myriad goods. Ben Franklin was a pharmacist, selling "commodities varied from needles and pins to horses and slaves," plus patent medicines and Seneca snake root, "with directions how to use it in pleurisy," as he advertised in his own *Pennsylvania Gazette* in 1730.[29]

While convenient, this jack-of-all-trades approach to pharmacy did nothing to enhance the standing of druggists nor to improve the quality of the care they provided. The inherent conflict between pharmacists and doctors was stirred anew when a famous pharmacist named John Morgan gave the keynote speech to inaugurate the medical school at the College of Philadelphia, which Franklin attended. "We must regret," Morgan stated, "that the very different employment of physician, surgeon, and apothecary should be promiscuously followed by one man: they certainly require different talents."[30]

The nineteenth century proved to be the beginning of a new age for the health sciences. In 1820, a physician named Lyman Spalding spearheaded the production of the first *American Pharmacopoeia*—the invaluable reference that listed all known drugs and how to prepare them.[31] The professionalization of pharmacy accelerated after the Civil War, when pharmaceutical boards, associations, and university programs sprung up all over the eastern half of the continent. Even in their embryonic states, these governing bodies proved helpful in establishing professional standards, forwarding the cause of pharmacy education, and working to keep some of the seedier elements out of the field—including addictive drugs like opiates and narcotics, which were not illegal or even regulated until the twentieth century. A committee of the recently formed American Pharmaceutical Association (APA) concluded, in 1901, that the data they had gathered on addictive drugs and their users was "appalling." The APA used its influence to help pass the Harrison Narcotic Act of of 1914, intended to "bring the opium and coca traffic and addiction problems under control."[32]

Despite the profession's tangible progress, by the end of the nineteenth century, the "drug business" still presented more questions than answers about the remedies it offered and still had plenty of room for snake oil salesmen, too. A photo taken sometime in the 1890s featured in Urdang's comprehensive history depicts the popular "Dr. Matthews Medicine Show" as it appeared during a tour of Wisconsin, a sort of "medical midway" that consisted of white canvas tents on the perimeter of the grounds, rows of benches in the middle, acrobats and musicians to attract a crowd, a chest of prepackaged medicines, and a speiler in top hat, presumably the good "Dr. Matthews" himself, on a stage, preparing to make his pitch. The photo caption of "Dr. Matthew's Medicine Show," read "Drug shops or stores did not have to be much more than a permanent habitation for such itinerant quackery until, through a publicly defined level of education and responsibility, a class of 'pharmacists' was created that could be expected to protect the public against it."[33]

Even the term "patent medicine" was something of a dodge, as the creators did not patent the *medicine* or its ingredients—which would have revealed how cheap and dangerous the contents often were, not to mention easily copied—but the formula's *name*, since the key to success was marketing, not medicine.[34]

As a result a true "class of pharmacists" was slow to develop. When both Dr. Holmes and Charles Walgreen Sr. arrived in Chicago, neither the government nor the profession asked much of anyone claiming to be a pharmacist. A brief examination of Dr. Holmes's professional life shows us much about the state of medicine and pharmacy when Walgreen moved to Chicago.

Dr. Holmes was born Herman Mudgett and was raised in New England. (For clarity, he is referred to here only as Dr. Holmes.) He attended the University of Vermont medical school. When Holmes entered medical school, the field was abuzz with the recent discovery of germs and how they functioned. Many had even begun to believe it was a good practice for the surgeon to wash his hands before amputating a patient's leg.

As Erik Larson wrote in *The Devil in the White City*, "In those days a doctor's office could indeed be a fearsome place. All doctors were, in a sense, amateurs. The best of them bought cadavers for study. They paid cash, no questions asked, and preserved particularly interesting bits of diseased viscera in large clear bottles. Skeletons hung in offices for easy anatomical reference." This apparently helped the practitioners to remember that the shinbone is connected to the thighbone.[35]

Dr. Holmes decided Vermont was too small a school, however; so after one year there he transferred to the University of Michigan in Ann Arbor, which could boast "one of the West's leading scientific medical schools," Larson wrote, "noted for its emphasis on the controversial art of dissection."[36] It was also home to the nation's first college of pharmacy, opened in 1868 by Dr. Albert Prescott, who had just finished his tour of duty as a military surgeon in the Civil War. Originally organized under the Literary Department, the college of pharmacy grew out of the medical school and earned both respect and criticism because Dr. Prescott stressed scientific understanding over the more practical vocational approach offered elsewhere, eschewing the need for an apprenticeship as a prerequisite for graduation.[37]

Michigan's college of pharmacy would graduate Charles Sr.'s son Chuck in 1928 and grandson Cork in 1959 and today features a wing donated by Walgreens. Charles's great-grandson Kevin, today a vice president for the company, also graduated from Michigan. The scientific rigor of Michigan's college of pharmacy would make its mark on the Walgreens and, through them, the entire industry in the years to come.

The shadowy nature of nineteenth-century medical education, however, cannot be ignored—especially as it impacted the field Charles Walgreen Sr. was poised to enter. On Monday, October 11, 1993, a backhoe had just begun excavating the foundation for the University of Michigan's new physics building. As it dug near the foundation of the decades-old West Engineering Building on Michigan's central campus, an odor suddenly arose, one so acrid that everyone nearby turned to cover their noses. Seconds later, the scoop brought up a fragment of a human skull.

What the construction crew had inadvertently discovered was a secret burial ground for cadavers—cadavers illegally obtained and disposed of— and with it, a glimpse into the unsophisticated and unregulated early years of medical education.

Michigan was ahead of most colleges, actually, when it started its own medical school in 1850. It did so simply by co-opting a three-man instructional outfit already up and running in town. Michigan was, indeed, noted for its emphasis on the controversial art of dissection.

One reason it was so controversial was the State of Michigan's ban on the two main methods for obtaining cadavers: buying them or stealing them. Michigan did the only thing it could do to fulfill its annual need for one hundred dead bodies: It broke the law. The "demonstrator of anatomy" authorized his agents to pay $30 to $40 per cadaver—enough to cover a third to a half of a medical school student's expenses. Anyone who has witnessed contemporary college students hauling bags of sticky, smelly beer bottles back to the party store on a hot Sunday morning for the 10-cent bounty each container represents can guess what happened next: The students got into the business of procuring cadavers, packing them in barrels labeled "fresh paint" or "pickles," and disposing of them when they were finished. This dirty little secret apparently wasn't much of a secret at all by the 1870s, when a piece in the yearbook defined "medic" as someone who "preys on both the quick and the dead," "never whistles when 'going through' a graveyard at night," and "is never happier than when he findeth a fellow-man 'in a pickle.'"[38]

In addition to the ethical questions that such practices should have raised, the medical ones were probably more serious—if less understood. In the cramped medical building, "patients and cadavers . . . co-mingled in the disease-ridden atmosphere," the *Ann Arbor Observer* reported. "The same lecture room and table used for dissections during the week were used for clinical demonstrations of living patients on Saturday mornings."[39]

The university would not open its new (and newly legalized) Anatomical Laboratory until 1887—three years after Holmes graduated. Given his future deviance, it's not hard to imagine him playing an active role in the bustling cadaver trade during his time at Michigan.

Holmes enrolled at Michigan's school of medicine on September 21, 1882, and impressed his professors as "a scamp"; but he graduated on time, just 21 months after he enrolled, as a Doctor of Medicine. In June 1884, he set out to find some favorable location in which to launch a practice, but he found it harder than expected.

With apparently little or no reservations, Dr. Holmes decided to leave the practice of medicine for pharmacology. What would seem a very strange move today made a lot more sense a century ago. Medicine, at best, was an unstructured, undisciplined field, which relied more on aggressive (and often disastrous) guesswork than on science.

Many doctors killed as many patients as they cured. In his history of the

Coca-Cola company, *For God, Country and Coca-Cola*, Mark Pendergrast describes the state of the profession during the Gilded Age, when Coca-Cola's creator, Dr. John Pemberton, was practicing pharmacy in Atlanta. "Cheap nostrums sometimes provided a safer alternative. Furthermore, there were few doctors in rural areas, forcing the country folk to use patent medicine . . . which were often taken to relieve the symptoms of overeating and poor diet, which went hand-in-hand in that period."[40]

And although pharmacology certainly attracted more than its share of charlatans a century ago—including Dr. Holmes—pharmacists more frequently offered the kind of practical, proven advice that doctors could not. For starters, the practice of pharmacy had been around much longer than the practice of medicine, insofar as the world's first "doctors" were really herbologists and chemists, not surgeons. Pharmacy was more structured and regulated, and there were many more pharmacists than doctors.

After Dr. Holmes bounced around pharmacies in Minneapolis and up-state New York, he settled in Chicago, a town that already had 1,500 pharmacies licensed under the state's new licensing system. Pharmacies seemed to pop up on each street corner the way gourmet coffee shops do today. Reading the various histories of Chicago of the era, it's tempting to conclude that everyone and his cousin were in the pharmacy field, including Daniel Burnham's father, who ran a successful wholesale drug business, and at one point Burnham himself, who started out his professional life not as a promising architect but as a failed druggist.

By the late 1880s, Dr. Holmes was running one of those 1,500 Chicago pharmacies. In fact, it was the visibility and the aura of professional respect that his new pharmacy lent him that allowed Dr. Holmes to lure attractive young women to enter his store, conveniently located a few blocks from the Exposition on Chicago's South Side, as both customers and clerks. To raise extra money, Dr. Holmes also started a mail-order medicine company. "In a parody of Aaron Montgomery Ward's fast-growing empire in central Chicago," Larson wrote, "Holmes had begun selling sham drugs that he guaranteed would cure alcoholism and baldness," the latest crazes.[41]

Like Holmes, Walgreen was also lured to the City of Big Shoulders during the Columbian Exposition and to the field of pharmacy. His approach to the profession would be as noble as his competitors' was shameless.

walgreen does chicago

If Holmes represented the darkest possible sides of pharmacology—from his spurious salesmanship, to his exploitation of the intimacy his position offered, to the ultimate betrayal of a professional's trust—Walgreen represented all that people admired about pharmacists: He was a knowledgeable, empathetic, and, most important, honest professional. But it must be said that, like Holmes (and many other young pharmacists, undoubtedly), Walgreen initially showed little passion for hard work, for following orders, or even for pharmacology itself, for that matter.

On that cold Saturday morning in the winter of 1893, when Walgreen took a small bag and the $20 his sister gave him and hopped on the train headed from Dixon to Chicago, he studied the *Tribune* classified section en route. By the time he got off the train, he already had a job opening targeted, just a few blocks from the station. He walked into Samuel Rosenfeld's drugstore at Quincy and Wells, not far from a block-long Marshall Field's store, and walked out with a clerking job that paid a healthy $5 a week.

Walgreen decided to celebrate his sudden success by spending the weekend shooting pool with some old buddies from Dixon who had moved to town, burning through the remainder of his $20. And that was the problem. When he walked through the door of the drugstore that Monday morning for his first day of work, he had to ask his new employer for an advance just to eat that night and get a room at a transient hotel nearby.

"The experience must have made an impression on him," Myrtle wrote, "because after I knew him he certainly kept his books balanced; and I never remember a single time that he took on anything, either in the line of business or pleasure, that he didn't know ahead of time he could pay for."[42]

But Walgreen's sense of responsibility wouldn't emerge for a few years. Like most of Walgreen's jobs, that one didn't last long. Despite economic tremors like The Panic of 1893—which forced 192 railroads to fail, including such legendary lines as the Northern Pacific, the Union Pacific, and the Santa Fe—Walgreen never seemed to have any trouble finding a new job in the drugstore business whenever he needed one. With 1,500 drugstores in town, it seems they needed him more than he needed them.

None of Walgreen's stints lasted more than a couple years, and most much less, including tours of duty in a handful of stores on Chicago's North Side. One shop owner there, Max Grieben, liked Walgreen's Aryan looks "and soft-spoken manner but told him he would have to learn German," which he did.[43]

But after leaving yet another job, Walgreen realized he was squandering his future in piecemeal fashion, with no focus or ambition to direct his search. Sensing that he needed to do something dramatic to wake himself up, he looked over the Chicago River one night, pulled out the remaining pennies in his pocket, and threw them into the water to force him to "cease his dawdling," as Myrtle recalled him telling her.[44]

Walgreen struck out this time for the South Side, which seemed to suit him better. Since the neighborhoods there were still booming with post-Exposition transplants, "he felt the South Side held the greatest possibilities for the future," Myrtle wrote. "He kept looking for a drugstore where he would feel as if he belonged."[45]

When charting Walgreen's peripatetic journey through Chicago's drugstores, you get the impression that the young man stuck with pharmacy not because he had a great passion for it but because it was convenient. It was simple work for him and an easy field in which to find a new job whenever he got the itch. In hindsight, however, Walgreen's "drifting" served him very well. Instead of glomming on to one mentor in one store in one neighborhood for his entire apprenticeship, Walgreen's clerking career exposed him to many methods of running a drugstore, not to mention the myriad neighborhoods into which he would soon be expanding after he started his own chain. When the time came for him to run his own empire, the lessons learned in these early years would give him a great advantage over his competition.

In 1896, Walgreen eventually settled at William G. Valentine's drugstore on Cottage Grove Avenue and 39th Street. The site was ideally located on the first floor of the Thacker Building, one of hundreds of city structures finished right before the fair, with cable cars stopping on both streets of the intersection. Thanks to his years as a drugstore journeyman, Walgreen's knowledge and skills had improved, earning him a decent $35 a month. Valentine, however, was in the habit of criticizing him for the smallest infractions, which didn't sit well with the young man who was now putting in almost 80 hours a week and living with two roommates over the store in a bedbug-infested apartment. (It's a testament to living conditions in nineteenth-century Chicago that a four-year-old building could already be infested with bed bugs.) He'd had enough.

While trying to decide just what to do—and having grown weary of bouncing from job to job—Walgreen liked to take his mind off his problems by going to the ballpark and the racetrack with his roommates. One afternoon at the horses, he hauled in some $70, twice his monthly salary, and was so giddy he played hooky the next day by telling Mr. Valentine he had a "pressing appointment." He then returned to the track and proceeded to lose all his winnings from the previous day, and then some. A few more trips like that cured Walgreen of betting what he couldn't afford to lose; but for a man with such conservative instincts, his gambler's nerves would prove a great asset when he started his own business.

Seeing no way out of his predicament, Walgreen concluded he had little choice but to quit, yet again. But before he walked out the door once more, a bit of long-dormant pride kicked in, and he decided to reform. Not for its own virtue, mind you. He wanted to become a model employee just long enough to make Valentine regret his leaving.

Walgreen's plan worked—maybe too well. Valentine was so impressed by the suddenly invigorated Walgreen's efforts that he bumped his monthly salary from $35 to $45, and then again a little while later to $55—pretty good money for a drugstore clerk.

Valentine also began mentoring the young man in earnest, urging him to study the pharmacology bibles—the *U.S. Pharmacopoeia*, the *National Formulary*, and *Remington's*. Walgreen probably surprised both Valentine and himself by taking the bait, poring over those dense tomes well enough to pass the Illinois State Board of Pharmacy examination in 1897 and become a registered pharmacist. This meant that for the first time in his life, Walgreen was free to own and operate his own store, if he ever had the urge and the opportunity.

to live and almost die in cuba

Whatever aspirations Walgreen might have harbored at the time were interrupted in February 1898 when the USS *Maine* exploded in Havana Harbor. To this day, no one knows how or why the ship blew up, but that didn't stop the United States from declaring war on Spain on April 25, 1898. Walgreen signed up with the Illinois National Guard the next day, happily informing Mr. Valentine that he was "giving up the drug business for the army so he would have shorter hours and could sleep later in the morning," Myrtle recalled.[46] It didn't quite work out that way, of course.

Walgreen might have been a bit apathetic about the daily grind, but he was a passionate patriot, "convinced that a man should contribute to his country's well-being in every way he could," Myrtle wrote.[47] When Walgreen's company commander asked him to take a day trip across the island of Cuba to map enemy positions, Walgreen hopped right to it. What might have been a tedioius task turned into a breezy exercise when he came across an officer in another unit who had already created detailed maps of the Spanish forces and invited Walgreen to copy them.

So, while Teddy Roosevelt was leading the Rough Riders up San Juan Hill, Walgreen calmly traced his new friend's maps and then spent the afternoon swapping stories and smoking fresh Cuban cigars—all to make sure he killed enough time to make his final results seem plausible. When Walgreen returned to his camp that evening, he was received by his commanding officer as a hero for producing such great maps. It would not be the last time Walgreen would demonstrate the fine art of working smarter, instead of harder—one of his trademarks.

There's an old saw that young generals focus on combat strategy, whereas older ones stress logistics. Walgreen was a whiz at logistics, from an early age. The Army wisely recognized this and put Walgreen to use in the dispensary of the Sibony Hospital. Every bed and hallway was filled with dying men—not from Spanish bullets but from microscopic enemies. The three-month war claimed 5,462 American lives, but only 379 from battle-related wounds. The rest died from malaria, typhoid, and yellow fever, which ran rampant on the tropical island.

Due to doctors' rudimentary knowledge of diseases at the time (they were only beginning to suspect that mosquitoes were the source of yellow fever), their practices frequently resulted in spreading diseases instead of containing them. The medics themselves often came down with one of the deadly bugs, including Walgreen, who contracted yellow fever and malaria simultaneously. He fell into a coma, "so far gone," Myrtle recalled the understated Walgreen telling her, "that the doctors held no hope for his living through the night. He knew this was the verdict, but it seemed like a fact about someone else."[48]

Paul Harvey, the legendary radio talk show storyteller, picked up the narrative from there in one of his classic "The Rest of the Story" segments in 1996. "Charlie was dying. . . . One of the physicians took Charlie's pulse, shook his head. 'Good as dead,' he said. Charlie's name was entered on the casualty list. It would appear in the next day's newspapers as yet another fever victim.

"It was just at that moment that Charlie felt free. It was as though he were poised at a corner of the ceiling, looking down at his own apparently lifeless body, looking down at the doctors and nurses, watching everything they did, hearing everything they said. But then he was overcome by an inexplicable awareness that if he did not return to that ravaged body, it would be as though he had failed some sort of an examination. He heaved a sigh. One of the doctors jumped, actually frightened, then called to his colleagues, 'He's still alive!'"[49]

Myrtle recalled her future husband telling her that when he was in the coma, "he knew there were things he also wanted terribly to learn. Whatever he glimpsed brought him back. . . . When he was able to talk, he related every move that had been made in that long room while he was supposedly unconscious. After that experience, he knew that immortality was not just a theory and that the soul was not bound to the life of the body."[50]

Too much can be made of these experiences, but Walgreen was an extraordinarily objective man, not given to exaggeration. There is no doubt this experience made quite an impact on him, allowing him to discard his fear of the future and imbuing him with the urgency to do something special before his time was done.

walgreen returns

Walgreen came home in November 1898, with an $8-a-month medical pension, some lingering symptoms of his illness, and the strong desire to downshift from Valentine's busy store. He walked three blocks south on Cottage Grove to the Bowen Avenue intersection, through the doors of a store on the first floor of the Barrett Hotel—which had been built for the Exposition in 1892—and asked the owner there, Isaac W. Blood, if he needed an experienced worker. Good help was still hard to find, so Valentine happily hired the 25-year-old veteran.

It wasn't much of a store, even by the standards of 1898: just 20 feet by 50 feet, much smaller than Valentine's. Mr. Blood's store was dank and dingy, lit by dangerous and shadowy gaslights, with narrow aisles and cracked and dirty tile floors. "The general atmosphere was uninviting," Herman and Rick Kogan wrote, a sentence that presents a simple contrast to the very effect Walgreen would always seek to achieve.[51]

The products on the shelves were of uneven quality, and Walgreen himself could honestly not vouch for all of them. This was the store where Walgreen worked, an almost perfect example of what pharmacy was like at the time, for better or for worse. But it didn't have much to do with the store Walgreen would create. That would be something altogether different. What probably looked like a step backward at the time would prove to be one of Walgreen's smartest career moves.

Bit by bit, Walgreen was getting the feel for what it would be like to actually own and operate a store, taking on larger responsibilities at each stop. Before Isaac Blood went on vacation, he asked Walgreen to sell his (Blood's) second, smaller store if he could. When two men offered $1,250 for the shop, Walgreen knew Blood would accept the offer. But Walgreen was a shrewder negotiator than his boss and told the men that the offer was too low. They called Walgreen's bluff, asking him to wire his boss their offer in the belief that Blood would happily sell at that price.

Walgreen believed they were right, so he outfoxed them again. He wired Blood their offer but added a kicker the buyers never saw: "If you want to sell store for $1,250, wire [back that] you won't take a cent less than $1,500." Blood did as his underling instructed; and sure enough, the buyers blinked first. Blood sold his unwanted second store for $1,500—20 percent more than what he had asked. Despite Walgreen's key role in the transaction, Isaac Blood didn't give him a cent for his help.

By this point, Walgreen had seen enough pharmacists to know what worked and what didn't. He now believed he could do it as well or better than most, and he was certain he'd much rather work for himself than for someone else. But when he approached Mr. Blood about buying the Cottage Grove store, Blood replied that he wouldn't take a cent less than $4,000. Obviously, Blood had learned Walgreen's lessons on negotiations too well, presenting Walgreen a seemingly impossible standard to reach.

As always, Walgreen saved his best efforts for any achievement that might grant him more independence. The only way he could ever pay off such a steep loan, he figured, would be to make the store more profitable so he'd be able to make his monthly payments from the proceeds once he took over.

Once again, Walgreen's strategy worked too well. As Walgreen's extra efforts began to produce extra revenue, Blood realized the store had more potential than he had at first thought. In 1901, when Walgreen's tireless efforts raised just enough capital to buy the store, Blood informed him the price had just gone up to $6,000—50 percent more than it was when Walgreen asked just two years earlier. Walgreen was floored, but he became even more determined to see it through.

Paradoxically, Blood's hard-to-get strategy might have been just the thing to stir Walgreen to commit fully to becoming a drugstore owner. He decided to drain his life savings; borrow an additional $2,000 from his father, who had been doing well in the growing Dixon real estate market; and signed a note for the remainder. The name "Blood-Walgreen" would appear in the directory until he had paid off the loan.

Walgreen was in deep—he knew he would not be getting out of debt any time soon. But by buying the modest store at 4134 Cottage Grove Avenue, he had something he valued more than anything, something he'd never had before: his independence. He had become his own boss and was finally in business for himself. The neat, gold-lettered sign above the door said it all: "C. R. Walgreen, R.Ph."

Thus, 2 years before the Wright Brothers launched their biplane at Kitty Hawk, North Carolina, Henry Ford started his automobile company, and the National League played the upstart American League in the first World's Championship Series; 4 years before Albert Einstein formulated the theory of relativity; 5 years before Willis Carrier invented air-conditioning; 6 years before Leo Hendrik Baekeland invented plastic; 51 years before Sam Walton opened his first Wal-Mart; 54 years before Ray Kroc opened his first McDonald's; and 61 years before Sebastian S. Kresge opened his first Kmart—before all these events, Charles R. Walgreen Sr. opened his first pharmacy.

No, Walgreen's first store didn't provide customers self-service, drive-thru photo processing, or the Intercom computer system. He couldn't offer his two employees pension plans or profit sharing—just long hours for an honest wage and a pat on the back. And the store itself was small enough to fit comfortably inside the cosmetics section of a modern Walgreens. But that first store was definitely a Walgreens. And a contemporary customer would have no difficulty recognizing or appreciating what Charles Walgreen was offering, including immaculate floors and crystal clear glass counters; straight, honest advice delivered in the customer's best interest; and unequaled customer service, the kind that brings customers back, again and again—whether it's 1901 or 2004.

the most important merger

It used to be said that behind every great man you'll find a great woman. Myrtle Walgreen was in many ways a traditional wife, with little ego to speak of; but no one who knew her would ever say she merely stood behind her husband. Without her support, Walgreen himself would not have dared to be so ambitious; and without her direct contributions—including baking the pies and making the soups and sandwiches that opened the food service division and fueled the chain's early expansion—the Walgreens chain never would have become the business empire it is today.

"The first key to our success," said former CEO Dan Jorndt, "was Mr. Walgreen Sr. hitching up with Myrtle. It's amazing what a team they were. Everyone says he was successful; but really, it's that *they* were successful. She was a Rock of Gibraltar and backed him up any way she could. He never had to check to see if she was with him, and vice versa."[52] Myrtle was her husband's equal, and no one knew this better than Walgreen himself.

It makes sense that the two got along so well from the start, given their similar backgrounds. Both were raised on Illinois farms by no-nonsense parents who nonetheless weren't afraid to roll the dice and very much valued having fun. Myrtle wrote of her husband, "He had a happy home, too, just as I did."[53]

She was born Myrtle Norton on July 5, 1879, to a resilient mother and a hard-working father. When her mother, Nellie, knew she was soon to give birth to Myrtle, she gathered her belongings, plus some fresh flowers, preserves, and handmade aprons for gifts, and traveled by horse-drawn wagon to stay with her mother 40 miles away in Carbondale—then came right home as soon as she could to tend to her husband and farm. "That was mid-America in the late 1870s," Myrtle wrote, "good neighbors, hospitality, but stand on your own feet."[54]

Her mother certainly embodied those traits and did so with flair. "Baking was an art at which no one excelled my mother. . . . Things always hummed when she was around."[55]

Although they were a quintessential farm family, the Nortons had more than a little history and culture. Myrtle's great-great-grandfather Ichabod Norton was killed by the British for making bullets for the Revolutionary army. Her grandfather Kennedy fought nobly in the Civil War, and her aunts included a professional artist, a piano teacher, and a University of Chicago alum. This might not seem like anything out of the ordinary today; but in the era of Stanley and Livingstone, the Boer War, and the assassination of President Garfield—a half century before the "Walton" years—such a refined background for a rural family was most uncommon.

Myrtle's favorite memories, however, were simple ones of family life. "In my childhood we had a good time at home," she wrote. Her father played the violin and would serenade her mother with an eponymous tune, "My Gal Nell." "Papa's pride of mother was very forthright," she said in her book. "What a wonderful atmosphere for a child to grow up in. . . . He always said that the day my mother brought home a daughter was the first time it ever struck him that when a man had a wife, a son, a daughter, and a farm there wasn't much left to wish for."[56]

It is not difficult when you read Myrtle's descriptions of the virtues her parents stressed to see how those morals were passed on to her son Chuck and to subsequent generations of Walgreens, providing the timeless basic values on which the entire company is based to this day.

Her father, Myrtle wrote, "took his responsibilities as trusts, and he had a keen sense of honor about obligations. He made us feel that if we took

Mention a little of his wife

on a job of any kind, it was our duty to do it in the best possible way, no matter how tired of it we might become. It is still almost impossible for me to leave any task unfinished, even though I may wish I had never begun."[57]

When Myrtle was four, the family moved to Chester in Southern Illinois so her father could get a more stable job as a guard in the state penitentiary, overlooking the Mississippi. "A big [jail] break was frustrated by father's men who refused to join in because he had been so square with them," she wrote late in her 84-year-long life. "The pride I felt when people spoke about the way Papa's men saved the day has stayed with me."[58]

Unfortunately, it was also the prison that gave Myrtle her most painful memory, too, that of her father dying of "lung fever," brought on by the fine dust from the quarries he guarded while the prisoners crushed rock. He was only 38, his young daughter just 7.

Through Nellie's strength and warmth, however, the family stuck together. The Nortons retained their sense of fun and adventure, too. "By August, attendance [at the 1893 Chicago Exposition] was averaging two hundred thousand a month," Myrtle recalled. "Down in our part of the state farmers were mortgaging their farms, teachers taking out their savings, merchants borrowing on their inventories, and some bankers even foreclosing mortgages in order to have the money to 'take the family to the Fair.' Mother certainly scraped the bottom of the barrel when she decided that [my brother] Paul and I were to go to Chicago."[59]

The trio rode on the Ferris Wheel, listened to John Phillip Sousa's famous band and—most exciting of all—drank ice water. "In those days," Myrtle explained, "ice was not taken for granted. Mr. Drake, the founder of the Drake Hotel, had honored Columbus by donating a fountain of ice water kept cold by three tons of ice every day. . . . It was a great Fair! What makes a fair great if not the mind stretching of the young and the fun that outlasts the decades."[60]

After Myrtle graduated from high school in 1898—the same year Walgreen shipped off to Cuba—her brother, Paul, decided he wanted to go to Chicago to become a registered pharmacist. He thought he would be striking out on his own, but Nellie Norton would hear none of it.

"Mother agreed at once. Chicago it would be," Myrtle wrote. "It was years later I realized what an intrepid soul my Mother was. She had many friends in Normal and Bloomington [Illinois]; her life was full, busy, and happy. But she never once spoke of *sending* Paul to school. She was the homemaker as well as the provider, and off we went."[61]

Paul enrolled at the Chicago College of Pharmacy, while Myrtle zoomed through her coursework at the Gregg Secretarial School, which allowed students to go as fast as they wanted, once they satisfied the requirements for each level. That's all Myrtle needed to know. She woke up at five each morning to work on the typewriter at home, walked to class, then came home at night to work on her shorthand skills by having Paul read the paper to her aloud. Her single-minded determination would prove essential to Walgreens' early success.

The working world, however, could be a dangerous place for a young woman in Chicago. The environment could be so unsavory for them, in fact, that an officer of the First National Bank felt compelled to run an ad in the help-wanted section of the *Chicago Tribune* to warn female stenographers of "our growing conviction that no thoroughly honorable businessman who is this side of dotage ever advertises for a lady stenographer who is a blonde, is good-looking, is quite alone in the city, or will transmit her photograph. All such advertisements upon their face bear the marks of vulgarity, nor do we regard it safe for any lady to answer such unseemly utterances."[62]

Miss Norton wasn't in the workforce long before an unscrupulous boss targeted her for such treatment. "Just let me kiss you," he told her one day, after he got her alone in his office. "What's the matter with one kiss?" Myrtle replied resolutely, "If you come an inch nearer, I'll throw this chair through that glass door," and took her boss's momentary pause as her opportunity to escape down the hall. Despite her courage under pressure, when she found her brother Paul, who worked in the same building, she was sobbing, too scared to speak.[63] And that marked the end of her stenography career.

About the same time, Myrtle made some changes in her love life, too.

In high school she briefly dated a young man named Earl, the son of (surprise) a pharmacist, of sorts. He was a "dashing fellow who played the banjo," she wrote, but "his father was known as the medicine man; that is, he went from town to town selling patent medicine. His family had a big fancy wagon which today would be called a trailer. When they let down the back of the wagon and pulled open the curtains they presented the audience with a ready-made stage." It is not surprising that Myrtle's upright brother "did not like Earl. . . . Besides, Paul felt that the drugstore was the place to buy medicines."[64]

Earl didn't last long, but she did have a "best beau" throughout high school, a popular young man named George. "No party seemed to get under way until George breezed in," Myrtle wrote. Even after the Nortons moved to Chicago, George kept coming around, all the way from Normal, Illinois. Myrtle, Paul, and Nellie all liked George, but "I was a shade worried when I began to hear that he had been seen with girls who were not the kind we always went around with. Finally certain rumors reached Paul's ears that George was stepping out a bit too fancily."[65]

By June 1900, Myrtle had no job or boyfriend, but she seemed content. She was always far more independent than needy in all her relationships, but she was also open to possibilities. "I can't remember a dull day," she wrote. "New interests were always popping up and everything I did I went into with my whole heart."[66]

When Paul, who had become a sales rep for a surgical supply house, went on a Lake Michigan junket paid for by the pharmaceutical companies, she happily went along. The companies gave the guests plenty of promotional trinkets and trash to wear on the boat ride, and as Myrtle said, with disarming directness, "I weighed 165 pounds with 45-inch hips and a generous 38-inch bust; so I must have made one of the larger displays." Apparently at least one young pharmacist noticed. "That was the day I met Charles Walgreen," she said. "Later he told me that whenever he heard me laugh [that day] he felt unaccountably like laughing, too."[67]

But Walgreen let his chance slip away. It would be months before

Myrtle's brother Paul asked her to come along with him to Mr. Blood's drugstore. Myrtle recalled:

> While Paul was talking business with Mr. Walgreen, I was walking around the store looking at everything on the counters, and I came upon a box of bath tablets. I had no more idea of buying those bath tablets than I had of buying hair tonic; but just to make conversation, I picked up one of the packages and said, "Mr. Walgreen, are these bath tablets any good?" He walked over to me and said, "Miss Norton, I couldn't recommend them personally because I have never used them, but I sell a great many."
>
> When we went out of the store I said to Paul, "Well, that certainly is an honest druggist. You would have thought he'd say, 'Certainly they're good!' thinking I was going to buy some, but he didn't." That made a real impression on me. I kept thinking how forthright that young Mr. Walgreen was.[68]

Honesty

Yet Walgreen again let the opportunity slip away. Months later, Paul and Myrtle were planning an August fishing trip to Wisconsin with a dozen or so friends when they happened to visit Mr. Blood's store again. While browsing the selections, Myrtle overheard her brother ask Walgreen, "Do you like to fish?"

"I admit I was hoping this friendly young druggist was going to answer 'Yes,' although I never thought of Paul's suggesting he come on the trip," Myrtle wrote. Walgreen replied, "Sure I like to fish," but failed to take the bait once more. Paul tried to invite him yet again a few weeks later, but again, no definite answer. Finally Mrytle returned for some stamps and told him she had almost completed her fishing outfit, trying to gauge his interest—but maddeningly, no response. Whether Walgreen was dense or merely modest is hard to say, but the communication gap between the Nortons and the young druggist was downright comical to observe.

On a warm Friday night, on the eve of the long-awaited trip, Paul and

Romance

Myrtle Norton visited Mr. Blood's drugstore one last time to spell out their invitation in no uncertain terms. "Well, Walgreen," Paul offered with a sigh, almost resigned to his friend's reluctance—or obliviousness—"we leave tomorrow night; and if you decide you want to go, just be down at the Northwestern Station at ten-thirty."[69]

"Mr. Walgreen seemed to be turning the idea over as if he had just taken it in that he could join our camping trip," Myrtle wrote, amused. Sure enough, at the appointed hour, Walgreen walked down the platform at the Northwestern Station—the same spot where he had first arrived in Chicago seven years earlier—ready to go on another life-changing adventure.

Two weeks in the Wisconsin woods put their relationship on a new course. As luck would have it, they were playing partners during the card games on the train ride up north. "My!" Myrtle wrote. "We found it easy to laugh that night."[70]

After a few days in the Great White North, Walgreen noticed that everyone was calling Myrtle "Sis," so he asked if he could, too. She agreed, and replied, "I'll call you Sonny."

"In those days the use of first names marked an advanced friendship," she said. "Women didn't even call their husbands by their first names in public."

"When we were alone he told me about his family and some of the serious times in his life. We eased our way into a lifelong friendship. From the first we were completely comfortable together."[71]

There was, however, the little matter of Walgreen's engagement to a woman back in Dixon. But near the end of the Wisconsin sojourn, he confessed to Myrtle that he was trying to gather the courage to break it off. The connection between Walgreen and his girlfriend wasn't strong, something even Walgreen's fiancée acknowledged when she complained that his letters to her "were like icicles." After meeting Miss Norton, Walgreen concluded he had to break up with his fiancée in person, telling Myrtle before the trip ended, "You may not think much of me [for breaking off my engagement], but I'm going to try to win you if I'm free. I've fallen in love with you. You're simply the girl I've been looking for."[72]

Soon enough, the deed was done, and Walgreen was a free man. Now, to win Miss Norton's hand, Walgreen took an aggressive approach that his first fiancée would not have recognized. Every evening, after a 16-hour day working on his feet, Walgreen stopped by the Nortons' apartment and then walked a few more blocks to his place to write the object of his desire a handwritten letter, which he had "special delivered" to Miss Norton the next day. These letters, it is safe to assume, did not remind Miss Norton of icicles or of any other frozen creation. She was as smitten with him as he was with her. The romance moved swiftly, culminating in their wedding on August 18, 1902—just a year after their camping trip.

Not only did the date mark the beginning of a very happy home life, but it would also prove to be the most important decision anyone ever made in the history of the Walgreen Company.

diving in—together

The 1902 wedding of Charles Sr. and Myrtle secured the Walgreens' family life forever. By all accounts, their marriage was a happy one, made stronger by the birth of Charles Jr. (or "Chuck," as he was soon known) in 1906 and Ruth, with bright red hair, in 1910. Despite working long, arduous hours, Charles Sr. would come home and get on all fours to thrill his young children, barking like a dog and bucking like a bronco to make them laugh.

Walgreen's happy family life didn't answer the questions in his professional life, however. Although he had just taken out a heavy loan to become a co-owner of Blood's store about the same time he met Myrtle and was only a year and change into paying off the loan when the two were married, he still appeared far from committed to a lifelong career in pharmacology.

Walgreen's restlessness manifested itself the day after their wedding in Seattle, where Myrtle had family. Walgreen spent their "honeymoon week" scouting the area for potential store sights, settling on one appealing corner—a corner the company would revisit decades later—before finally deciding the time wasn't right.

The Walgreens returned to Chicago, determined to pay off the store loan as soon as possible. Through their frugality, the Walgreens were able to put half his salary toward the loan payment each month. The young couple allotted themselves only $25 per month for rent. The best place Myrtle could find, however, was a tiny apartment a half mile west of the store for $27.50; so they had to scrimp elsewhere, with Myrtle doing all their washing, ironing, and cooking. In the early years of their marriage, Myrtle was a truly traditional wife, rarely asking about her husband's business, especially when he came home bone-tired after a 16-hour day.

Though Walgreen was committed to following through on his first store, he still hadn't dedicated himself to the pharmacy business itself. While toiling on Cottage Grove, he dabbled in a Los Angeles wrapping paper company, an Idaho mining outfit, and a Chicago grain commodities firm. He also tried opening new stores with friends in Dixon, Illinois, and Hot Springs, Arkansas; but these expansions proved premature. Instead of strengthening Walgreen's new-born company, these side interests proved a distraction from his core store; so he decided to sell off his holdings to the partners involved.

Since he had tried just about everything to avoid what seemed inevitable, Charles Walgreen Sr. finally concluded that his calling was to be a pharmacist, based in Chicago. Once he committed to this idea, things changed dramatically.

Walgreen didn't waste any time refurbishing Mr. Blood's dark and dusty old store. He replaced the cracked tile floor, converted the dangerous gaslights to electric, widened the aisles, and added a new front awning that said, "Drugs and Surgical Dressings." He was more vigilant about the quality, variety, and value of the products he displayed on his shelves. And he made certain every customer was cheerfully greeted by him or his sole employee when he or she walked in.

That last improvement might have been the most important—and one of the traits that has separated Walgreens from the rest for over a century: customer service. As with IBM, McDonald's, and FedEx in their heyday, the difference usually isn't the product but the people. Simple professionalism—especially in a field broad enough to accommodate snake oil salesmen like the deadly Dr. Holmes, "Dr. Matthews' Medicine Show," and Myrtle's old boyfriend Earl, who traveled from town to town with his father's vaudevillian "elixir act"—quickly separated Walgreen from the charlatans surrounding him, including many among those running the 1,500 drugstores operating in Chicago at the time.

Remember, this was a time when pharmacists didn't simply order and distribute pills from the manufacturers. They produced most of the customers' prescriptions themselves. So the drugstore customer back then had to put a lot more faith in the pharmacist than we do today.

All these painstaking tasks, however, didn't generate much revenue. Only 2 percent of Walgreens' profits came from the pharmacy department in the company's first decades, whereas two-thirds of the store's intake was from tobacco and soda fountains.

While other proprietors required customers to walk to their stores and wait for the pharmacist to get to them, in due time, Walgreen encouraged his patrons to call their orders in. He developed an impressive routine he called the Two Minute Drill. When a customer called, Walgreen would repeat the customer's name, address, and order as he wrote them down to ensure accuracy; then he quietly pass the slip to his assistant, Caleb Danner.

Walgreen would keep the customer on the line by discussing everything from the climate to the Cubs—who were then the dominant team in baseball—while Danner collected the items, dashed over to the customer's house, and knocked on the door. The customer would tell Walgreen that someone was at the door, find Danner there with their order, and come back to the phone to ask Mr. Walgreen, "Just how did you do that?"

It was a neat trick, one that helped spread the word that Walgreen's store was a cut above the competition. Walgreen's ability to provide such efficient service while forming friendships with his customers quickly established his place as the new standard-bearer in the neighborhood.

As Goethe, the nineteenth-century German philosopher, promised, once Walgreen committed himself, fortune started working on his behalf; and Walgreen took full advantage of the opportunities presented to him. One day, for example, a cooking pan salesman walked in to ask where he could find a good hardware store. It seems that one of his regular customers had just backed out of a 300-pan purchase, and he had to unload them. Walgreen remembered his wife's delight with her aluminum kitchenware, so he figured he might be able to sell them to other women in his drugstore better than the salesman could to the men at the hardware store. They agreed on a price, and Walgreen went to work setting them up on a table in the middle of the store. At 15 cents each, the handsome pans went fast, earning Walgreen a tidy profit and more customers. The successful gambit encouraged him to take more chances in the future to expand his merchandise selection and marketing methods.

The Walgreens were able to make their final payment on the store loan to Mr. Blood in early 1907. Decades later, Myrtle still remembered the night her hard-working husband came home, "late as usual," but this time proudly waving the final check.

"He put it in an envelope addressed to Blood, and the two strolled to the mailbox," the Kogans wrote. "Walgreen pulled down the [mailbox] flap. His smiling wife inserted the envelope, and he kissed her soundly. On the walk home, they talked of what they would do with the extra money now that no more monthly payments needed to be made. 'One of these days,' Charles said, 'I'll buy you a fur coat, Myrtle.'"[73]

The same year, the Walgreens bought their first store outright. William Valentine, Walgreen's old boss, told him he planned to sell his bigger store at Cottage Grove and 39th—the same store Walgreen left after he returned from Cuba because it was too busy and hectic to accomodate his convalescence—and move back to Terre Haute, Indiana, to buy a com-

purchased another store.

pany that made clocks. Valentine asked $15,000 for the store, 150 percent more than Walgreen paid for his first store. Walgreen protested that he simply didn't have that kind of money.

"Charlie, you were the best clerk I ever had," Valentine replied, no doubt enhancing his memory of Walgreen in light of his recent success. "And I really want you to have that store. Think it over."[74]

Walgreen had finally reached the point of no return. He could continue dabbling in this or that, looking for a quick hit or a way out of the pharmacy business, or he could decide that his future was in pharmacy and make a run of it.

"To make a down payment on a second drugstore," Charles Jr. said, "Dad had to sell a half-interest in his first store. His friends advised against it. 'Chicago has too many drugstores already,' they warned. And Dad said, 'Chicago may have too many drugstores, but it hasn't enough Walgreens drugstores.'"[75]

Walgreen's resolve was firm. "He now realized more firmly than ever that the time had come for him to move ahead in the drugstore business," the Kogans wrote. "He had no wish, as he would say again and again in later years, to drift along with a single store and continue to engage himself in outside business endeavors."[76]

Walgreen signed another loan in 1909 to buy Valentine's store. Because it stretched his finances so far, however, he could only wangle the deal with the help of Arthur C. Thorsen, a former colleague and now a pharmacist at the Armour Company pharmaceutical products plant. Thorsen agreed to buy half of Walgreen's first store. Walgreen took this money, plus some savings, to cover the down payment on Valentine's store. The two partners agreed that Thorsen would manage the first store, which was incorporated under the name "Walgreen-Thorsen," and Walgreen would own and operate the second himself, under the title "C. R. Walgreen & Company."

No one—not even Walgreen himself—could have realized it at the time, but a chain had been born, a chain that would become the greatest in drugstore history.[77]

the start of something special: 1910–1929

on his own

After opening his first store in 1901, it took Charles Walgreen Sr. a full 8 years of hard work to secure his second small store, but only 20 more years to create the foundation for an empire.

The 1910s and 1920s were probably the most demanding decades in Walgreens' history. All four family members (Charles Sr., Myrtle, and offspring Chuck and Ruth) worked ungodly hours to feed the chain's burgeoning growth. But those might have been the company's most exciting years, too, filled with boundless optimism, energy, and inno-

43

vation, without the complications and pressures future expansions would present.

Like other U.S. corporate giants—such as McDonald's and IBM—Walgreens' initial growth was built on a lot of old-fashioned values mixed with a few newfangled ideas. McDonald's grew on a foundation of friendly service and clean bathrooms, while offering something new: "fast food" and drive-thru service. IBM boomed not only because of its top-quality typewriters, but also because of Thomas Watson Jr.'s insistence that his service people wear coats and ties when visiting clients—a symbol of the respect IBM exuded for its customers, which business guru Tom Peters believes was one of Watson's greatest contributions.

Likewise, Walgreens started with attentive clerks and helpful advisors—unusual among druggists in that era, who tended to be austere and distant, standing behind their elevated counters and forbidding partitions—and offered a few things you couldn't get anywhere else.

Almost a century before business books gushed about Walt Disney employees calling their customers "guests," Charles Walgreen Sr. wrote, "Every customer is a guest in our store and should be treated as such. It is unusual service, uncommon thoughtfulness, that makes customers remember a store, brings them back, leads them to speak favorably of it to others. . . . If you can serve your customers with the same thoughtfulness, interest, courtesy, and friendliness that you would show if they were guests in your own home, then you will have satisfied customers and find greater enjoyment in your work."[1]

And as usual, he meant it.

the secrets of the second store

Walgreen's first store established him as an independent businessman, but it was his second store that set up Walgreens as something special. The shop at the corner of 39th and Cottage Grove served as a laboratory for trying out soda fountains and lunch counters; as a training ground to recruit and develop Walgreens' future leaders; and as a workshop to define and refine the fundamental functions that are the foundation of any sound business. All these components comprised the formula for success that Walgreen perfected at his second store before duplicating it all across Chicago, and then the nation.

The grand experiment almost ended before it started, however, when Walgreen heard rumors that a drugstore might be moving into a vacant storefront across the street from his second store. He was concerned enough to purchase the site of his third store—at Michigan Avenue and 55th Street—as insurance in case the rumors proved true. Walgreen was relieved to learn that, in fact, the slot across the street from his second store would be leased by a Chinese restaurant called King Joy Lo; and although Walgreen didn't care for Chinese food, he was so grateful for the early break that he made it a point to visit the restaurant regularly to make sure it stayed afloat.[2] Walgreen's fear, however, had served him well, bringing him a third store and a nice lunch.

In the 1910s, Walgreens' "world headquarters" was not the million-square-foot (actually 948,000), nine-building complex in the Chicago suburbs where Walgreens' executives have worked since 1975, but a wooden desk and two chairs near the front of Walgreens' second store.[3] It was there Walgreen concocted the ideas and hired the employees who would make that sprawling headquarters possible—even necessary—decades later.

Walgreen's second store featured handsome window displays—which Walgreen considered so important that he hired an artisan to design them, despite his shoestring budget—and glass cases filled with cigars, chocolates, and free perfume samples, more akin to a jeweler's display than anything customers expected to see in a drugstore at the time.

In the back of his second store, Walgreen installed two pay telephones that were cleverly designed to work with special slugs that customers could only get from the cashier at the front of the store. Thus, to make a simple phone call, most visitors walked past Walgreens' entire inventory three times—to the back of the store to see the phones, to the front counter to buy the slugs, and to the back again to make their calls—making any number of impulse purchases along the way.

The most impressive thing customers passed was the soda fountain. It's an anachronism today, but 90 years ago it was as unthinkable for a drugstore to be without a soda fountain as it is today for a major bookstore to be without a gourmet coffee shop.

Drugstores and soda fountains were first linked in the early nineteenth century, when pharmacies sold all manner of elixirs (many of them pure nostrum) and shots of bottled soda water, all purportedly to improve their customers' health. It's hard to fathom today the faith people had in fizzy water to cure their ills, but it explains why people traveled for hundreds of miles to visit health spas like Hot Springs, Arkansas. It also explains how something as bland as bottled seltzer water—a steely, slightly salty drink—became a staple of drugstores nationwide. While seltzer water can provide slight relief for indigestion—think Alka-Seltzer—its value might have been greater as a mainstay of vaudeville comedy.

Drugstore proprietors replaced bottled seltzer water with charged water and finally in-store soda water dispensers. They stored the bubbly water in a canister under the counter, then sent it through a tin pipe leading to an ornate spigot, similar to the systems pubs use today to serve draft beer.

"The soda fountain was a uniquely American phenomenon," Mark Pendergrast wrote in his history of Coca-Cola. "With so many new drinks available [including Coke and Dr. Pepper, created in Texas in 1885], the soda jerks had to become virtuosos at mixing drinks with grace and speed. . . . The busy late-nineteenth-century soda fountain first satisfied the American demand for fast food and drink."[4]

Though the soda fountain was popularized in the hot South, Walgreen, always looking for something to set his stores apart, had a hunch that soda fountains were the future up north, too, and decided to go all out to make his the best in the neighborhood. He acquired the space adjoining his second store, cut an archway door through the wall to connect the two rooms, installed eight booths and eight small tables, and spared no expense constructing a soda fountain on the far side with a 16-foot-long marble counter. Silver spigots dispensed the drinks; Tiffany lights illuminated the scene; and all was reflected in a 12-foot mirror framed in rich, ornately carved wood. The grand design proved so popular that he duplicated it in

Merges with Coca-Cola

each new store he opened. The work of art lent the entire room a sense of style uncommon for corner drugstores.

"For as long as he lived," Herman and Rick Kogan wrote, Walgreen "held to the firm belief that a clean, attractive, well-operated soda fountain was one of the best business-building assets a drugstore could have—a magnet that operated every hour a store was open, drawing customers who would come back again and again."[5]

Walgreen's decision to expand and enhance the soda fountain proved a very wise one indeed, generating profits and a good buzz around town. He eagerly expanded the fountain's repertoire to include ice cream cones, sundaes (so spelled to avoid offending religious customers), banana splits, carbonated drinks with flavored syrup, and a new drink that was sweeping the nation—Coca-Cola.

Like other enterprising pharmacists, who were a notoriously creative lot at the turn of the century, Walgreen started stocking his shelves with the company's own brand, including Walgreens' coffee, cod liver oil, and something called Bug Pizen, which, the package assured buyers, was "extremely efficacious in exterminating bedbugs," a product Walgreen undoubtedly wished he had had years earlier to combat the insects who ruled his flophouse apartment. But it was the introduction of Walgreens' own ice cream that transformed the nascent chain in ways no one could have anticipated.

i scream, you scream

Our love of frozen sweets started with the Romans, who created treats we'd probably categorize today as flavored ices or sorbet.[6] It took England's King Charles I to make the dairy treat we call ice cream a mainstay of the royal diet; but he loved it so much, he kept his recipe a secret from his subjects. When he was beheaded in 1649, his ability to retain the recipe for himself diminished substantially, and the formula got out. George Washington paid some $200 for a version of it, and James and Dolly Madison offered guests a dish of the sweet stuff at their second inaugural ball in 1809.

But ice cream didn't catch on with everyday citizens until three advances made it easier to make, store, and eat. (1) Nancy Johnson invented the first hand-crank ice cream maker in 1847. (2) The spread of safe and cheap electricity in the nineteenth and twentieth centuries allowed ice cream makers to refrigerate their goods (Fridgidaire introduced the first self-contained refrigerator unit in 1923).[7] And (3) the ice cream cone—invented during St. Louis's combined Olympics and World's Fair in 1904 when an ice cream vendor ran out of paper dishes and asked the waffle maker working next to him to roll a few up so he could keep selling his cold confection—made ice cream easier to sell. Small wonder that the children's song, "I Scream, You Scream, We All Scream for Ice Cream,"[8] was recorded in 1928.

Add it all up, and you have the Golden Era of Ice Cream. When Walgreen bought his first store in 1901, Americans consumed some 5 million gallons of ice cream annually; but by 1919, demand had increased 30-fold to 150 million gallons a year. Walgreen correctly sensed that the time was ripe to indulge America's sweet tooth.

When Walgreen was still focused on his second store, everyone might already have been screaming for ice cream; but Walgreen—and perhaps only Walgreen—thought it could be better. Long before people worried about fat grams, calories, or cholesterol—or even knew what they were—Walgreen wanted to make an ice cream with more butter fat than his suppliers offered. "So he installed an electric freezer in the basement of his store and made his own."[9]

Walgreen guessed right. The company's own ice cream drew customers who otherwise had no desire to enter a drugstore—but they had to, because only Walgreens sold such superrich ice cream.

the hot lunch program

The cold creations were immensely popular all summer long, but they couldn't attract customers once the weather turned chilly, which rendered

Walgreens' fancy room superfluous for the frigid half of the Chicago year. In Walgreen's first year in the second store, 1909, he closed the soda fountain from October to May, using the luxurious counter to display dry goods like soap, talcum powder, and cold cream.[10]

After another great summer watching the soda fountain draw thousands of customers, Walgreen approached his second winter in the new store with dread, confessing to Myrtle, "I never thought what a barn that [second] room would be in winter time."[11]

Walgreen decided he had to do something to make that extra space pay year round, so he once again decided to break with conventional wisdom. "I think if we served a few good sandwiches and something hot—maybe some soup—and a little dessert, we could keep that room open all winter," he said to Myrtle. "Would you help me?"[12]

Naturally, the answer was yes. Myrtle woke up each morning at dawn to buy the supplies she'd need and returned to their apartment's tiny kitchen to make one kind of sandwich, soup, cake, and pie for each day of the week—from egg salad to tongue sandwiches, chicken soup to cream of tomato, chocolate to coconut cake, and lemon cream pie to apple. She would deliver the food to the store by eleven to feed the hungry lunch crowd. "We didn't have automobiles in those days," recalled Charles Jr., who started delivering the food for his mother when he was old enough to do so, "so we always lived within walking distance of the [second] store."[13]

When Charles Sr. put a sign in the store window announcing "Home Cooking," it wasn't false advertising. The myriad delights emanating from Myrtle's kitchen drew workers from the stockyards and the switchyards, as well as housewives looking to pick up a fresh dessert for that night's family dinner—a service that, in characteristic Walgreens' style, benefited the customers as much as the company. It didn't hurt that, before World War I, Walgreens was the only drugstore to offer hot food on Chicago's South Side.

Myrtle kept up this manic effort for two years; but after the birth of Ruth in 1911, it was decided that they should hire a woman to do the cooking. But Myrtle's loyal—and fickle—clientele could taste the difference and complained. So Charles had to let the woman go and asked his wife if she could keep cooking just a little while longer.

A "little while" turned out to be three more years, until finally the demand for Myrtle's "Home Cooking" was so great—especially after Walgreen opened his fourth store in 1913—that Charles decided it was time to open a company commissary to whip up Myrtle's popular fare for all his stores. Walgreens' food division, which started in Myrtle's cozy kitchen, would produce fully a third of all company profits for a half century—and probably generated more affection and loyalty for the corporation than any other division.

Myrtle had made her mark. "Work was as natural to me as breathing," she wrote in her autobiography, at age 84. "I cooked as happily as I ate, and I swept and dusted with the same verve I had for dancing. . . . A lot of happiness was stirred, beaten, and rolled into that food."[14]

You could argue that the pharmacy has always been the soul of Walgreens, the bedrock of intellectual integrity and community service—especially during the first half of the century, when Charles and Chuck Walgreen emphasized the importance of maintaining a professional pharmacy department, even though it didn't make any money to speak of. Then the soda fountain was Walgreens' heart—the friendly, fun side that made people smile and created an emotional bond with generations of Americans, one strong enough to endure and grow even after Walgreens closed the food division.

cultivating leaders

Not only did Walgreens' gradual early growth give Charles the space to install the soda fountain and lunch counter that became Walgreens' calling card, but the new stores provided enough opportunity to allow Walgreen and Thorsen to hire and develop the core people who would direct the company's stunning growth through the mid-twentieth century.

Roland G. Schmitt's path to and through Walgreens would become a well-worn one, and it is still traveled today. The very day he enrolled in the Illinois School of Pharmacy in 1910, he noticed a "help wanted" announcement on a bulletin board at the school for a part-time apprentice at Walgreen's first store at the corner of Cottage Grove and Bowen avenues. In the same youthful spirit that Walgreen demonstrated when he hopped on a train from Dixon to Chicago 17 years earlier, Schmitt stepped on a streetcar that afternoon, introduced himself to Arthur Thorsen—who was impressed by the young man's wit and warmth—and accepted Thorsen's offer of $8 a week (just $3 more than Walgreen earned after he got off the train almost two decades before).

Schmitt worked at the store every morning for an hour and a half, took the same streetcar back to school for a day of classes, then returned to the store to work from 6 P.M. to midnight—then got up and did it again after a few hours of sleep. After graduation, Schmitt became a full-time employee, a store manager, and finally the vice president of store operations—an unusually well-liked man with an easy smile. He retired in 1960, after putting in a very productive half century with Walgreens.[15]

Like most of Walgreens' freshman class of executives, James E. Ward began his tenure at the bottom and learned about the company from the ground up on his way to the executive level. Ward struck Walgreen as an energetic, bright-eyed young man; so he hired Ward as a general utility boy at the second store on 39th Street in 1910, charging him with organizing the stockroom, making deliveries, and operating a medieval-looking machine that sharpened customers' used razor blades, if you can imagine.

A few years later, Ward was felled by a thorax ailment so puzzling that doctors of the day couldn't diagnose it, even as Ward lay wasting away in his bed. Determined to help his young understudy beat the odds, Walgreen asked a friend, Northwestern University's Dr. N. C. Gilbert, for another opinion. The resourceful doctor stopped Ward's demise by devising a way to drain the young man's lungs, starting Ward on his way to recovery. Near the end of the decade, Ward was well enough to serve in World War I. Walgreen's only recorded disappointment in Ward was his refusal to study pharmacy, though Walgreen apparently forgave him because he named

Ward his director of purchasing, a job Ward fulfilled to great acclaim for over three decades.

Walgreen's third store, at Michigan Avenue and 55th Street, not only served as a hedge against the possible failure of the second store when Walgreen heard rumors of another drugstore coming in across the street, it also attracted two young workers who would become Walgreens legends: Alphonse Starshak and Harry Goldstine.

Alphonse "Al" Starshak came in as an assistant manager and pharmacist in 1912, and Harry Goldstine came aboard the next year as a clerk. Their recruitment and rise speaks volumes about the Walgreens' approach to personnel generally. "Each man possessed qualities Walgreen admired in potential managers," the Kogans wrote, "a penchant for organization, a willingness to work long hours without complaint, a desire to increase sales and profits for the company as well as compensation for themselves, an ability to confront problems without undue stress, and, above all, a zeal for unstinting service to customers of every sort and maintenance of good relationships with employees on every level."[16]

Starshak became Walgreens' top trainer for new store managers, while Goldstine made a name for himself by developing training programs for everyone else. Both men thereby dramatically influenced the character of the company at every level long after they retired as vice presidents decades later.

growing like topsy

By 1912 the three Walgreens stores each had a professional pharmacy, a festive soda fountain, a popular lunch service (later expanded to serve three meals a day), and skilled, ambitious people to make them all hum. It was time to copy the recipe and spread it around.

Walgreens opened its fourth store in 1913 at Calumet Avenue and 43rd Street , putting the young Goldstine in charge; and its fifth store opened two years later on Cottage Grove and 35th Street, just four blocks down from its first two stores, with Starshak running the new site. Both new stores quickly proved to be as successful as their predecessors, convincing Walgreen to give the green light to more expansion plans.

The incredible growth to come and the remarkable risks Walgreen and his team would take to create it would be breathtaking to anyone but a Chicagoan living at the dawn of the twentieth century. The company's leaders had been born in Chicago or drawn to the specter of its unequaled rise as a world-class city. Since they could remember, they had seen miracles occurring all around them on an almost daily basis: the reversal of the Chicago River to better serve the young city; the town rising rapidly from the ashes of the Great Fire to become far bigger and better than before; the Columbian Exposition's fabulous White City emerging from a fetid swamp in just 18 months to wow the world; skyscrapers popping up every month, then every week, drawing neck-craning tourists from around the globe; and the growth of the city itself, from a backwater river town to one of the world's great cities in mere decades, arguably the most dramatic development of any city, anywhere, at any time.

Walgreen and his colleagues not only saw all this happen—or read about it—they felt it in their bones, breathed its spirit, and believed in its lessons. In Chicago in the early twentieth century, more than in any other place or era, anything was possible if you were willing to work for it.

In short, Walgreens would never have become the Walgreens we know today if Chicago hadn't been Chicago. At this fortuitous nexus of time and place existed the perfect storm of preconditions for a sensational success, including ambition, innovation, and confidence, coupled with the Midwestern work ethic and bedrock values that made Walgreens' early growth possible.

With the success of the first three stores, Walgreen and his management team's outlook shifted from cautious optimism to voracious enthusiasm, snapping up every promising new location they discovered. The company exploded from five stores in 1915 to nine the next year and to nineteen by

1919—every one of them at densely populated intersections on the South Side. Walgreen's predilection for busy corners remains a central tenet of the company's philosophy today, as it is making expansion decisions in the middle of another building boom.

When he reflected on the company's early success, Walgreen liked to reply, "We just grew like topsy!" Though it's unclear today what that word means (even unabridged dictionaries don't include it), it's a safe bet that Walgreen intended to express a positive assessment of the chain's acceleration.

Most of Charles Walgreen's reasons for growing so rapidly are pretty obvious—more income, profit, and security, for starters, especially when the timing was clearly right to take advantage of its winning formula—but others are less so, including increasing opportunities for the first wave of eager employees it had recruited and trained.

Of all the positions Walgreens' employees have filled over the past century, you could easily argue that the post of store manager has always been the most crucial to the company's success—and the most revered, accordingly, by underlings and superiors alike. Chief executive officers (CEOs) from Charles Walgreen Sr. to David Bernauer today have all recognized that the store manager position is the pivot point for the entire company. When managers are hired, trained, and retained properly, the rest of the company hums. But if they fail to understand their customers, employees, or the drugstore business itself, there is not much anyone in headquarters can do to save them.

Best-selling business guru Peter Drucker once observed, "Whenever anything is being accomplished, it is being done, I have learned, by a monomaniac with a mission."[17] At Walgreens, those "monomaniacs with a mission" have been the store managers more than anyone else.

From the beginning, the Kogans wrote, Charles Walgreen considered store managers to be the linchpin in the chain and encouraged them "to think of themselves as independent retailers with a large and worthwhile organization behind them—not, in contrast to the policies of other chains in or out of the drug field, above them."[18] This sense of ownership and independence inspires the best effort from store managers to this day—and is one reason turnover at that level is virtually nonexistent.

Walgreen put systems in place to ensure managers' job satisfaction. When the company opened a new store, it would install a "veteran" manager (which back then meant simply someone who had already been a Walgreens store manager previously) to get it started and then hand over the reins to a youthful go-getter like Goldstine or Starshak. The practice of putting such young, relatively inexperienced people in charge of important stores, which recent CEO Dan Jorndt calls the "quantum leap" approach of promotion, remains a central strategy at Walgreens.[19] At Walgreens, ability still trumps seniority.

To give the managers a stronger sense of ownership in their stores, from the start Walgreens gave managers bonuses based on their stores' profits, with which they were strongly encouraged to buy Walgreen stock. Roland Schmitt loved telling the story of how Charles Walgreen would present him with his regular bonus check but hold on to it tightly, refusing to hand it over until Schmitt agreed to invest it in company stock. This might seem coercive today, but as Schmitt watched his portfolio multiply over the years, he saw Charles's persuasion as excellent fiscal advice and was justly appreciative of it.

the pepper pod

As the company grew, Charles Walgreen's original "world headquarters"— a table and two chairs in the front of his all-important second store— quickly proved too small for the job. He opened his first separate office at 3470 Cottage Grove Avenue, with some manufacturing facilities attached, before moving the company headquarters to 768 Oakwood Boulevard, not far from his first store, with four offices for him and his executive team.

Communication is the key to any good organization, but when Charles was starting out, it was easy. He was always a naturally outgoing, engaging, and glib man, eager and able to develop strong personal relationships with his colleagues and his guests. By 1919, however, it became clear that the company's rapid growth was making it difficult to spread the gospel among the chain's 19 stores, hundreds of employees, and thousands of customers.

Charles combined his flairs for marketing, writing, and relationship building to come up with a creative solution: *The Pepper Pod*, a monthly publication produced to keep the "Walgreen community" connected. In December 1919, a few months after the Treaty of Versailles was signed and the Cincinnati Reds won the World Series over Walgreen's beloved White Sox in the famed "Black Sox" series, Walgreens published 50,000 copies of *The Pepper Pod*, a free publication for employees (called *Walgreen World* since the early 1970s).

The first issue ran 12 pages long, in tabloid style, with the table of contents on the front. The range of subjects listed there closely mirrored the professional priorities of the Walgreens chain and those of Charles Sr.: helpful health tips, lighthearted amusement, and, always, savvy marketing.

"In presenting the first number of *Pepper Pod*," Charles wrote on the first page, "we are perfectly frank in stating that it is issued for the purpose of increasing the business at Walgreens Drug Stores. . . . We want the *Pepper Pod* to make you more familiar with our methods of doing business. . . . It is our idea to show you that you will be better served, for less money, at our stores, than elsewhere." But, Walgreen added, "We hope to make it different from any other store paper, so that you will want it each month."[20] In other words, there was method to the madness in printing even the fluffiest features, to generate more customer loyalty.

The advice offered says a lot about the state of health care in 1919. People were just becoming self-conscious enough (and wealthy enough) to care about their appearance in a way farmers decades earlier did not. Tips on how to "Relieve Bad Breath" appeared on page nine, assuring readers they could rid themselves of halitosis "by diluting a little Golden Seal Antiseptic with eight or ten parts water, using it as a garble and swallowing a few drops." To soften your skin, the *Pepper Pod* suggested that sprinkling oatmeal in your bathwater should do the trick. (This was obviously written before the advent of instant oatmeal.)

The medical advice of the day seems foreign to a modern reader for two reasons: (1) It tends to be simultaneously more formal and earthy than we are accustomed to. (2) It is filled with equal parts scientifically sound information and *Farmer's Almanac*–style superstition. In the piece on "Constipation and How to Prevent It," for example, the Walgreens experts advise "exercise in the open air, sleep and proper ventilation of bedrooms, with abundance of nourishing food, including plenty of green vegetables and fresh fruits."

Before the Food and Drug Administration (FDA) and dietitians (the term had only been coined a few decades earlier) studied such things, Walgreens offered its views on "Purity in Candy" on page three—getting a shameless plug for its offerings in the process. "All the candy we sell can be eaten with perfect safety, in moderation, and we would not advise an immoderate use of the very best we sell. Use goods temperately and conserve your health by abstaining altogether from any edible or confection about which you have the faintest suspicion."

The newsletter justified its liberal approach to proferring medical advice as follows: "As purveyors of health-giving merchandise, we feel it within our sphere to disseminate knowledge as to natural or, we might say, common sense measures of maintaining health." In doing so, Walgreens added to the centuries-long debate over who, exactly, should be giving out medical assistance to customers. The company's stated position in the inaugural *Pepper Pod* would be radically revised after World War II by Charles's son Chuck.

To attract a wider range of readers, the *Pepper Pod* also included some lighter fare, such as rhyming, perky poetry written by an employee named Marie Geiger, riddles and jokes, like the following.

HOKUS: Is it true that bleaching hair causes insanity?
POKUS: "Well, I know many a fellow who is simply crazy over a blonde."

You get the idea.

For the kids, the *Pepper Pod* printed a story, probably written by Charles himself—an experienced bedtime story teller—titled "Trotty Twinkletail's Thanksgiving."

Charles's fervent patriotism and strong political opinions—he was a card-carrying Republican throughout his life, a true example of compassionate conservatism—also found voice in the *Pepper Pod*. The first issue featured an essay on tax money being wasted by the sluggish Chicago courts and a letter from a Walgreen friend in post–World War I Berlin, who admitted to being, "homesick as a pup . . . because, believe me, everything is nothing beside the good old U.S.A. You hear that kind of talk in songs and in poetry, but you don't know what it means until you go up against it." As proof, Walgreen's friend discussed the German Railroad system, which was "almost at a collapse—like everything else—and the trains are few and very crowded." The correspondent's train ride from Hanover to Berlin took an excessive five hours, with hundreds standing up the whole way.

The messages weren't subtle, nor was the commercial intent of the publication, which Walgreen had made disarmingly clear on page one. With Walgreens' manufacturing plant going full speed, Charles was eager to push their in-store products. The *Pepper Pod* advertised cold cream, vanishing cream, citrus cream, and cucumber lotion for 25 cents to 35 cents a jar. (Charles's "focus group" for these products, and many others, was a one-woman team named Myrtle, who once found herself sampling 10 tubes of toothpaste for the purchasing department.) For the men, Walgreens offered Cuban cigars, decades before they were outlawed in the United States, and aftershave lotion for 35 cents a tube, purported to be "soothing, cooling, and healing, easy to apply, never sticky, and much to be preferred to plain bay rum or witch hazel."

Charles also put in a good word for Walgreens' own "Plum Whip Ice

Cream . . . to make your Xmas dinner complete . . . a Real Confection, a Delightful Novelty," consisting of chopped plums and whipped cream, mixed, "and all frozen together into a brick of unalloyed enchantment," for 60 cents.

Many items listed, however, are still familiar to a contemporary consumer, such as Colgate toiletries, Waterman fountain pens, and Kodak cameras. The fabulous folding model sold for $29.36, with the basic Brownie going for $2.86.

Gillette blades cost a dollar at most stores, but only 69 cents at Walgreens, which Charles felt compelled to defend. "Gillette Blades is not the only item we sell so cheaply as to invite skepticism," he wrote. "Take our Coffee—we sell tons of it—but many people will not even try it because it seems too cheap to be any good. But it IS good—as good as any at any price, and better than 90 percent of that sold for me. Don't be afraid of anything sold at a Walgreens store, for quantity buying permits low prices."[21]

The *Pepper Pod* served its purpose; and in the early 1970s, Walgreens changed the name to *Walgreen World*. Walgreens has produced 70 volumes of the *Pepper Pod*—650 issues, millions of copies' worth—confirming the wisdom of yet another Charles Walgreen innovation.

steppin' out

Like his newsletter, Walgreen believed that "all work and no play" made for dull boys, so he had no qualms about diverting some of his expanding fortune for fun. The family bought a new home on Drexel Boulevard catering to all Walgreen's favorite pastimes, including rooms for reading, ping-pong, billiards, and a bar.

In 1910, the Walgreens joined the Waupansa Club on Drexel Boulevard, a respected social club, so Charles could frequent a more refined setting to play his favorite game, billiards, than the neighborhood halls. (However, he never stopped visiting the local pool halls altogether.)

The Waupansa Club also featured bridge nights and dancing. Charles taught Myrtle how to play bridge, and she returned the favor by teaching her husband how to dance. Both learned the other's specialty passably well, but Charles disavowed ever dancing with anyone but his wife because, he said, "I would never inflict myself on another lady."[22]

With the Walgreens' elevated income bracket came elevated tastes. The family joined the comprehensive Calumet Country Club in 1916 inspiring Charles to take up golf, which he did with his characteristically earnest, systematic approach, taking lessons, reading books, studying each club's function, and practicing constantly. He soon was as proficient on the fairways in his forties as he had been on the sandlot diamonds as a kid, playing regular rounds with people outside the Walgreen Company to expand his network of friends. Even leisure time was often used to forward the company's interests—and since Walgreen always wore a suit and tie when he played, it might not have been that leisurely, either.

Although Charles's daily schedule was naturally jam-packed, he found time to take a course to improve his memory and got it down well enough to entertain his friends by memorizing the sequence of a deck of cards, which they then took with them, and reciting the correct order of the cards a month later. Any salesman can tell you how valuable it is to have a sharp memory, especially one for names, and Charles honed that advantage.

In his remaining free time, Charles liked to spin bedtime stories for Chuck and Ruth. During the national influenza epidemic of 1918, when the Walgreens were quarantined in their beds for three weeks, Charles rose to the occasion by telling long stories every night, many of which Chuck can still recall today, in his late nineties.

On Walgreen's bedside table, he kept a rotating stack of books. A voracious reader, Walgreen loved popular history and biography—the preferred genres, it seems, of successful executives, generals, and football coaches—but he had a weakness for *Robinson Crusoe* and its lesson of "the middle way." "The middle station of life was calculated for all kinds of virtues and all kinds of enjoyments," Daniel Defoe wrote in 1719, "that temperance, moderation, quietness, health, society, all agreeable diversions, and all desirable pleasures were the blessings of attending the middle station of life."[23]

"It means," Walgreen explained it to his children, "that if you're too poor, you can't be what you want to be nor do what you ought to do, and if you're too rich, you get worried about losing your money and belongings."[24]

By following the virtues extolled by the book, ironically, Walgreen would break his own rule and become "too rich"—though it must be said the family has, on the whole, handled it much better than have other American dynasties.

At the dawn of the new decade, the Walgreen Company owned and operated 20 stores in the Chicago area, all but one on the South Side; but even that impressive growth, accomplished in just 10 years, was about to be dwarfed in the next decade by an explosive expansion program—one fueled by milk shakes.

chicago in the roaring twenties

To anyone who lived through the 1990s, a thumbnail sketch of the Roaring Twenties will sound very familiar, indeed: a decade of unprecedented peace and prosperity, fun and frivolity, which came crashing down at the decade's close. The landing in the 1920s, however, was a lot rougher than that in the 1990s.

Fatigued by the drudgery of farm life and worn out by the horrors of the Great War, young Americans moved to cities like Chicago by the millions. There they discovered hair bobs and hip flasks, jazz clubs and ball clubs.

The decade marked the Golden Era of Sports. Fans flocked to see Babe Ruth, Bobby Jones, Bill Tilden, and Jack Dempsey. A brand new circuit, the National Hockey League, started a franchise in Chicago called the Blackhawks, in honor of the tribe Abraham Lincoln's unit fought outside Dixon, Illinois, in 1832.[25]

The public's immense interest in college football justified the construction of colossal stadiums at Ohio State, Michigan, Notre Dame, Northwestern, the University of Chicago (which was a charter member of the Big Ten under Amos Alonzo Stagg), and the University of Illinois, where Red Grange ran wild before signing with the Chicago Bears to play in sparkling new Soldier Field, which many believe saved the embryonic National Football League (NFL) from extinction.

It was an era when anything seemed possible, from Lucky Lindbergh's trans-Atlantic flight to Hollywood's first "talkie" (Al Jolson's *Jazz Singer*) to a fundamentally new form of literature—direct, spartan, and scandalous for its adult themes—ushered in by Oak Park, Illinois, native Ernest Hemingway. Margaret Sanger introduced the diaphragm to the public, while drugstores like Walgreens began selling condoms, the only thing proven during the Great War to stop the epidemic spread of venereal disease.

The Twenties acted like a flask of bootleg whiskey on the American psyche, reducing inhibitions and inciting silliness, but also creating a climate that cultivated misconduct—not to mention spawning the national hangover that followed.

The Harding administration's troubles only confirmed the public's feelings of betrayal, which peaked in 1922 when investigators discovered Harding's Secretary of the Interior had been selling drilling rights on federal lands in Teapot Dome, Wyoming, in exchange for hundreds of thousands of dollars in kickbacks, stock, and cattle.

Nothing encouraged widespread lawlessness, however, like the Nineteenth Amendment: Prohibition. Even average, otherwise law-abiding citizens, including Charles Walgreen himself (he definitely broke this law), found it impossible to follow this edict every day. Terms like "moonshine," "bootlegging," and "organized crime" all entered the American lexicon.

People would go to incredible lengths to get their lips on a few sips of alcohol, in just about any form they could get it. The production of legal sacramental wine, for example, increased by hundreds of thousands of gallons, suggesting either an amazing upturn in the number of church-goers or an epidemic of illicit alcohol use among everyday Americans.[26]

And they became increasingly creative in finding and exploiting loop-holes, including prescriptions for the "medicinal use" of alcohol, particularly whiskey. This naturally led to pervasive abuse of the law in drugstores, many of which popped up as mere fronts for selling liquor, often with counterfeit prescription blanks.[27] The State of Illinois tried to stop these manipulations in 1925 by requiring people who owned and operated drugstores to be licensed pharmacists. Walgreens kept its nose admirably clean; but like all drugstores, it still had alcohol in every store, and it was not the pharmacist's job to judge the customer, only to fill his or her prescription. And sometimes the problems occurred after hours. Charles Jr. remembers that whenever there was a fire in one of the stores—which almost always started in the kitchen, far from the pharmacy in the back—his father "wanted the fire department to get in as fast as possible and get out as fast as possible, because whenever they came in we'd always lose a case or two of liquor" from the back.[28]

Chicago found itself at the epicenter of the Roaring Twenties, from its unequaled reputation as a sports-crazed town to its central role in the illegal alcohol trade. When infamous Chicago mobster Al Capone was accused of smuggling whiskey from north of the border, he replied, "Canada? I don't even know what street it's on."[29]

Like so many Chicagoans, Capone was a Walgreens regular. He lived near the Hotel Woodlawn, which had a Walgreens on the first floor. According to Charles (Cork) Walgreen III, the store had a secret passageway through the pharmacy department that went down into the stockroom and from there "out somewhere." Capone apparently found it to his liking and used it more than once.[30]

For his part, Charles Walgreen was not a teetotaler, but he was no faux-pharmaceutical rum runner, either. Walgreen liked to shoot billiards at the pool hall across the street from his second store, to bet at the track, and to play poker with friends. Like virtually every other resident of Chicago—arguably the world's most thoroughly corrupt city in the 1920s—Walgreen enjoyed an occasional drink, and he wasn't going to let Prohibition change his habits much. He had a recipe for a drink called the

"Thunderbolt," which consisted of the remains from all the bottles on the bar, some ice, and a little champagne, "and that's it," Cork said. "If you have two of them, you're on the floor!"[31]

Around this time, Walgreen bought a cruising boat, the *Dixonia*, on which he had installed a secret bar—one designed to flip over, out of sight, if authorities happened to board. On the boat, Walgreen also had what looked to be a large, brass handbell; but instead of a hollow center for the clapper to do its work, the bottom was sealed to store a couple fifths of whiskey. The wooden handle screwed off to allow filling or emptying the container as needed.

Walgreen's personal life, which was otherwise above reproach, is one thing. His professional life was another. True, certain unethical customers (in concert with unethical doctors) might have slipped a Walgreens pharmacist an occasional prescription for "medicinal whiskey"; but there is no indication such behavior was countenanced by the company, which kept its sterling reputation throughout the era. When a devil's brew of dubious practices was washing over the city, there was never a whiff of institutional impropriety surrounding Walgreens, in this or any era.

It also simply wouldn't make business sense for Walgreens to become involved in the common "side business" of phony pharmacies. At the start of Prohibition, Walgreens was already one of the biggest chains in Chicago; and by the end of it, Walgreens had become *the* biggest chain in the country. The growth of Walgreens was partly due to its uncompromising approach to its pharmacy, the most professional around in an era rife with quackery. Risking a bust just didn't bear cost-benefit analysis. More important, Walgreen's demand for discipline among his troops was legendary. It seems highly unlikely for a CEO famous for stressing honesty above all in his troops to want to get involved in running whiskey on the side. Further, as we'll see, it wouldn't make sense for Walgreens to put so much effort into attracting customers through its marketing, its products, and its soda fountains to earn honest profits if it intended to use the store as a front for rum running.

Walgreen struck a blow for morality when he changed the design of his stores because of an impromptu visit he made. At the time, pharmacists had the luxury of working in privacy behind a tall partition. One day, Walgreen stopped in one of his stores and found the manager sitting on a stool behind the partition, with the cashier on one knee, the cosmetician on the other, and a bottle of "medicinal whiskey" being passed among them. Walgreen left without a word, but he fired the manager the next day and ordered carpenters to cut the partitions in half at all their Walgreens stores. "Everyone copied us," Cork said, "but they didn't know why!"[32]

on the lighter side

True to the spirit of the decade, Walgreens set up an endless series of promotions to dazzle and attract customers, giving them a reason to remember their visits. These promotions included Goldfish Giveaways, One-Cent Sales, and Surprise Package Sales of some secret merchandise. These marketing tricks caught the public's attention while moving a lot of unwanted inventory in a most clever manner.

"One reason for my dad's success was his belief in controlling inventory," Charles Jr. said in an interview, still lucid at age 97. "He'd get all his leftover merchandise and put on a One-Cent Sale or wrap it in a nice box and have a Surprise Sale. He'd sell it to the customer for a dollar, with the guarantee that whatever was inside was worth at least five dollars. You couldn't return it, but we never had any complaints, because it was always a surprise. This worked great for merchandise we were trying to get rid of. Everyone was happy."[33]

The Goldfish Giveaway worked just as well. Walgreen set up large aquariums filled with colorful fish in each store, which naturally drew people to the display, and offered them a free goldfish with every purchase of a dollar or more. "You'd get a goldfish in a little paper carton," Charles Jr. recalled, "and that worked out great, because then they'd want to buy a goldfish bowl, and that covered the cost for the goldfish."[34] The additional supplies customers bought for their new fish put Walgreens in the black for each Goldfish Giveaway.

Charles Walgreen Sr. caught the decade's economic boom, too, though only on Chicago's South Side at first. He had long sworn off starting stores inside Chicago's glamorous but pricey Loop, but ultimately he couldn't resist.

Walgreen made the leap in 1921 and located his first Loop store at 17 E. Washington, in the Venetian Building. To ensure the store's success, he sent a handful of his best people to work at the new branch, including fountain manager Ivar "Pop" Coulson. Walgreen's belief in the power of soda fountains to give a store personality and charm ran deep, indeed. As he told *Chain Store Age* (now *Drugstore News*), "Fountains are the magnets drawing customers into the stores."[35]

A key to Walgreens' success was a two-pronged approach: (1) The pharmacy gave the chain credibility, which explains why Walgreen was such a stickler for integrity behind the counter when others were selling snake oil and why he insisted on having the best pharmacies in town even when they were losing money. The pharmacy was always the foundation of the business, Walgreens' soul. (2) The soda fountain, however, was pure fun. If most drugstores of the day couldn't match Walgreens' reputation for professionalism, those that could surely could not match Walgreens' soda fountain excitement—the heart of the business, the side that reached out to customers and made them feel welcome. While the pharmacy fostered trust, the soda fountain generated warmth. It was a tough combination to beat.

This explains why Walgreen spared no expense on his soda fountains. When you entered a Walgreens in the 1920s, you'd walk along the immaculate wooden floors to the booths built from sturdy hardwood, or to the tables in the middle of the room covered in white linen, or to one of the stools lining the long, gleaming, white marble counter (including a 78-footer in Milwaukee). You'd see another white marble counter running along the wall for the clerks to do their work, with a seemingly endless supply of confections neatly ordered on mahogany shelves and in glass cabinets, rows of bright lights suggesting a dressing room mirror, and even vaulted ceilings, with ornate carvings and tiles trimming the work.

A Walgreens soda jerk—dressed in white pressed pants, an apron, white dress shirt, tightly knotted bow-tie, and a white cloth hat—would ask, "How're you doing?" with the kind of energy that gave you a little boost and would then take your order. He'd work the brass taps to draw you a Coca-Cola, or he would mix you a malt in shiny steel blenders along the wall and pour your treat into fluted, crystal clear glasses, specially designed for this purpose.

And that's where Coulson was born to work. Like so many Walgreens' cognescenti, Coulson started at the chain's second store, a star of the Chocolate Annex, 1914. Coulson was a natural behind the counter, the kind of guy who could engage whoever sat down at his soda fountain— young or old, rich or poor—like a seasoned bartender. Coulson loved it when the traveling vaudeville stars stopped in while taking a break from their work at the theaters nearby. Coulson would laugh at their jokes and then pass them on to his customers.

But Pop Coulson made his greatest contributions at the controls behind the counter. Some people have green thumbs for making plants grow or a knack for making cars hum. Coulson had a natural affinity for the soda fountain and a love for creating new concoctions with all the goodies available behind the counter.

In the 1920s, many drugstores served malts, which consisted of milk, chocolate syrup, and a spoonful of malt powder, all mixed in a metal container and served in a fancy glass. But on an especially hot summer day in 1922, Pop Coulson hit upon his "eureka" invention and added a quintessential item to the American culinary repertoire in the process. To the tried-and-true malt recipe, Coulson added a generous scoop of Walgreens' famous Double Rich Ice Cream (manufactured in its own plant on East 40th Street in Chicago), then a second scoop, stirred it together in the mixer, and served it with two vanilla cookies (from the company bakery) on the side—all for just 20 cents.

The milkshake was born!

Customers lined the block around Walgreens' Loop store, waiting to try Coulson's creamy creation. Walgreen noticed the tumult and quickly spread Coulson's recipe to his other stores—now numbering over 20. The sinful sensation was raved about in newspapers and talked about in every city where there was a Walgreens. But most of all, it was the object of much adoration. It was not at all unusual to see long lines outside Walgreens stores and customers standing three and four deep at the fountain waiting for the new drink. Suddenly, "Meet me at Walgreens for a shake and a sandwich" became bywords as popular as "Meet me under the Marshall Fields clock" at State and Randolph in Chicago.[36]

Once again, Charles Walgreen's prediction that his soda fountain would be absolutely essential to his stores as a source of revenue, company growth, and increased customer satisfaction (which translated into even higher levels of customer loyalty and patronage) came true. In its own way, Coulson's malted milkshake was the fuel for Walgreens' dramatic growth.

While Walgreens' Double Rich Chocolate Malted was taking the city by storm, a young man named Frank Berlin, just out of high school, was working at a soda fountain in a Duluth, Minnesota, drugstore chain called Liggett's. He'd heard of Walgreens' new drink from salesmen making their rounds, who told him demand was so great they had 500 mixers working at once. Naturally, he wanted to see what the fuss was all about; so he took a train trip to the shake's birthplace. There weren't 500 mixers, of course, but Walgreens did have six mixers at eight different soda fountain stations, whirring nonstop to churn out shakes for an insatiable public. "You couldn't hear yourself think, there was so much noise," Berlin recalled. "That was some drink, that double Chocolate Malted. Very, very popular!" He was so impressed that he embarked on a successful career at Walgreens before becoming a successful plastics manufacturer.[37]

"One of our regular customers was a big, tough-looking guy with a scar on one cheek," recalled Hubert Wolfe, a fountain clerk at the Walgreens at Clark and Jackson. "Whenever he came in, he had two equally tough looking guys with him. He always ordered a Double Chocolate Malted with a raw egg in it. And he always left a dollar tip. I later found out he was none other than Al Capone."[38]

fundamental values

Charles Walgreen's stores might have been known for milk shakes and goldfish, but they endured by adhering to the timeless values of honesty and respect toward Walgreens' employees and customers. In this over-heated decade, when sensations disappeared as fast as they arrived—with flappers, the Charleston, and pole sitting just a few convenient examples—Walgreens stood the test of time.

Walgreen first sought to treat his employees well, and he believed that they, in turn, would treat the customers like guests. Although we have no record of Walgreen's views on the Haymarket Affair, in which six workers striking for an eight-hour workday were fatally shot by Chicago police in 1886, or of the deplorable working conditions at the Chicago stockyards, it is easy to believe that Walgreen's unusually enlightened approach to labor relations—especially for his time—was shaped partly by Chicago's notorious reputation as the nation's center for labor unrest.

Walgreen sought to hire the best people available for every opening he had, utterly unthreatened by talented underlings. He had a keen eye for ability and character, and he had enough humility to help it flourish in his company.

"Mr. Walgreen was a wonderful man, [but] a stern man," recalled retiree Lester Schaffner, of Oak Lawn, Illinois. "As long as you did your work, you had no problem with him." Early in Schaffner's career, Walgreen came into his store. "I wanted to make points, so I called out, 'Hello, Mr. Walgreen.' [But] he wagged his finger telling me to come over and said, 'When I come into this store, I don't want you to announce me.' He wanted to see what was going on."[39]

Myrtle observed:

Charles always said the reason the business grew was because he was lucky in the men who came to manage stores. I don't know how many times he used to come home and remark, "Well, today I hired another man who is smarter than I am." I would make the wifely comment about nobody being smarter than he was, not in the drug business. But he would say, "You're dead wrong; the only really smart thing about me is that I know enough to hire men who are smarter than I am." He certainly did get capable men: men who were far-sighted, loyal, hard-working, and capable. They all helped to make Chicago and the business grow."[40]

While other companies were still practicing the old-school style of management—browbeat your employees until they quit, then get new ones—Walgreen tried to make his stores the kinds of places where he would want to work. His checkered history as a desultory store clerk prob-ably taught him better than anything else what not to do to get the best performance out of his staff.

For starters, Walgreen made it a point to pay his employees better than his competitors did. His motives were probably equal parts business strat-egy and altruism (he was an unusually generous man, with friends, family, and colleagues). He knew if he wanted the best people, he had to pay them like they were the best. But he also knew the only way to avoid being handcuffed by a workers' union telling him how to run his business was to treat his people well enough so they wouldn't be tempted to unionize in the important service jobs. As Chuck put it:

Dad did not disbelieve in unions, and he didn't mind recognizing them, like the carpenters and electricians and tradesmen who worked on our stores, just as long as it didn't include the pharmacists or other people who worked *in* our stores. We paid well, better than the union rate, so I thought it was stupid for our employees to con-sider union membership when the [union members'] pay and benefits weren't as good as ours. I guess they [thought it stupid], too, because we really never had a movement to unionize. . . . Treating our people right was embedded in me pretty much by my dad, his philosophy. We treated the employees well, and still do."[41]

Walgreens' turnover rate, then and now, remains among the lowest in the retail sector.

More important to Walgreen than saving money was preserving the culture he worked so hard to establish, a culture that set his people up for success, not failure. As early as 1916, when Walgreen consolidated the nine existing stores under the Walgreen Company umbrella, he sought to protect the entrepreneurial approach that drove the chain's initial growth: providing his employees with plenty of incentives to stay with the company. These included opportunities for partnerships at each store, bonuses and stock offerings, promoting from within, and giving employees the autonomy necessary to make their mark. This simple but effective philosophy has been a central plank in the company platform since the beginning.

putting out fires

DIFFICULTY WITH CUSTOMERS but make it !

In addition to all the intangibles, including goodwill, that accrue from treating employees right, Walgreen understood clearly that the main purpose of such treatment was to ensure that employees would treat their customers right.

There is no better example of Walgreen's philosophy of customer service than his advice on how to handle unhappy customers. It is a treatise of sound thinking on a tricky but vital topic for almost anyone dealing with the public—which is to say, everyone—but especially those working in the often aggravating world of retail. That Walgreen wrote this in late summer of 1923 in an internal issue of the *Pepper Pod*—decades before corporations habitually paid customer relation consultants thousands of dollars per day for half the wisdom contained here—is rather stunning.

Titled "Displeased Customers,"[42] Walgreen wrote:

> The business of handling displeased customers is simply a matter of a little tact and a lot of common sense.
>
> A customer who has been inconvenienced for some reason or other by an unsatisfactory purchase will often lose his temper and perhaps be quite unreasonable in his arguments. In handling such a customer, always bear in mind that if you were in his position, you might be angry, too, and don't forget that no matter what attitude he takes, he is a Walgreens customer and must be treated courteously and with respect.

You'll note that Walgreen quickly dismisses the "customer is always right" philosophy for something more realistic (not to mention more sympathetic to his clerk): The customer may well be very wrong, even insulting, but it won't help you to point it out. Walgreen counseled:

> Never argue. Don't even talk until your customer has told his whole story. Don't interrupt. After he has finished his story and is relieved, tell him in a quiet, controlled voice that you are very sorry that he has been put to any trouble. Say that you understand how he feels about the matter, etc., and don't blame him for being exasperated.

Another sage morsel: Interrupting or objecting to a customer's rant—no matter how unjustified—is tantamount to trying to stop a running chain saw with your hand. You'll only get your fingers sliced off, and the chain saw won't notice. Better to let it run itself out of energy, in its own time, before taking remedial action.

> It sometimes happens that a customer's complaint is unjustified. In such a case, explain your side of the matter quietly and calmly, reminding your customer that there is this or that to be taken into con-

sideration, too; but even though the customer does appear to be wrong, make an exchange or the adjustment he asks, at the expense of the store. And such expense will amount to nothing as compared with the goodwill created.

Walgreen wanted his employees to understand that even if the customer was not right, they shouldn't be afraid to help the customer understand the larger picture, and they should make sure he or she went away feeling good about the exchange, in any case. Notice also Walgreen gave his employees carte blanche to "give away the store," to borrow the terminology of those who take a penny-wise, pound-foolish approach to customer service. To allow his employees to dip into the company's supplies or cash registers to rectify the situation not only eased the customer's anger but also let the employee know that she or he was a valued member of the Walgreens' team, one trusted enough to make such decisions without first consulting with the boss or filling out forms while the customer seethed. This is crucial, because handling upset customers is often like putting out a fire: The sooner you get to it, the smaller it's going to be and the less likely it is to spread.

And there was something else to be gained. "Displeased customers, if handled diplomatically, can be converted into strong boosters." The most fervent believers, after all, are converts. Characteristically, Walgreen was thinking of the future, with optimism and an eye on the bottom line. He'd rather see his employees return a few bucks than lose a repeat customer.

Remember that Walgreen wrote this long before Americans knew anything of the Better Business Bureau, Ralph Nader, or class action lawsuits. No, this was the era in which Henry Ford displayed the retailers' contempt for the public when he stated that customers could buy his cars in any color they wanted, so long as it was black.

When it came to customer service—and, by proxy, employee relations—Walgreen was way ahead of his time.

the walgreen creed

In 1922, the same year Pop Coulson came up with his earth-shattering shake, Charles Walgreen Sr. did something far less splashy—but far more lasting—when he finally published in the chain newsletter the company creed he had composed when he started his first store.

> We believe in the goods we merchandise, in ourselves and our ability to render satisfaction. We believe that honest goods can be sold to honest people by honest methods.
>
> We believe in working, not waiting; in laughing, not weeping; in boosting, not knocking; and in the pleasure of selling products. We believe that we can get what we go after and that we are not down and out until we have lost faith in ourselves.
>
> We believe in today and the work we are doing, in tomorrow and the work we hope to do, and in the sure reward the future holds. We believe in courtesy, in kindness, in generosity, in cheer, in friendship, and in honest competition.[43]

Decades before hollow "mission statements" became a national fad, this simple, sincere declaration laid down the fundamental values that Walgreens would follow to the present.

"Every dot-com starts out and says, 'What's our corporate culture?' Well, you don't have one!" exclaimed Dan Jorndt, who served as a Walgreens pharmacist, store manager, district manager, treasurer, and CEO in his 40-year career. Jorndt continued:

> You can't just adopt one or manufacture one. This culture here is real, and it goes back a long, long way. It's something solid, something tangible.
>
> The original Walgreen was an affable, able, effective, and honest guy—how's that for alliteration?—the kind of guy who knew what he wanted his company to look like, the kind of guy you can build a

company on. He had the kind of values that last. You've probably seen the Walgreen Creed, something he wrote years ago. Well, we read it at our store managers' meetings, and we get goose bumps. It's that good."[44]

the knight report

65 Stores.

Walgreen's approach caught on with his people, who in turn captured his customers. From 1920 to 1925, the chain expanded from 20 to 65 stores, all but six of them in Chicago.

Such rapid growth, coupled with Walgreens' noticeably consistent, principled approach to customer service, naturally started drawing attention from professional observers of such things. The University of Chicago (U-C) found itself surrounded by Walgreens' South Side stores by mid-decade, so it was only a matter of time before someone there decided to take a closer look.

In 1925, a business professor named James O. McKinsey, who later served as chairman of Marshall Field and Company, became increasingly curious about the well-run company and suggested that one of his protégés, Robert Knight, make a formal study of the chain for his master's thesis. What started as a casual office-hour chat became a report that would help shape the company far beyond World War II.

Robert Greenwell Knight was born in England and raised in Canada, where he starred in the classroom and on the debate team—two skills that would serve him well throughout his life—at the University of Manitoba in Winnipeg. He migrated to Chicago to study for his master's degree at U-C's Department of Commerce and Administration (now called the Graduate School of Business), where he met Professor McKinsey.

Once McKinsey unleashed Knight on the Walgreens assignment, the young graduate sunk his teeth into it like it was red meat, spending most of 1925 dissecting everything from individual window displays to corporate accounting practices; interviewing clerks, soda jerks, and executives; and producing 127 pages of transcripts and statistics, observations and suggestions—the first comprehensive analysis of the chain by an outsider, and still one of the few ever conducted.

Knight opened his report by addressing the issue of chain stores, a hot topic at the time because chains had only recently begun to challenge the mom-and-pop operations that still claimed the vast majority of retail business. (Chain restaurants and hotels—the first thing we think of today when we consider chain operations—would not be seen for decades.) All things considered, Knight wrote, the chain store was "the most effective medium for supplying consumer wants at fair prices." (The debate would not end there, as we'll see, but Knight's conclusion was obviously shared by most consumers of the day.)[45]

Having taken care of the chain issue for the time being, Knight then went on to address Walgreens in particular, dividing his study between the microeconomics of the operation of the typical Walgreens store and the macroeconomics of operating the entire chain.

On the micro side, Knight gave Walgreens very high marks. Unlike most chain retailers, Knight observed, which stressed the importance of adhering to centrally determined procedures at the expense of the individual judgment of its store employees, "The Walgreen Company believes in the exact reverse and refuses to put into practice many of the methods of close central control."[46]

Despite the premium Walgreens placed on autonomy, however, there were plenty of points of consistency across the chain, including excellent customer service ("Strongly believed and rigidly enforced") and a commitment to a professional pharmacy department in each store ("whether it pays or does not pay—a policy which is by no means universal with chain drugstore organizations"). Knight reasoned that such measures contributed to "the development of the drugstore from the old fashioned chemist's emporium to the modern convenience goods department store."[47]

Although Knight described the company's store operations procedures as "few and informal," he felt the chain could get away with it because communication between the central office and the outlets was constant. One way Walgreens negotiated this tricky balance between its desire to keep motivated, largely autonomous store managers while maintaining consistent presentation across the chain was to send Harry Goldstine's two "traveling agents" to the stores every day to see how they were doing, to collect their best practices, and to share those of other stores with them.

The traveling duo also served as talent scouts, just as Walgreens traveling zone and district managers do today. When they visited a store facing a particular problem, the company reps helped fix it. If the problem proved intractable or if the employees were genuinely incompetent or "uncoachable," the agents had the power to recommend closing a store or firing a staff member, though Knight noted such drastic steps were too rare to impinge on the spirit of friendly cooperation that existed between the stores and the central office. The approach was visit, share, and monitor, but avoid dictating—much like Walgreens' approach today.

The central office reached out to the stores in other ways, too. At the time of Knight's report, the company produced a daily, one-page *Pepper Pod* for its employees, containing all manner of marketing advice, price notices, and managerial tips—plus an occasional motivational pep talk—every word written or reviewed by Charles and printed on a single mimeographed sheet by Walgreen's secretary, Florence Lynch. (Current employees might recognize this as a forerunner to retired CEO Dan Jorndt's weekly "Jorndt's Jolts," which were so good that the company had them collected into a volume. They have been succeeded by current CEO Dave Bernauer's "Dose of Dave.")

Knight gave other aspects of the macroeconomic side of the organization mixed reviews—strong on central marketing and purchasing, inefficient in accounting practices.

Knight confirmed what everyone already knew—that marketing was one of the company's greatest strengths, from the beginning—but he shed some light on why: the remarkable dedication Walgreens had to presenting a good store image and promoting it.

Always a firm believer in advertising—a legacy of the patent medicine business, the first American industry to fully exploit the tactic—Walgreen once told an interviewer, "No business can prosper without letting the public know of its existence and the values it offers."[48]

He put the company's money where his mouth was and consistently spent 2 percent to 3 percent of his revenues on newspaper ads. It might not sound like much, but that figure represented the profit margin for many stores and, in real dollars, adds up fast: $54,887 in 1922, up to $245,788 just two years later, thanks to the increase in both the number of stores and the revenues per store.

On November 16, 1922, Walgreens took a bold step when it bought its first full-page ad in the *Chicago Tribune* to announce "Chicago's Leading Drug Sale" for that Thursday, Friday, and Saturday, the most popular shopping days, Walgreens had learned. Among the attractions offered that a modern reader might recognize were Listerine for 67 cents a bottle, Pepsodent at 31 cents a tube, and Ivory soap for 7 cents a bar. Walgreens also peddled a few items not commonly found on its shelves today, including Enoz moth spray, Norwegian Cod Liver Oil, and Fairyfoot, which "stops bunion pain" for just 89 cents. The campaign was such a big hit that Walgreens did it again a month later, in another three-day stretch a week before Christmas. Almost always, Charles's faith in advertising paid off handsomely.

Of course, getting people to visit your stores won't count for much if they don't like what they see when they get there. While other drugstores, chains or otherwise, were often careless with their window displays, Walgreens had established a veritable army of 25 men whose sole job was to create the most appealing and effective window displays possible. They accomplished this by making posters, drawing up sketches, trying different angles on the easels that held up their signs, and experimenting with various looks until they hit on a winner. Then they sent the recipe on to their stores, which were expected to improvise the centralized design but not dismiss it.

If all this seems like overkill for a 10-by-20-foot window space, well, you just have to see what they came up with back then, something more akin to a jeweler's display than a drugstore window. Before the era of advertising bombardment on television, radio, and the Internet, people walked downtown to do their shopping, making window displays one of the sole means for stores to market themselves—and arguably the most important.

The purchasing department, Knight stated, was also at the cutting edge.[49] Jim Ward—who had joined the company as a boy and who, you will recall, almost died before Walgreen brought in a specialist from Northwestern to save him—received high marks for his running of the division that bought all but 10 percent of the merchandise sold in the stores, most of it nationally advertised products like Coca-Cola, Kodak, and Procter & Gamble (when such national brands were a new phenomenon) because Ward found they sold much more briskly than smaller, lesser-known brands.

"The company buys goods only from high-grade vendors," Knight wrote, "produces only quality goods in its factories, and never purchases 'seconds' upon any terms." Knight was surprised to discover Ward was in the habit of purchasing most products in small quantities, which seemed to squander one of the advantages of being a chain. But Knight discovered that whatever economies of scale Walgreens would have realized by making larger purchases would often be quickly lost—and then some—if the company ended up stuck with outdated stock, too much capital tied up in inventory, or overburdened warehouses, which were already feeling the growing pains of Walgreens' expansion. Ward's methods reduced the need for clearance sales, which were "regarded with disfavor," Knight wrote. "And the word itself—clearance—is an admission of bad merchandising methods."[50]

Ward was way ahead of his time, practicing an early version of the "just-in-time" delivery practices Japanese companies popularized in the 1980s and 1990s, and reaping many of the same rewards.

Knight discovered, however, that some of Walgreens' strengths were also the source of its weaknesses. Although Knight praised the uncommon autonomy given Walgreens store managers, "standing on their own feet," as he wrote, in an attempt to "keep centralization and formal methods to the barest minimum consistent with efficiency," he also felt the policy, carried as far as Walgreens did, led to wasteful duplication of tasks, since systems designed for small companies "are not necessarily good ones for much larger enterprises."[51]

Knight suggested, for example, that the CEO name a general manager to take over many of the CEO's administrative duties, giving him more time to devote to larger concerns. Knight wrote that if that was not possible—accurately predicting Walgreen's refusal, on the grounds that such a move would risk the loss of "family feeling," as Knight described it—the company could at least consolidate the dozen or so divisions into just three or four umbrella departments, reducing layers of bureaucracy and saving the CEO time by consulting only with 3 or 4 people each day, not 10 or 12.[52]

For example, Knight offered, merchandising, soda fountain service, window displays, marketing, and personnel could all be placed together under "Store Administration," with a single executive responsible for them all. Likewise, Knight wrote, accounting, insurance, taxation, leasing, and the treasury could all be overseen by a single comptroller. Reengineering the corporation, Knight believed, would create greater efficiency throughout the company.[53] For example, instead of the CEO having to read the balance sheets of every store every morning (each store kept its own accounting books, as if operating independently), Walgreen would merely have to read a single report outlining the sales of all the stores, with especially hot or cold ones flagged for his attention.

On the whole, however, Knight couldn't help but commend the company he had spent a full year studying. The final proof of the wisdom of the Walgreen Way—bedrock values coupled with bold ventures—was the bottom line. The numbers couldn't be ignored, starting with stores: 2 by 1910, 20 by 1920, and 65 by 1925.

More important, Knight felt, was the fact that "the average volume of sales per store has shown a remarkable increase." For comparison, Knight used the Great Atlantic & Pacific Tea Company (which we would later know as A&P), partly because Walgreens had already surpassed the other chains in town.[54]

Sargent's had been Chicago's most venerable chain since Ezekiel H.

Sargent opened his first shop on Lake Street (the city's main drag before the Chicago Fire) in 1852, just 19 years after the incorporation of the town itself. Sargent's stores could count Abraham Lincoln, Marshall Field, and *Chicago Tribune* owner Joseph Medill (for whom Northwestern's acclaimed school of journalism is named), plus all of Chicago's first generation of mayors among their repeat customers.[55]

By the time Knight started researching his thesis, however, Walgreens was growing at Sargent's expense, putting the once-popular chain in retreat. Knight therefore decided that A&P, which was innovative and on the rise like Walgreens, made for a more apt comparison.[56]

Started in 1859, A&P sold $25,000 worth of goods per store in 1915 and almost doubled that figure to $45,000 by 1919. It was an impressive accomplishment by any standard—except Walgreens', which generated $30,000 in sales per store in 1916; $67,400 in 1920; and $138,000 in 1925, dwarfing A&P's figures.

Knight considered this "perhaps the most solid development, for to increase sales per store is both more difficult and more useful than merely to increase their number,"[57] a strategy the company surely follows today, even as it expands to record dimensions.

Knight's thesis was well received by the school, which conferred its master's degree on him. In the wake of his dissertation, Stanford University, a New York accounting firm, and Walgreens all offered Knight permanent positions. Charles Sr., however, was the most insistent. "I just must have that young man with us," he told his executive team. Knight accepted Walgreen's offer to fill the new position—a position Knight had recommended creating—of "comptroller" and promptly enacted his suggestions for consolidating the accounting department's tasks to avoid the unnecessary duplication of duties.

Walgreen's initial impression of the young man proved, as such impressions usually did, to be true. Five years into the job, Knight became a company director; he retired in 1961 as a vice president and treasurer.

"He would approach a subject from many viewpoints and develop many angles," Chuck Walgreen recalled. "He was like a dog with a bone—wouldn't let go until it had been gone over most thoroughly. Most folks did not drop into his office after 4 o'clock because they learned they would be tied up until at least 6:30 and would be having a late dinner at home."[58]   *KNIGHT imitator.*

"absolute dominance"

When Robert Knight started his thesis, Walgreens had already blossomed to 59 Chicago stores. When he finished, Walgreens had 69 in the city alone, adding almost one a month, with plans to accelerate the expansion plans dramatically. By 1926, the year Knight became Walgreens' first comptroller, Walgreens had opened 33 more Chicago stores, for a total of 92.

According to a brochure Walgreens put together to coax manufacturers to pool their resources on advertising, all Walgreens' Chicago sites were "centrally located. . . . Dotted along every boulevard entering or leaving the city, they prevail at principal elevated stations, they dominate the downtown shopping area, and [they] cover main suburban points."[59]

It might have been a sales pitch, but Walgreens could back up every claim. As Dizzy Dean once said, "It ain't braggin', if it's the truth." And it was. By the mid-1920s, Walgreens ruled Chicago's drugstore business, including "absolute dominance in the Loop area," a region it had entered only five years earlier.[60]

The explosion required the company to create its own "SWAT" (special weapons and tactics) team for store openings, which occurred monthly by the mid-1920s, then weekly by the decade's end. In typical Walgreens' style, the company found a champion to head up the unofficial "store opening" team, who was eager to dive headfirst into the task: Elmer E. Reuckert.

Reuckert signed on as assistant manager under Harry Goldstine at Walgreens fourth store, at 43rd and Calumet, in 1914. "A robust sort, Reuckert achieved a kind of celebrity, even after becoming a top-flight manager, by donning work clothes to work with store opening crews for the rest of the decade and beyond," the Kogans wrote. "By 1934, when he was named a director of the company and its secretary-treasurer, he told a *Pepper Pod* reporter that he had thus aided in opening no fewer than 105 stores, most of them in Chicago and environs."[61]

Opening store after store might have been exciting, but Chuck Walgreen recalled the other side of the boom: all the blood, sweat, and tears that the seemingly endless grand openings required. While taking a year off in the middle of his studies at the University of Michigan in 1925–1926, Chuck was a central member of Reuckert's team. "We were opening a store a week," he recalled, "but they were tiny, only about 2,000 square feet. The carpenters would have the store ready for us, and we'd move right in. The soda fountain took up half the space, merchandise the other half. We would stock [shelves] and work out window displays. We'd start Monday morning and finish up Friday night, working 10 or 12 hours a day. We'd have the opening Saturday. Sunday, we'd sleep all day and get ready [to open another new store on] Monday."[62]

After Chuck returned to his studies in Ann Arbor, Reuckert and friends had no trouble staying busy, opening a store a week throughout 1927. Though still very much a Chicago-centric company, by that time Walgreens had already dipped its toe into Hammond and Gary, Indiana; Milwaukee, Wisconsin; and St. Louis, Missouri. Walgreens' executive team believed they were ready for a much riskier move: New York.[63]

if they can make it here

When Charles decided to dive into something, he usually opted for the deep end. And so it was that Walgreens opened its first New York store right in the middle of it all: at 1501 Broadway and 44th Street, in the Paramount Theater Building. The new store was stocked with one of the best perfume counters in the city to ensure its survival until, the executives hoped, the rest of the store caught on with the neighborhood.

The New York franchise was more than just another store. Located in the heart of the theater district, the store become a favorite stop for famous writers, singers, and particularly actors, who bought their sundries there, ate in the basement restaurant, and admired the caricatures of famous patrons adorning the walls. Those who longed to join them on the "Wall of Fame" often worked for the store on their way up or whiled away the afternoons with their fellow starving artists in the soda fountain booths, dreaming of great days ahead.

With so many future stars having worked there, the site earned a place in acting lore. Long after she had become a household name, Lucille Ball liked to tell the story of her brief tenure as a waitress there in 1938, when she was fired for forgetting to put the bananas in a banana split—a little detail the store managers apparently stressed.

Legendary columnist Walter Winchell called these aspiring thespians "Walgreen actors" and the Walgreens basement "Ham Cellar," "Sardi's Basement," or "The Banana Split Club."

Two decades later, the Kogans reported—and years after Walgreens opened a larger store in the Times Square Building just two blocks south— a feature writer for the *New York World Telegram* in the 1940s described Walgreens' Paramount store as "one of the major institutions of the theatrical world."[64]

The spot inspired writer Ruth McKenney to pen a series of *New Yorker* "Talk of the Town" stories, which were adapted for a stage play called *My Sister Eileen* in 1941, which in turn became a popular Hollywood movie musical of the same name in 1955.

Loyalty to Walgreens' flagship Manhattan store was not limited to the famous or famous-to-be, of course. John Oveian, a Yugoslavian immigrant who worked in the Paramount Building as a maintenance man, set a record that, undoubtedly, still stands. From the time Walgreens' first New York store opened in 1927 to 1957, Oveian said in his letter to Chuck Walgreen that he ate every breakfast, lunch, and dinner in the Walgreens' basement restuarant. For that reason, Oveian wrote, he felt he deserved a gold watch from Walgreens.

Chuck asked Russell Plummer, who worked in Walgreens' food service department, to fly out to New York to see if Oveian's story was on the level. Plummer discovered that Oveian, a lifetime bachelor who rented a modest apartment near the Paramount, had naturally become something of a local legend with every Paramount Walgreens' store employee, past and present, and had more seniority than all of them. As far as he could, Plummer verified Oveian's claim—no one there recalled him missing a single meal—and recommended to Chuck Walgreen that he grant Oveian's request. Walgreen agreed.[65]

The store's fountain manager, Joseph Pape, and his supervisor, Fred Sparks (who remembered Oveian from the days Sparks worked there in the 1930s) presented the loyal customer with his gold watch in Times Square, as reported in the *New Yorker*'s "Talk of the Town" section and Walter Winchell's nationally syndicated column. When a *Pepper Pod* reporter asked Oveian if had ever grown weary of Walgreens' menu after eating 31,799 meals there, he said, "No, I had to stop because the store closed."

It should not come as any surprise that after Walgreens shut the doors on its Paramount Building shop, Oveian quickly switched his allegiance to the Walgreens at Times Square a few blocks away. He and Chuck Walgreen continued their Christmas card correspondence every year until Oveian's death in the mid-1980s.

Walgreen had entertained the idea of taking the company public for some time. The chain's incredible growth convinced him that they needed to go public to help fund the expansion underway, and the success of the first New York store convinced him they were ready.

On the morning of February 15, 1934, Walgreens could boast 483 stores (25 percent of which were outside the Midwest), 12,000 employees, and, for the first time, the letters WAG on the New York Stock Exchange.

Walgreens was on the board.

If you had bought a single share that day for $24.625, it would have split nine times into 512 shares, each valued at $36.25, by December 15, 2003—and would be worth a total of $18,560.

read all about it

As the company's profile rose, so did its exposure, attracting outside observers who wrote for larger audiences than professors reading graduate dissertations at the University of Chicago.

Four months after Walgreens went public, in the September 1928 issue of *Chain Store Review* (now called *Drug Store News*, the industry's principle publication), Charles Walgreen explained the philosophy behind the chain's great expansion. "Growth in business is largely multiplication," he said, sounding much like a recent Walgreens' CEO describing the chain's amazing growth in the last quarter century. He continued:

Small, a pattern is set, which, with growth, remains substantially unchanged. Provided the person is correct in substantial details, the business can multiply itself a thousand-fold without altering the paramount task of management, which is keeping all phases of essential details in correct relationship to the whole.

But if there are uncertainty and doubt in that original pattern, these elements are simply magnified by growth—size possesses no magic for overcoming defects—and the fear of bigness is probably largely a fear that something like this may happen. . . . I had the fear of bigness once—but no more. A successful business, like a tree, grows rhythmically, uniformly in all its essential parts. I entertain no fears for the future of that business which starts out with fundamental proportions right and keeps them right even when events require computations to be made in the millions instead of the thousands. However big the figures may be, the percentage will never outswell 100![66]

In the June 1929 issue of the same publication, Walgreen outlined the company's approach to hiring and training new employees—what we would call personnel issues. "We like to hire young men just as they come from the schools of pharmacy, and we maintain vigilant contacts with schools to that end," Charles explained. "Whenever we hire a man, we bear in mind that we are hiring a prospective manager. We do not want a man unless we have reason to believe that he has the ability and ambition to become a store manager, or better." When they found their man, he received $50 a week, better than most equivalent jobs, but only a "starting point," in Walgreen's words.[67] A good manager could earn substantial performance bonuses and enhance his portfolio with plenty of Walgreens stock.

When Walgreens went public in 1928, the company required all private shareholders to cash in 7 percent of their stock. That earned one lucky employee $102,000 for his 7 percent; another manager got $68,000; and a soda fountain manager got a check for $24,000.

"I regard it as a pleasant obligation," Charles said, "and also as the soundest business policy to be constantly creating conditions such that any man with the necessary capacity can advance to millionairedom within the organization as readily as if he were in business for himself alone—if not, perhaps, more readily."[68]

Walgreen's position—you worked for it, you invested it, you deserve it!—might not seem exceptional to anyone unfamiliar with the world of salespeople and sales managers and the commissions they haggle over. Most seasoned salespeople can tell all-too-familiar horror stories that go like this: They achieve so much under their companys' incentive plans that their boss feels their bonuses have grown too big to bear, prompting the boss to slash salespeople's pay to get their income "in line" with others who achieved far less and to restructure the pay plan so it can't happen again. This happens every day in the car business alone.

So, although Walgreen should not be praised for simply honoring his word, it's worth noting that Walgreens' policy of celebrating, not punishing, such successes, distinguishing the company from many others that were not so trustworthy.

In the next installment on Walgreens for *Chain Store Review* (August 1929), the publication laid out Walgreens' marketing strategy. In it, Charles maintained that the most effective ads were simply "newspaper copy packed with facts about merchandise and prices that will bring people into the stores."[69]

Despite Walgreen's almost religious belief in the power of good customer service, Walgreen advised against bragging about it: "Do not talk about service; let it speak for itself. Give the service, to be sure, and strive to make it better than any competitor's, but let the customers discover it themselves."[70]

Even the magic of Walgreen's famed two-minute drill, which he and Caleb Danner conducted in the first store's first years to make a splash, would be spoiled if it was officially promoted by the company. Doing the drill was a great way to spread the word about Walgreens' excellent service, he explained, but advertising it would raise expectations to impossible levels and create negative publicity whenever they fell short. "Let the advertising copy concern itself with getting customers into the stores," he cautioned, "not to be served in just a certain way, but to get the merchandise they want at a proper price—perhaps an advantageous price. Talk to the main issue."[71]

Walgreens did just that, to the tune of $84,000 in 1924, $905,000 in 1929 (the year the preceding story was published), and $1.093 million in 1933, in the depths of the Depression. Walgreen's faith in advertising was absolute.

chain fight

Beware of what you wish for, as they say, because you just might get it. With Walgreens' increasingly public success, it was inevitable that detractors would emerge to take their shots.

Walgreens was not a juicy target then, nor is it now; but if you were looking for something to criticize in the 1920s, you would probably do what Walgreens' competition did: argue that chains of stores were evil.

Antichain proponents, then and now, have made several negative arguments—including quality of community life, variety of consumer choices, and the like—but their main point is simply that chain stores are bad for the country because independent stores can't compete against them.

In the late 1920s, chain store opponents—consisting primarily of independent businesspeople—urged their state and federal legislators to contain the chains' growth. They found sympathetic listeners in Iowa Senator Smith Brookhart and Louisiana Governor Huey Long, among others. When several states tried to impose special taxes against chain stores, however, the courts quickly declared them unconstitutional. These rulings only seemed to anger Senator Brookhart, who then prodded the Federal Trade Commission (FTC) to investigate the chains to determine if the critics' concerns were well-founded.

In 1929, a year after the FTC started its investigation that would last six long years before being completed in 1934, Walgreen decided to take the initiative and wrote an essay titled "There's No Monopoly in Selling" for *Chain Store Review* to make one chain's case.

Walgreen started by assuring independents that the U.S. economy had enough space for all merchants to survive. "There is, and will be, ample room for the live, progressive, independent merchant using modern methods in location, the selection of stock, arrangement of fixtures, training and personnel, and cooperation with other independents to mutual advantage," he wrote. "The wide-awake independent merchant who operates his business in a scientific manner need have no fear of being forced out of congested retail trade areas."[72]

The independent, Walgreen argued, had considerable advantages over the chain operations in knowing the local market, providing a personal touch, maintaining closer supervision of his store, and conducting more detailed stock control. Despite these edges, Walgreen wrote, "We have

CRITICISM,

often found when buying out an insolvent business that the failure resulted first and last from carrying dead stock rather than any difference in prices of merchandise." In other words, James Ward's carefully crafted purchasing strategy gave Walgreens the upper hand over those stores—chain or otherwise—who bought too much and found themselves holding the bag later on. And, just to underscore his belief that the best man usually wins in U.S. capitalism, Walgreen couldn't resist saying, "No successful chain has ever been a dowdy, hodgepodge store. Invariably, there has been order, cleanliness, atmosphere."[73]

Walgreen believed that customers didn't care if a store was independent or part of a chain, only if it looked clean and sharp, with good selection and excellent service—an argument with which most customers would agree, in any era. And, it goes without saying that even the world's biggest chains started out as single stores—neat, well-run independents. They didn't become bigger by being bad and unpopular.

In 1934, after the FTC spent six years and $1 million at Senator Brookhart's behest to confirm the many ills he believed chain operations beset on the country, the report stated that the investigators found just the opposite to be true.

> If ability to undersell based on greater efficiency or on elimination of credit and delivery costs is destroyed by [special] taxation, it is the consuming public which will really pay the tax and not the chains. To tax out of existence the advantages of chain stores over competitors is to tax out of existence the advantages which the consuming public has found in patronizing them, with a consequent addition to the cost of living for that section of the public.[74]

Despite the FTC's rather sweeping dismissal of the chain opponents' arguments, 28 states tried to assess special taxes on chains through out the Depression anyway; but all of them failed in the legislature, in the voting booth, or, most commonly, in the courts.

Walgreens was not deterred. Pop Coulson's famous chocolate malted milk shake combined with the modern marketing methods and old-fashioned morals that Walgreens instilled in each store through its growing core of True Believers stimulated the most ambitious expansion in Walgreens' century-long history.

Walgreens started the 1920s with 20 stores and closed it by entering Utah, Idaho, Wyoming, Nevada, and California when it bought up the 28 stores of the Schramm-Johnson chain, thereby bringing the company's total holdings to 397 stores in 87 cities across the country—an almost 1,000 percent increase in the number of stores in just 10 years. Revenues and profits soared with the growth. In 1923, the company reaped $3.6 million in sales and $192,000 in profit, creating a profit margin of 5.3 percent. In 1929, Walgreens brought in $47 million in revenue—a 13-fold increase from just six years earlier—and $4 million in profit, for a profit margin of 8.5 percent. The young Robert Knight was right: One of the chain's most impressive accomplishments was increasing the yield per store, even as it spread across the country, establishing the 1920s as one of the most successful decades of the company's long history, any way you slice it.

As the decade entered its final months, John Nickerson and Company, a prominent New York investment house, issued a report titled *A Chronicle of Progress*, in which it discussed, among other things, the virtues of Walgreens' management and, by extension, its stock.

> Among all the chain stores of the country, the one which we regard as outstanding at this time as an attractive medium for investment is the Walgreen Co. It operates in the most favorable of all the major chain store fields and has a management [team] which has proved itself competent and experienced. . . . As chains go, it is comparatively young, but already it owns nearly ten percent of all chain drugstores of the country. Its growth has been little short of phenomenal, exceeding even the rate of growth of most outstanding chains in other fields.[75]

The Nickerson report proceeded to explain Walgreens' success, citing many of the same attributes Robert Knight had noticed four years earlier, including carefully selected locations, clean stores, attractive displays, powerful marketing, and, not least, an unusual dedication to customer service—the exact same basic formula the company follows today.

Interestingly, the report went out of its way to make special mention of two aspects of the Walgreens operation that didn't have a direct impact on the bottom line—employee relations and the pharmacy division—but were vital to the chain's success: "Without the loyal cooperation of its entire personnel," the report said, "particularly those who are in constant touch with the public, it would not be possible for the company to show the successive annual increases in volume of business."[76]

The Nickerson people were sharp enough to recognize the important role the pharmacy played in fostering customer trust and loyalty: "Particular attention has always been devoted to the prescription department, and the company's high reputation in this regard has been a large factor in the successful building up of the business."[77]

It is a bit surprising that a financial house would notice the pharmacy division, as it only brought in a few small percentage points of revenue each year—just a tenth of what the company made from the food service division alone or from tobacco sales. But the Nickerson researchers recognized that the professional reputation of the division separated Walgreens from the thousands of other drugstores on street corners across the country that had untrained or unscrupulous people behind the counter selling snake oil for top dollar. Although the soda fountain might have been the friendly face Walgreens showed the public, the pharmacy department was its soul, the repository of the bedrock values of honesty, integrity, and customer care when it mattered most.

the good life

Having already succeeded beyond his wildest dreams, Charles was now well-prepared to make good on the promises he'd made to Myrtle early in their marriage.

Years before, he had told her that once they had $20,000 in the bank they would buy a nice place in the country. In March 1929, just months before the stock market crash, Charles purchased a gorgeous 15-acre tract of land outside Dixon, his hometown. The lot was heavily wooded, with a clearing on the bluffs overlooking the Rock River.

On this clearing stood a log cabin, a large barn, a few smaller buildings, and all that remained of a once glorious mansion in woeful disrepair, a sort of postbellum "Tara." Almost a century earlier, about the time the Black Hawk War was fought in the same woods and fields, a man named Alexander Charters had bought and named the estate "Hazelwood," in honor of a treasured park in Belfast, Northern Ireland, his former home. Charters had opened Hazelwood to Abe Lincoln, Stephen A. Douglas, and other dignitaries of the day until his death in 1878, after which the property gradually fell apart due to neglect.

Walgreen fulfilled one other promise, too. On that brisk winter evening 22 years earlier, after the young couple had walked down the block to drop the final payment of the loan for his first store into the mail box, he had turned to his wife and whispered, "One of these days, I'll buy you a fur coat, Myrtle." Years later, Charles Walgreen provided his hard-working wife with everything she wanted.

The Walgreens' dreams had come true.

It might have taken Walgreen 15 years to realize he was a pharmacist, but it only took 20 more to make Walgreens one of the largest drugstore chains in the world. The Walgreen Way was spreading fast; and thanks to its foundation of bedrock values, it was built to last.

CHAPTER 3

nothing
to fear:
1929–1945

[handwritten annotation: Simply Name them Challenges]

facing fear itself

On Tuesday, October 29, 1929, stockholders dumped a record 16.4 million shares on the trading floor, opening the floodgates for $50 billion in stock losses and sparking the Great Depression. A few months later, workers finished the Empire State Building; but the world's tallest structure remained almost completely empty until after World War II because no one could pay the rent.[1]

When a reporter asked Babe Ruth, who signed a contract for $80,000 in 1930, if he felt it was unseemly to make more money than President

Herbert Hoover, he replied, "Why not? I had a better year than he did." Few argued.[2]

It is not surprising that the American people voted to oust Herbert Hoover in the 1932 election in favor of an unheralded—and underestimated—presidential candidate named Franklin Delano Roosevelt.

By the time he took office in 1933, FDR had his work cut out for him. Five thousand banks had failed—and this, in the days before the Federal Deposit Insurance Corporation (FDIC) protected investors from losing everything—and unemployment had quadrupled to some 16 million people, roughly a third of the nation's workers.

In Chicago, from 1929 to 1933, employment had been cut in half, and payroll was one-quarter of its pre-Depression levels. Foreclosures quintupled, from 3,148 in 1929 to 15,201 in 1933. Land values plummeted from $5 billion in 1928 to $2 billion in 1933.

"Chicago in the thirties was a place which few people of the twenties could recognize, and a city hard to imagine even now."[3] In an *Amos and Andy* radio skit, a man walks up to a hotel desk and asks for a room. The clerk replies, "For sleeping or jumping?"[4]

FDR's first job was to calm his people, restore their confidence, and remind them that they had "nothing to fear but fear itself." Then he went to work to get the country moving again.

better days are coming

If Walgreens' Roarin' Twenties' salad days closely mirror those of the 1990s—both characterized by heady success coupled with the discipline to avoid getting dizzy with it—the company's performance in the Great Depression parallels Walgreens' resilience in the new millennium: a determination not only to press on but also to grow in the face of difficult times while reinforcing the virtues the company has always extolled.

After Black Tuesday, Charles Walgreen's job was essentially the same as FDR's: to reassure his employees that their company was equipped to weather the storm and to urge them to remain resolute because "better days were coming."

In an internal *Pepper Pod* worthy of one of FDR's fireside chats, Charles wrote:

> We are passing through the most unusual Depression in the history of our country. It is further emphasized by the fact that it closely follows our greatest peak of prosperity. General conditions have been, and still are, serious. Nearly everyone has a feeling of concern. Every person, every group, every class of society is affected.
>
> We, as individuals and as a group, can keep ourselves in a happier and healthier state of mind by adjusting ourselves to conditions as they are. Self-pity, pride, and vanity will not lighten our burden. More than ever, we need to be hopeful, energetic, and ambitious for, after all, present conditions are going to improve.
>
> It is my impression that we will—just how soon, I cannot say, but we will—enter into one of the longest eras of prosperity that we have ever enjoyed. So be courageous and be patient. Be your best! Do your best! Pass this spirit on to your customers. Give them cheer; encourage them. They like it; we all do! A smile is like a ray of sunshine on a dark day. It is even more helpful than the medicine you sell, and what is more, its benefits are contagious.
>
> And whatever you do, do not acknowledge defeat, for remember: as surely as the sun rises—BETTER DAYS ARE COMING."[5]

It helped Walgreen that his case was much easier to make than FDR's. In 1930, the first full year of the Depression, Walgreens' sales actually jumped $5 million to a record $52 million. Though the chain's profits had been cut in half from the previous year's high of $4 million, during the Depression, any profit was a good profit.

In another internal edition of the *Pepper Pod*, Walgreen stated his belief that the chain's remarkable resilience was not because of "one dominating idea" but because of the disciplined application of 10 simple practices, including greeting every customer with a smile; always keeping "the customer's interest at heart"; being "honest with your customers, the company, and yourself"; and always remembering to say "Thank you."[6]

(That this philosophy closely mirrors the company's philosophy today is no accident. "We have an expression," former chairman and chief executive officer Dan Jorndt explained. "'We're not looking for the silver bullet, the answer to all our prayers.'"[7] When faced with tough times, Walgreens historically has not gone looking for easy answers, instead focusing on the same simple traits that allowed it to succeed when times were better.)

Walgreen even laid it all out in a 118-page hardcover book for salespeople, *Set Your Sales for Bigger Earnings*. "Success is doing a thousand little things the right way—doing many of them over and over again," he wrote. Employees were expected not only to educate the customers about Walgreens' tremendous selection—"People should know by this time that we carry everything from Peau Doux golf balls to a native Algerian pickle"—but also to master the simplest elements of positive human interaction. "Avoid the artificial, forced smile, and do not stare," Walgreen advised. "Don't rush forward as though you were going to pounce upon her. . . . Stand erect, chest up and shoulders back."[8]

Optimism aside, the era's economic realities could not be ignored. Walgreens had to institute countless cost-cutting measures, from installing lower-wattage light bulbs in storage rooms to using both sides of the paper rolls in the adding machines. To avoid laying employees off, Walgreens cut workers' wages by 10 percent; Charles Sr. also cut his own salary by more than a third, from $60,000 to $39,000.

Although Charles was a staunch Republican who, like most successful businessmen of the time, opposed many of FDR's "New Deal" policies, he knew the company had to take care of its own. So he put aside over $30,000 as an emergency fund for Walgreens employees, retirees, and others the company felt could use a hand and sponsored raffle parties to raise money for food baskets to the needy.

Naturally enough, the harsh consequences of the Depression often hit very close to home. When Charlie Morris thought to write Charles Walgreen Sr. in 1930, it had been more than three decades since the two had worked together at William Valentine's store on 39th and Cottage Grove. After Walgreen had returned from the Spanish-American War weakened by yellow fever and malaria, it was Morris who took in his friend to bring him back to health. In the following years, however, as Walgreen began building his empire, the two old friends lost track of each other.

In 1930, a year into the Great Depression and before the days of the Occupational Safety and Health Administration (OSHA), workmen's compensation, the National Labor Relations Board, and the growth of the personal injury industry, Morris severely injured his hand at his job. He was flat out of luck, out of work, and—soon enough—out of money. Desperate, he decided to see if the "rich drugstore merchant" he had been reading about in the papers was his old friend from Valentine's store, and he sent him a letter. Walgreen answered promptly, inviting his former colleague to visit him at Walgreens' headquarters.

"The rich man grabbed the aged Morris and hugged him like a long-lost brother," one paper reported. "The two old pals had the time of their lives renewing their friendship." Walgreen covered Morris's medical care and gave him "a job for life."[9]

The most important thing Walgreen did for his employees, however, was not rescue them from disaster but direct a company that, incredibly, continued to grow throughout the Depression. In the long run, it's far more helpful to keep everyone fishing than to hand out fish.

Fresh from the success of the previous decade's unprecedented growth, Walgreen posted a sign outside his office that said, "Don't rest on your laurels." He followed the simple maxim religiously. Instead of backing off or being content to tread water until the trouble passed, the company's directors kept pushing ahead. "We expect to continue moderately to increase the number of our stores," Walgreen wrote to his employees, "as well as to develop new products . . . and all the facts within my knowledge justify a feeling of cautious but firm confidence in the immediate as well as in the long-range future of our company."[10]

Walgreen wanted to make this point with his top managers more force-fully, face to face. So he summoned the directors of Walgreens' 18 territo-ries—representing zone offices from New York in the East to Salt Lake City in the West, from Minnesota in the North to Houston in the South—their top assistants, and Walgreens' executives for the first company-wide meeting at Chicago's Stock Yard Inn (an irony Upton Sinclair would have appreciated) on April 6 and 7, 1931.

The speakers—most of them well-known Walgreens executives—of-fered advice, support, and motivation to surmount the obstacles that the Great Depression presented, covering everything from merchan-dising to hiring to advertising nationwide. In his lecture on the impor-tance of window displays, vice president Harry Goldstine maintained, "Precedent should not stand in the way of progress," giving the managers a free hand to try new approaches representing "the outgrowth of pro-gressive ideas."

Robert Knight weighed in on economizing. "Fine results have been at-tained," he said, "by eliminating unnecessary things and unnecessary peo-ple, by giving the honey makers more scope and letting the drones loaf elsewhere." It is not clear if he was advocating layoffs, but the Walgreens' workforce grew substantially during the Depression.

Robert H. Riemenschneider, the company's director of promotion and advertising, ended the two-day meeting with a crescendo by announcing that the company was less than two weeks away from launching a nation-wide, five-day sale, running from April 16 to 20, and would generate publicity for the first-time event by spending over $75,000 for ads in 122 newspapers, blanketing every one of Walgreens' 98 markets.[11] The managers were understandably thrilled to get such overwhelming backing and returned to their towns with great anticipation for the upcoming event. The sale's success encouraged similarly aggressive efforts through-out the decade.

At the end of the next fiscal year, at the very nadir of the Depression, Charles Walgreen Sr. received a personal letter from Arthur Andersen, fa-ther of the eponymous Big Five accounting firm, who felt compelled to write him with that rarest of things: good news from an accountant. Dated November 7, 1932, Andersen wrote:

My Dear Mr. Walgreen:

I have had the pleasure of reviewing the Walgreen Company statements for the fiscal year ended September 30, 1932.

In view of the fact that I have seen so much red ink this year, the performance of your Company is clearly an outstanding one. I wonder sometimes how you have been able to do it. I think it is all summed up in a statement of one of our managers who remarked to me that he thinks that the Walgreen organization is one of the best chain store set-ups he has ever seen and that everybody on the job is working for the best interest of the Company. No finer tribute than this could have been paid.

With kindest regards, Very truly yours, (signed) Arthur Andersen.[12]

Walgreens faced the Great Depression with the same simple philosophy with which it has approached every era in its 103-year history: an uncanny combination of timeless values and cutting-edge innovations. In the nation's toughest decade, that meant creating a mutually beneficial network of affiliated stores, creating a bold advertising campaign, increasing food service to previously unthinkable levels, and entering new markets while other chains shrank. In other words, while everyone else was playing defense, just trying to survive, Walgreens confidently went on the offensive, working toward a bright future few others dared imagine.

helping the mom-and-pop shops

Although Charles Walgreen was an unabashed capitalist, he occasionally backed positions and policies that had a certain collectivist bent. In 1911, just two years after he had opened his second store, Walgreen organized

the Velvet Club (eventually called Federated Drug Company) to help independent drugstores buy in bulk in order to compete with Louis Kroh
Liggett's omnipotent United Drug Company. The alliance was an effective
way to increase small stores' variety while decreasing costs, and it held together for over two decades. Walgreens enjoyed an unexpected by-product
in the bargain, because the association introduced the growing chain to
new stores, markets, and managers—many of which joined Walgreens in
the expansions that followed.[13]

In the wake of the antichain movement, Walgreens was understandably
sensitive to being perceived as a steamroller, but Charles and his assistants
helped a step farther than necessary for public relations purposes alone.
John D. Rockefeller and other "Robber Barons" had grown fat partly by
dropping their prices to unsustainable levels, undercutting the competition through a practice called *dumping*, until the smaller companies could
no longer bear such losses and went under, ridding Rockefeller's corporations of more competitors and freeing them to crank their rates even
higher than before without fear of a price war.

Walgreen was not at all squeamish about watching dusty, disorganized,
poorly run drugstores close their doors; but he opposed dumping as un-
necessarily predatory, believing that drugstores should succeed on their
merits, not through monopolistic means. California legislators passed a
statute called the Fair Trade Acts in 1931—which permitted manufacturers to set minimum prices that neither independent stores nor chains
could undercut—and other states soon followed. Walgreens supported
the measures, even though without it the chains might have taken advantage of an unregulated environment to wipe out independents,
Robber Baron–style.

Walgreen had little affection for a new wave of fly-by-night retailers
called "pine-boards," so named because these slap-dash stores stacked their
goods on unpainted pine-board shelves, which harkened back to the worst
elements of the nineteenth-century traveling medicine shows. Like any
trend, this one had some appeal, including low prices, aggressive marketing, and the facade of pharmacies, though few actually had prescription de-

partments. The last issue particularly grated on Walgreen because his stores had always offered its customers fully stocked pharmacies, staffed with certified professionals, from the day he opened his first store; and the company went out of its way to maintain these departments long before there was much economic incentive to do so.

Walgreens eagerly joined the National Association of Chain Drugstores, formed late in 1933, to fight the pine-board trend and even supported FDR's National Recovery Act (NRA) of 1933 because it was established, among other things, to monitor the practices of these pine-board stores. A few years later, the Supreme Court eventually ruled that the NRA was unconstitutional; but by that time, the ball was in motion, with numerous states and professional associations working together to enforce codes of conduct among drugstores—another step in the ongoing professionalization of the industry.[14]

Walgreen came up with a way to cut through the legal red tape and unsavory patina of unregulated snake-oil shops to help thousands of independent pharmacists directly when he conceived of the Walgreens Agency system in February 1929, just months before the stock market collapsed. The thought occurred to him when he considered the thousands of towns across the country that had fewer than the 20,000 people Walgreens required to start a new store. Walgreen knew his company created its population formula for sound reasons, but he also knew that the small stores in those small markets were still selling lots of merchandise—totals that added up fast.

To tap into this neglected sector of the industry, Walgreen decided to offer selected independent outlets in small towns great prices on over a thousand Walgreens products (from Epsom salts to stationery); store supplies, like napkins and signs; advice on store operations and merchandising, especially for financial planning and window displays; and the credibility and cachet that came with the Walgreens name, including a borrowed boost from national ad campaigns. In return, Walgreens received a relatively small but steady stream of additional income, enhanced name recognition in new territories, and—one of those unexpected by-products—a fantastic farm system for identifying talented young pharmacists and managers.

To head the new program, Walgreens made a savvy selection in Raymond E. Walker, who, as a former small-town banker from North Dakota, seemed perfectly suited to the position—and was. Walgreens started the Agency program in June 1929 with small stores in California, Washington, and Oregon and two traveling company representatives to help them; but the program quickly took off, fueled partly by the small druggist's desperate need for additional help during the Depression.

By 1934, the nascent program had grown to 17 Walgreens representatives in 33 states overseeing the performance of over 600 Agency stores, which generated $1 million of Walgreens' $54 million in revenue that year.

Management devoted special editions of the *Pepper Pod* to the Agency stores "to provide and maintain a closer coordination of thought and action," "to build a bond of sincere loyalty and friendship throughout the ever-growing organization," and "to rear from your daily work a structure which shall be known for all that is best in business." To those ends, the occasional editions included a page headed "Ideas That Work" with tips from around the country—what we would call "benchmarking" today—and testimonials, including a letter from Russell P. Iltis of International Falls, Minnesota.

In 1933, a year after Iltis switched his affiliation from another chain to Walgreens, his small store's sales and profits doubled. He wrote:

Any druggist who may be invited to avail himself of the many opportunities of an affiliation with the Walgreen Company should by all means consider himself honored. And if he will then follow the program as it is laid out for him and cooperate 100 percent, capitalizing on the almost inexhaustible amount of expert service and the experience of so rare and successful an organization, we are certain that his success and experience at the end of a year's time will by all means be parallel to or succeed ours.[15]

Granted, it sounds a bit Eddie Haskel–esque, were it not for Mr. Iltis's sincerity. He also had the numbers to back him up and plenty of small store affiliates who agreed with him. When Agency head Raymond E. Walker stepped down in 1950, his baby had over a thousand affiliates in all 48 states.[16]

The Agency system accomplished everything it had been designed to do, and then some. It spread the Walgreens name coast-to-coast; it saved small stores nationwide; it brought in some additional revenue for the company; and, under the category of unintended consequences, it also produced dozens of future stars who would become leaders in the decades to come—though not all of them in the drugstore industry.

Walgreens' Agency affiliates included a humble outlet in Huron, South Dakota, owned by Hubert Horatio Humphrey Sr. His son Hubert worked there as a clerk during high school and later as a pharmacist before embarking on his political career, which led to the U.S. Senate and to the White House as Lyndon Johnson's vice president. "That store was the meeting place for the whole town," Hubert Humphrey recalled in the 1960s, when his brother Ralph was the manager. "During the Depression, Dad canceled all his customers' debts because he said they didn't have any money anyway. People would trade chickens and eggs and meat for drugs, and we used the food at our luncheonette—25 cents for a full meal."[17]

The program would reach its peak in the late 1960s with some 1,900 Agency stores, about eight times more than Walgreens owned itself at the time. "This division was an important part of establishing the Walgreens name across the country," said John Rubino, who headed up the system in the 1970s. "Mr. Walgreen's 1929 idea served our company well."[18]

walgreens' own: from coffee to corn remover

Despite the Depression, Walgreens had the nerve to stretch not only horizontally, across the land through its Agency system, but also vertically, extending its connection to the customer from the factory to the counter. The company's line of private-label products, introduced two decades earlier, grew to include over a thousand items, from Columbian coffee to cod liver oil, hosiery to playing cards, cigars to sodium bicarbonate, and hair brushes to bay rum.

Walgreens was so encouraged by the consistent sales growth and profits of its store brands that, a month before Black Tuesday, the company started building a massive 224,000-square-foot state-of-the-art building on Chicago's southwest side to house the company's laboratory, factory, warehouse, and distribution center and finished it five months later.

The tablet room was equipped to make 6 million pills a month, which were then sent on to the bottle-filling and labeling machines, which could process four bottles a second. At a time when many pharmacists were still concocting their own prescriptions with mortar and pestle, this facility was way ahead of its time. The factory could crank out 750 jars of cold cream an hour, 3,000 pounds of talc and facial powders a day, and a million pounds of chocolates a year.[19]

During the Depression, Walgreens took on the additional duty of making Russell Stover candies, too. Russell Stover had shown an early knack for selling sweets in the 1910s when he and a partner created the country's first chocolate-covered ice cream bar, which we call an Eskimo Pie today. Stover managed to squander that fortune, however; so in 1923 he and his wife, Clara, decided to create a line of chocolates in their modest Denver home under the name, Mrs. Stover's Bungalow Candies.[20]

The treats were a hit; but once again, the Stovers' finances were run aground, this time by the Depression. Walgreens decided to absorb the company—on the strength of the product and the good name—until the 1940s, when the renamed Russell Stover Candies was ready to stand on its own. Today it is the nation's largest producer of boxed chocolates and remains a loyal Walgreens supplier.[21] Thanks partly to the factory's double duty, Walgreens' chocolate production rose from 1 million pounds in 1933 to 2.25 million pounds the next year.

The factory produced enough goods of all kinds to justify the spacious adjoining warehouse manned by 400 employees, ready to load 10 freight cars and 14 trucks at any one time.

Walgreens sold some of the toiletries—like shaving cream and talcum powder—under the name Peau-Doux (pronounced "Po-Doo"), French for "soft skin." On the morning of one of Walgreen Sr.'s birthdays, he was using the company's trademark shaving cream when his two young children surprised him with his present: a toy Boston bulldog, with characteristically soft skin. Walgreen named him Peau-Doux and soon added his likeness to the familiar trademark.

"It was amazing the number of products that could be developed with our own name and to our own specifications," Chuck said. "The number-one thing with all of them was quality. They had to be as good as or better than anything on the market, or else we wouldn't put our name on them. That was my Dad's view: that since we're not going to be advertising our products heavily, they have to be the utmost in quality to get repeat business."[22]

However, the company soon found that even the popular Peau-Doux name and logo had their limitations. When Walgreens started marketing its own golf balls, Chuck Walgreen quickly realized "soft skin" was "a rather foolish name to give a golf ball," especially since the duffers they were trying to sell to would often cut "smiley faces" and "half-moons" into their golf balls with their errant irons. A softer golf ball skin is not what they needed. As the company's sundries buyer in the early 1930s, Chuck was responsible for developing a number of company product lines, and he had a quick-and-easy answer to the golf-ball problem: "We just changed [the name] to Po-Do."[23] In the modern era of expensive focus groups, test markets, and "blue ribbon panels," it is rather refreshing to read of a manager who had a simple idea and acted on it. Walgreen's solution allowed the golf ball to keep the essence of the good name, without turning off any duffer who might know enough French to understand what it meant.

Of all the products Walgreens has sold under its own name over the years, the Po-Do golf balls, it seems, earned a spot in the nation's heart more than any other. *Wall Street Journal* sports columnist Frederick Klein wrote in 2000:

As a boy in Chicago, I used to dive for golf balls in the pond at the city-owned Waveland Avenue golf course. The course being populated mostly by duffers, I always got what I came for. The prizes were $1 balls; even a scuffed dollar ball would sometimes fetch a quarter. When I found a new ball, it usually was a Po-Do, the ball of choice for municipal golfers of the time. That was a mixed blessing, because while I almost always could sell a good Po-Do, it would rarely bring more than 10 cents. (Walgreens sold them three-for-$1 new.)

I also played golf at that time—nine holes for 25 cents—so I wound up keeping a lot of the Po-Dos I found. Sure, I was conscious of their plebeian status, and hitting one squarely didn't yield the same distance or satisfying click the dollar balls produced, but they went pretty much where you hit them.

And the Po-Do was more than just a cheap ball. In 1941, the pro Johnny Bulla endorsed it and went on to win that year's Los Angeles Open, a major PGA tour stop. Sales soared, and it became the nation's No. 1-selling ball.

Bulla . . . was quite a golfer, a runner-up in the Masters, U.S. Open, and British Open. [He'd endorsed the Po-Do, but he never used one in a tournament, preferring instead Walgreen's Golden Crown, a more expensive ball.] Walgreens and I were careful never to claim otherwise. [Bulla did take a dozen Po-Dos out to a practice range and drive them in front of witnesses, averaging 302 yards a drive—facts featured in the Po-Do ads.] The wind was behind me that day and the ground was pretty hard, but the yardage total was square.

Bulla would like to see the Po-Do come back. He thinks a good 35-cent ball would be good for golf, and for America. And—hey!—maybe there'd be an endorsement contract in it for him.[24]

Walgreens discontinued the Po-Do golf ball in 1965 but brought it back briefly in the mid-1990s. The timing couldn't have been worse for the return of a low-cost, low-brow golf ball. The U.S. economy and golf's popularity were both booming—the exact opposite of the conditions that spawned the Po-Do's original success.

But the Po-Do golf ball—and the hundreds of other Walgreens products that were rolled out during the Depression—did their job. In an era when money couldn't be tighter and brand loyalty still counted for something, Walgreens' line of "homemade" goods fit the times perfectly.

The decision to expand Walgreens' in-house product line provides an excellent example of the formula the company has used to stay on top for over a century: old-fashioned values of quality, customer service, and company pride combined with confidence, boldness, and the ability to adapt to the times. The Depression provided the acid test. While other companies were falling by the wayside, Walgreens grew.

getting the word out

Few things demonstrate confidence in your company and your future like advertising. Walgreen had been a clever and motivated marketer since he set up his stand of pots and pans in his first store and watched them fly out the door; but during the Depression, when most firms were cutting back their advertising budget because the economy was bad, Walgreen stepped his up dramatically—for the very same reason. People were going to be tighter with their money, he figured, so Walgreens had to show them the tremendous deals their stores offered.

Walgreen was right. In 1931, when Henry Ford was closing a plant that housed 75,000 jobs—seven times the number of total Walgreens positions at the time—while blaming the Depression on the laziness of workers, Walgreen was supporting his people with the $75,000 ad campaign to promote the chain's four-day sale that April. When others were backing off, Walgreens was jumping in, increasing its advertising expenditures from $905,000 in 1929 to $1.093 million in 1933. And it knew how to make a splash, too, at one time flooding 150 publications in 125 cities with massive ads, 54 of them full-page. To generate sales for the 1933 Christmas season, the company took out a four-page, four-color ad in the *Chicago Tribune*.[26]

When Americans started listening to the radio, Walgreens saturated that medium, too. In 1931, Walgreens became the first drugstore chain in the country to advertise on the "talk box," sponsoring popular shows from *Ben Potter, Boy Detective* (who was no relation to Harry) to *Hit Tunes of the Week* (a predecessor to *Kasey Kasem's American Top 40*), featuring such stars as Tommy Dorsey, Guy Lombardo, and Benny Goodman.[27]

Walgreens wisely recruited Bob Elson, the "voice of the Chicago Cubs," to become the voice of Walgreens, too. (His brother Charles enjoyed a long Walgreens career.) Elson's trademark delivery was smooth and monotone—perfect for the low-profile Walgreens corporation—and he used it well enough to earn his spot in the broadcasters' wing of the Baseball Hall of Fame. But it has to be said that Walgreens wasn't Elson's only "favorite store." Hall of Fame pitcher Jim Kaat, who grew up in southwestern Michigan listening to Elson's broadcasts, recalls the legendary announcer telling him, "Kid, when you're paid as lousy as we are, you gotta try the market." Elson persuaded Kaat to invest in Magnavox, which earned both a small fortune.[28]

Elson, later nicknamed the Old Commander because he served in the U.S. Navy during World War II, also padded his income by plugging just about any company, car wash, or corner barbershop that asked him—often during games, without the Cubs' knowledge of his financial arrangement. As fellow Hall of Fame broadcaster Lindsey Nelson recalled, "I've never heard *anybody* do as much shilling when he was on the air. We used to kid that Elson *had* to be on the take. Bob'd mosey along and say, 'There's ball two—and speaking of ball, did we have one last night at Rosa Mesa's Restaurant!' The [Cubs] never got a penny for Bob's shilling. . . . Say what you will about the Old Commander. If shilling was an art, Bob raised it to a new plateau."[29]

Perhaps Walgreens was lucky to catch Elson early in his career, when the money was above board, the ads were legitimate, and the baseball fans and teams weren't subjected to countless, shameless plugs.

damn the depression, full speed ahead!

In Walgreens' century-long history, the Depression was the company's toughest time, for both the stores and the employees. Yet, enduring the first four years of the Great Depression had little real impact on the company.

The company experienced a sea change in the middle of the Depression, however; and unlike most sweeping historical transformations, this one can be pinned to a single year, 1933, when the entire Walgreens corporation shifted its posture from merely surviving the Great Depression to thriving in spite of it.

In that one year FDR replaced Herbert Hoover, pushed through the New Deal (including the National Recovery Act Walgreens supported), and repealed Prohibition. Walgreens prepared its stores to take advantage of the good news by sending buyers to Europe before the final announcement to bring back all the Scotch whiskey and French wine they could the day it was declared. Walgreens was ready. The company also joined the National Association of Chain Drugstores in 1933, broke the million-dollar mark for advertising investment, expanded its Agency system dramatically, and paid the first dividend in company history (25 cents per share), a happy habit that continues to this day. Charles "Chuck" Walgreen Jr. became an executive vice president and married Mary Ann Leslie, his father's secretary. And, despite a cacophony of pessimism, the city of Chicago went ahead with its plans to host its second world's fair, titled "A Century of Progress," which enjoyed surprising success. All these events conspired to help Walgreens enter a bold period of expansion, one that outsiders thought impossible in that difficult decade.

Chicago's 1933 World's Fair had been designed to demonstrate man's mastery over his environment—which this vibrant city that men had made out of a swamp could fairly claim—and to celebrate the one-hundredth anniversary of the village's founding. Planned a decade in advance, in much flusher times, critics warned that the timing couldn't be worse and that the fair was bound to flop.

Once again, however, Chicago's dogged optimism overcame all, just as it had so many times before. Though the "Century of Progress" fair—which must have seemed more than a bit ironically named in the face of massive unemployment—was not as spectacular as Chicago's coming-out party in 1893, the 1933 version might have been more warmly welcomed by Chicagoans, who were hungrier for reassurance and relief from their daily struggles than were their ancestors.

The two fairs make convenient bookends for Walgreens' remarkable rise. When the previous one hit town, in 1893, Charles Sr. had recently arrived in Chicago on the train, looking for work as a clerk. His future wife—and food division pioneer—was then just a teenager awed by the bright lights of the White City. At the time, there were some 1,500 pharmacies in town—none of them Walgreens.

Forty years later, Charles had graduated from store clerk to the most prominent pharmacist in the nation, and one of the most successful businessmen in his adopted hometown. As proof, Walgreens was the "official pharmacy" of the fair, with two futuristic "art deco" stores on the fairgrounds that quickly proved inadequate to meet the tremendous demand of the fairgoers.

Unlike most of the official fair vendors, Walgreens did not raise its prices to gouge the visitors, but it still managed to turn a decent profit. Business was so brisk, in fact, that the company decided it had to expand its presence at the fair—immediately. "Beno" Borg, Chuck Walgreen's college roommate, called in all manner of tradesmen one minute after midnight on a Sunday, and six days later opened a 175-seat addition to the nearby 23rd Street plaza store, with 100 stools surrounding the soda fountain and a huge aquarium for a back bar. On Labor Day 1933, Borg's expanded store served 19,000 customers, which remains the company high;

the following year the chain reaped a record $54 million in revenues and realized $2.6 million in profit. Though not a record, in the depths of the Depression, any profit was noteworthy.

The fair's popularity defied the skeptics, generating $10 million in gate receipts alone and $26 million in gross revenues for the vendors, enough to convince the sponsors to re-up for a second equally successful summer in 1934. For Walgreens, the fair was especially fruitful. The "Century of Progress" drew 887 vendors, yet Walgreens alone pulled in fully 4 percent of gross revenues—about $1 million of the $26 million the fair raised, or 36 times more than the average vendor yielded.

Charles believed that the fair's real benefit to the chain, however, would be longer lasting than a few more dollars in the till. While the *Pepper Pod* allowed that Walgreens would make a "satisfactory profit" from the fair, the more important statistic to Charles was the 4 million customers served, many of them for the first time, gaining the company "substantial goodwill and advertising value," in Charles's words. "These millions of people are going to be your everyday customers from now on. What they think of Walgreens in the future will depend entirely on your treatment of them."[30]

Walgreens knew how to hit the iron when it was hot—or even just warm enough to make a good dent. While Walgreens' expansion during the Depression couldn't come close to the stratospheric growth it enjoyed in the Roaring Twenties—from 20 to 397 stores, a leap of almost 2,000 percent—Walgreens grew from 397 stores in 1929 to 493 in 1939, a rate of 24 percent, which could fairly be called robust and, given the times, even astounding.

Walgreens' Depression era expansion was harder than those numbers suggest because it wasn't simply a matter of taking the 397 stores with which it started the decade and adding 96. In 1933, for example, Walgreens opened 24 units but closed 25; the next year the chain opened 44 but closed 31. Thus, increasing the total fleet by 96 probably required opening 200-some stores and closing 100 or so, with all the extra effort and tough decision making that goes with such a strategy.

(This vetting process might have been what Robert Knight had in mind when he mentioned, at Walgreens' first nationwide conference in 1931, the necessity of getting rid of lazy drones and replacing them with worker bees. He did not seem to be advocating that Walgreens reduce the already stressed labor force—there is no evidence that Walgreens sought to do this and quite a bit of evidence to the contrary—but that the company could ill afford to carry deadweight for the sake of it. If you were lucky enough to be wearing a Walgreens smock while your neighbors stood in breadlines, you were expected to justify keeping it.)

Emboldened by the Columbian Exposition's success and encouraged by the chain's subsequent growth, Walgreens dared to dream big again, with the kind of romance that created the chain's elaborate soda fountains a decade earlier. Instead of being content simply to add more stores, Walgreens sought to make something special, something that would stir souls, starting with the chain's first "Super Store" in Tampa, Florida. Finished in 1934, in the heart of the Depression, the glamorous, 4,000-square-foot art deco building offered customers twice the size—and selection—of the typical Walgreens, including a grand soda fountain, always a popular attraction in the sticky South. Walgreens proudly termed the groundbreaking store, "The most efficient modern retail drugstore yet devised" and soon duplicated the design in Salt Lake City, Milwaukee, and Rochester, New York.[31]

Three years later, Walgreens took it a few steps farther—and four floors higher—when it opened another stunning store at 200 E. Flagler, Miami's main drag. The air-conditioned five-story colossus had an 80-foot-long soda fountain of solid white oak, a banquet hall, a 700-seat restaurant served by four kitchens, and an in-house ice cream factory that could produce 600 gallons a day. The success of the store's comprehensive restaurant prompted Walgreens to install full-service cafeterias nationwide.[32]

The most unusual feature of this million-dollar store, however, was the basement—the only one in South Florida at the time—originally built to house the store's own power plant. This became unnecessary when the local energy company reduced its rates, allowing Walgreens to convert the space to the chain's first "sports department," replete with golf clubs, tennis rackets, and fishing gear.

"This store was built for service [and] convenience," Charles said, sounding like his successors commenting about drive-thru pharmacies and one-hour photo processing years later, all designed to provide customers with maximum convenience. "There is no drugstore in the world as modern or as complete."[33]

Apparently the media agreed, with the three local papers competing to see which could give "the largest drugstore in the country" the most extravagant coverage.

The most impressive Super Store might not have been the biggest, but it was the stateliest. Although its restaurant sat a relatively paltry 375 people, the Walgreens' Oak Room restaurant and tea room inside the Super Store at Randolph and State streets in Chicago made a bigger splash when it opened in 1940, with one of the world's largest soda fountains and an escalator to take you there—something special at the time. By the middle of the decade, food service accounted for half the floor space in most Walgreens stores and a third of the profits.

"When we opened these large stores," Chuck recalled, "we found we didn't have enough [merchandise] to put in them." That, of course, was the problem Walgreens wanted to have—and one that was easily solved by simply producing more of its own products, including 2.4 million malteds in 1934 alone.[34]

In the midst of this unlikely uptick, Walgreens' success once again drew outside observers curious to see just how the company was pulling it off. In 1934, Paul H. Davis and Company, a top-rated investment advising firm in New York and Chicago, issued a report on the drugstore chain that almost echoed the analysis John Nickerson and Company had produced just five years earlier, a few months before Black Tuesday. That one was written at the peak of the Roaring Twenties and the other at the depths of the Depression speaks volumes about the stability of the firm.

Davis and Company praised Walgreen's "foresight and merchandising genius as well as an exceptional judgment in selecting men of ability to assist in the company's management." The report concluded that the company's secret, such as it was, boiled down to "30 years of aggressive yet conservative management"—in other words, bedrock values coupled with bold ventures, the very same equation Walgreens has relied on for over a century.

No sooner had the analysts from Davis and Company departed than the reporters from *Fortune* magazine arrived to produce the lead story for the September 1934 issue on the chain.[35] Titled, "500 Corner Drugstores," the piece extolled Walgreens' merchandising prowess. "A druggist's technique nowadays is to put before you everything that you can conceivably need in your home, at a price calculated to attract you." Walgreens' decision to sell much more than drugs, which began when Charles first put together his display of pots and pans years earlier, had caught on.

"Across the fountain [of the average Walgreens store] each year flow 455 gallons of chocolate [and] 45 gallons of vanilla syrup," the author said. Tables for food service alone, the magazine reported, accounted for half the floor space in many stores. Although the pharmacy department brought in a paltry 3 percent of profits, Charles remained committed to staffing a full-service pharmacy in every store.

The *Fortune* staffers were smart enough to look beyond the soda fountains that hooked readers and customers alike. Walgreens' success, they said, was due in part to some very smart financial decisions that customers never see. The once powerful Liggett chain and the United Drug network were in trouble, *Fortune* explained, because they had locked themselves into long-term leases in the 1920s that had become oppressive in the 1930s. Walgreens executives, in contrast, signed much more favorable leases and only leased what they needed without taking on extra space they would then have to sublease to others, putting the onus on the chain.

Fortune gave particular credit to Robert Knight, whom it called the "financial brain" of the outfit, who had "analyzed, trimmed, and coordinated Walgreens financial methods to weather the storm that broke in 1929." In other words, Mr. Knight had done exactly what he'd promised to do 10 years earlier after he finished his master's thesis.

For all these reasons, *Fortune* concluded, during the darkest days of the Depression, Walgreens "sits at the top of the retail drug business."

finding time for fun   *Balanced life*

It is a Walgreen family trait to find time for fun, even in the toughest times. During the Depression, the family enjoyed some of its happiest days at their Hazelwood estate in Dixon.

Having purchased a run-down Shangri-la, the Walgreens threw themselves into the project wholeheartedly, restoring and expanding the central home (which grew from a cabin to something more closely resembling a castle), building an in-ground swimming pool, and planting elaborate gardens, which Myrtle cultivated the rest of her life, thereby transforming the once decrepit estate into an Illinois showplace.

The town of Dixon, as depressed as any of the era, especially with its centerpiece in ruins, was thrilled. "To have strolled over Hazelwood and to have noted the physical destruction," wrote an anonymous person, in "Hazelwood: Its Masters," in 1937, "would have forced one to agree that nothing but sordid revenge of some unnatural character could have caused such cruel wreckage." But, "Anonymous" continued in the breathless style of the day, "When it had become known that [Charles] had made the purchase of Hazelwood, what a feeling of relief and pleasure pervaded every avenue of business and social life in Dixon! The Dixon boy had returned to save Dixon and Hazelwood! No one but the resident of the old home town and the lover of Hazelwood, even to this day, can appreciate the feeling of relief and gratitude that followed."[36]

The Walgreens often invited the "Walgreens girls"—office secretaries, numbering over a hundred—out to Hazelwood for relaxing summer weekends as a reward for their hard work. And, when Charles decided to play a round of golf at the nearby course, another Dixon boy named Ronald Reagan frequently caddied for him. (He and Nancy would return to Hazelwood at Chuck's invitation in 1978, during Reagan's presidential campaign.)

Hazelwood's guest list over the years has been studded with celebrities, including, in the early days, Carl Sandburg and explorer Rear Admiral Richard E. Byrd. Charles had long been an admirer of the famous pilot; he donated a ton of Walgreens powdered milk for Byrd's 1933 expedition to Antarctica. He could appreciate the Admiral's efforts more than most, perhaps, because he, too, was a pilot. Charles bought the nation's first corporate "aero plane" and earned his pilots' license. (Even Myrtle learned to execute loop-de-loops.) But he had never met the explorer until 1938, after Myrtle attended one of Byrd's lectures in Chicago and invited him to Hazelwood for the night.

By the next morning's breakfast, Myrtle recalled in her autobiography, her husband and the Admiral were "deep in a friendship that was like picking up in the middle of years of common interests."[37] They remained in close touch until Charles's death.

Most Walgreens employees derived their greatest satisfaction from having a good job in a good store working for good people—none of which were to be taken for granted in the 1930s—and the simple pleasures that arose during the day. Delbert Adkins, for example, recalled years later:

> I was in the big city of Dallas in 1940, fresh off the farm. The Texas Employment Commission sent me to Walgreens, said they needed a busboy. I had no idea what a busboy was; I thought maybe I'd go out to the curb and take orders from people on a bus. I got the job: ten hours a day, $10 a week, seven days a week.
>
> Just before I got married they promoted me to soda dispenser. The first day I worked at the fountain, a gentleman came in and said, "Cherry Coke fizz." I had no idea what that was. So the manager showed me—cherry syrup, Coke syrup, and a fine stream of carbonated water. The man said, "Boy, they're sure hiring 'em dumb these

days." Next day I saw him come in, I had his cherry Coke fizz waiting. He said it was still fizzing and tipped me 50 cents [big money in
those days].[38]

the son also rises

In hindsight, it seems a given that Charles and Myrtle's son, Chuck, would
lead the company one day; but as he was growing up, it looked like anything but a sure thing.

Chuck helped his parents from early on, doing everything from delivering his mom's apple pies on his bike as an eight-year-old to working on the
store-opening crews that christened a new outlet almost every week as a
college student.

Chuck and his younger sister, Ruth, attended the University of Chicago
(U-C) laboratory school just down the street from the Walgreens' home.
The U-C lab school was among the first of its kind, led by pioneering ped-
agogue John Dewey. During Chuck's senior year, headmaster Dr. Revis,
who later served as president of the university, asked each student where
he or she planned to go to college. Chuck had no idea. "Some families live
and die about where their kids go to college," he said, "but that didn't
mean too much in our family."[39]

For graduation, Chuck's parents presented him with a brand new Model
T Ford. Chuck took the shiny car and a tattered old tent and hopped on
the back roads (there were no other kind in the 1920s) to tour college
campuses around the country, stopping at Harvard, Dartmouth, and
Middlebury, among others. On the way back to Chicago, Chuck remembered one of his favorite lab school teachers, Dr. Virgil Lohr, telling him
to stop by the University of Michigan in Ann Arbor, if his travels took
him that way, and look up a woman named Miss Buntin.

Chuck did just that. "And that's the first time I ever gave a thought to
the University of Michigan," he said. After Miss Buntin examined the
young man's transcript, she politely pointed out that he lacked the two

years of foreign language Michigan required, but she was so impressed by his grades—and his new-found passion for attending the school—that she made an exception and admitted him for the fall term.

Miss Buntin could never know that her simple decision would eventually reap the university millions in gifts from the Walgreen family, which would send three generations (and counting) to the campus. The donations have helped Michigan's College of Pharmacy retain its place among the nation's elite. In fairness, there was no way Miss Buntin could have guessed, because Chuck decided to enroll in the school's college of architecture.

"'So,' she told me, 'be sure to study well,'" Chuck recalled. "My first blue book exam, I thought the whole thing was a big mistake, because the professors asked questions about the beginning of the subject, which I'd never learned, and I didn't think that was a very nice thing to do. All I did was play poker, instead of review. I didn't do so well on the final exams—two As and two Bs."[40] Not bad, of course, but not nearly as impressive as the A-pluses Chuck had earned at U-C high.

"After I got the grades and my dad saw them, he said he knew I could do better," Chuck recalled. "'Chuck, we have to talk seriously,' he said. 'If you think you'd like to get into the drug business, there are a couple things you have to do, and one is pass the state board exam for pharmacology.'"[41]

Thanks to Prohibition, the rules had changed since Charles Sr. worked as a clerk when he first arrived in Chicago. To prevent pharmacies from selling alcohol under the guise of "medicinal purposes," the State of Illinois mandated that all drugstores be run by state-licensed pharmacists, who risked losing their licenses if they made any backdoor prescriptions.

Chuck decided to take the year off school, work for his dad's company, and see if he liked it. Despite being assigned to the rigorous store-opening team, Chuck liked the work just fine and decided to follow in his father's footsteps. He returned to Michigan in the fall of 1926, this time as a student in the College of Pharmacy. After graduating in 1928, he returned to Walgreens' Chicago headquarters, where he met his future wife, Mary Ann Leslie.

Miss Leslie had started at Walgreens a few years earlier as a three-week temp in the purchasing department, but she had managed to turn that into a permanent job as Charles Walgreen Sr.'s personal receptionist, earning accolades for her ability to handle all comers with aplomb.

A good example: One day in 1933 a man carrying a revolver walked up to her desk and asked to see her boss. Leslie assessed the situation, then calmly replied, "Sir, Mr. Walgreen is busy now, so you'll have to take a seat on the waiting room bench with the other gentlemen who are waiting and take your turn."[42]

Perhaps soothed by Leslie's smooth demeanor, the troubled man, incredibly, did as instructed, affording Leslie the opportunity to tell Mr. Walgreen about his unscheduled visitor. Walgreen was as cool as his receptionist. He picked up the phone and called for a security officer, who kindly escorted the man downstairs, where the police were waiting. At Walgreen's request, no charges were filed.

Back when company headquarters was still a pretty compact space, it was inevitable that Chuck would meet the poised young receptionist. The two hit it off and married in 1933. Two years later they gave birth to Charles III. When Charles Sr. laid eyes on his grandson for the first time, he exclaimed, "That's my little corker!"[43] A nickname was coined, and former CEO Cork Walgreen has carried it ever since.

Chuck worked his way up from opening stores to leasing real estate, working on the front lines of the company's never-ending quest to find a good corner. He proved especially effective at renegotiating store leases, a vital skill during the Depression, as the *Fortune* story mentioned earlier had attested. Chuck plied his craft mainly out West, in Utah, California, and Oregon, with a simple but effective approach: He persuaded the landlords to set the rent lower than the pre-Depression rates so the store could stay above water, but higher than the current market price so the landlord could keep making a profit. Walgreen almost always got what he wanted, partly because the deal made sense for both parties, partly because he sought only "a fair arrangement," and partly because of his engaging "million dollar smile," as his dad put it.

As one California landlord recalled, "Walgreen came in with that smile of his and put the books on the table and kept smiling [until] I took off $40,000."[44] (that's more than $500,000 today). Such deals covered a lot of workers' wages.

When asked to name the highlight of his 51 years at Walgreens, Chuck quickly cited the day in December 1933 that he was named a company vice president, "because," he explained, "you get so many privileges—including an office next to my father's."[45]

While Chuck was working his way up the company ladder, Charles was weaning himself from Walgreens to allow more time for flying, refurbishing Hazelwood, and giving away his money. Charles had always been generous with his employees, his pay plans, and his charitable giving, but one of his biggest gifts started out with an argument.

the accidental benefactor

An investigation of Walgreen's highly public conflict with the University of Chicago may seem, at first blush, to be of only incidental importance to a history of the Walgreen corporation. But the values at stake in this debate were of the utmost importance to him—and his company. What customers experienced when they walked into a Walgreens store was a direct outcome of the beliefs on which Walgreen based the company decades earlier.

The entire imbroglio started when Myrtle's niece Lucille Norton—daughter of her brother Paul, whose family had moved to Seattle—wanted to attend the University of Chicago. She naturally moved in with the Walgreens, who paid her $300 tuition.

All was well until she began engaging Charles in testy dinnertime debates over socialism, communism, and "free love," among other hot topics. When Charles remarked, "Lucille, you're getting to be a communist," she replied, "I am not the only one—there are a lot more on campus." This alarmed Charles. "Do you realize," he asked, "that this means the abolition of the family, the abolition of the church, and especially do you realize it means the overthrow of our government?"—all the things that Charles believed in most. "Yes, I think I do," Lucille said, "but doesn't the end justify the means?"[46]

Charles became more concerned when Lucille said she had been exposed to these ideas primarily by her professors, one of whom assigned Karl Marx and Friedrich Engels's *The Communist Manifesto* (1848) and another who advocated "free love," an idea far more shocking in the 1930s than it would be when it resurfaced in the 1960s.

In hindsight, it would be easy to dismiss Charles's fears as those of an "establishment reactionary," the kind of person who might support Senator McCarthy in the 1950s. But in the 1930s, Americans—and especially students—were wondering if the American way of life could survive, or even if it should. Unemployment was high, bread lines were long, and optimism was low indeed. In a 1933 survey of 1,000 students attending nine Eastern colleges, 50 percent said they were "willing to try socialism," 40 percent were opposed to free enterprise system, and 13 percent favored "communism and revolution." One student strike attracted 500,000 supporters, followed by another of 1 million students. The majority of Americans were opposed to any involvement in a foreign war.[47]

Although we know how both the Depression and World War II turned out, Charles Walgreen didn't have the benefit of foresight. (The Bolshevik Revolution in Russia had succeeded just 18 years earlier, while the Fascist revolution in Spain was headed the same way.) Furthermore, Charles had attended what amounted to glorified trade schools—for accounting and for pharmacy—whose sole purpose was vocational preparation. So the idea of high-powered professors espousing such beliefs was understandably foreign and threatening.

On April 10, 1935, Charles Walgreen sent a letter to University of Chicago president Robert Maynard Hutchins to inform him that Walgreen was withdrawing his niece from the school because he was unwilling "to have her absorb the communistic influences to which she is insidiously exposed. . . . Why one of our country's leading universities, sound and substantial in the majority of its teachings and activities, with its fine opportunity for teaching and advancing a higher and finer standard of American Citizenship, should permit, even to a limited degree, seditious propaganda under the guise of academic freedom, is something I cannot understand."[48]

A cynic might point out that all business moguls are keen to maintain the status quo because they have been rewarded so handsomely by it and must protect the system to protect their own wealth. But that would not be fair to Walgreen. His patriotism ran deep and stretched far back in his life, long before he was a millionaire or even a store owner. In fact, patriotism was the second thing in Walgreen's life about which he was truly passionate, the first being baseball. (His love of Myrtle came next, with his passion for work emerging years later.)

Once the conflict was put in motion, it didn't take long for William Randolph Hearst's *Chicago Herald-Tribune* to pick up the story and spread it across his network of papers around the country. Looking at the documents, one senses that this embarrassed Walgreen, who was not afraid to give his opinion and stand by it but was constitutionally indisposed to making a scene. Just eight days after his letter to President Hutchins, Walgreen responded to a woman who had apparently sent Walgreen a supportive letter; he replied that while he "greatly appreciate[d]" her comments, he merely "acted as an ordinary citizen in removing my niece from the University of Chicago, for reasons which I considered proper. In doing so, I unwittingly precipitated the general question of Communistic influences at the University."[49]

But the ball was already in play. The Illinois State Senate set up a five-man panel to conduct a month-long investigation of the university, culminating in public hearings.

Once matters were in the open, it seemed that perhaps things had been a bit overblown, due partly to Lucille's interpretation of events. Although it was true that one professor required his students to read Marx and another made what he claimed was a joking reference to free love, the university made a plausible case that the radicalism of the campus had been greatly exaggerated—55 percent of students in 1932 supported Herbert Hoover over Franklin Roosevelt—with many student leaders presenting evidence in corroboration.[50]

For his part, Hutchins played the dicey situation like a pro, first defending the importance of academic freedom in order to soothe his professors, then providing reassurances to outsiders like Walgreen. A member of the faculty, Hutchins said, must be allowed to "join any church, club, or party, and think, live, worship, and vote as he pleases." But he added that "the University would . . . dismiss any professor who, before an appropriate tribunal, was proved to have advocated the overthrow of the government by violence."[51]

The controversy had been settled to everyone's apparent satisfaction, but Hutchins wisely didn't stop there. To court Walgreen and to convert him to the university's cause, he enlisted the help of William Benton, a wealthy Yale graduate who had recently retired from his advertising firm. Benton established a friendship with Walgreen over several months. Knowing of his passionate belief in the American system, Benton asked Walgreen, "Why don't you give money to the university to help the university correct the defect which you feel is in it?" Walgreen replied that he "would be glad to consider this." He felt some remorse that the imbroglio might limit donations to the university and, perhaps, that his concerns might have been fanned by Lucille's partially inaccurate assessment.[52]

Hutchins took it from there, enjoying long conversations with Walgreen at the company headquarters at Bowen Avenue and at the school's Quadrangle Club. He also encouraged the CEO to visit any lecture and classroom he wished, to see for himself the university's mission.[53] If Charles Walgreen was a master at converting upset customers to loyal patrons, President Hutchins was his equal.

Hutchins's efforts soon bore fruit. On June 5, 1937—over two years after Walgreen first wrote Hutchins—President Hutchins announced the creation of the Charles R. Walgreen Foundation for the Study of American Institutions "to forward the development of good citizenship and the improvement of public service" with a gift of $550,000 in

Walgreen stock. "In establishing this foundation," Walgreen said, in a prepared statement, "I am not interested in promulgating any special view. I do desire a fair and impartial study of our institutions. My confidence in our way of life is such that I believe to understand it will be to cherish it." The next day, the front page of Hearst's *Tribune* called Hutchins's role "an outstanding feat of academic salesmanship."[54]

Part of Walgreen's gift was earmarked for a lecture series by people of accomplishment, including Walter Lippman, Carl Sandburg (a close friend), and Archibald MacLeish. The foundation was included in the social studies department until 1958, when it was moved to the business school, where George J. Stigler was named to head the foundation as the first Charles Rudolph Walgreen Professor of American Institutions. Stigler would go on to win the 1982 Nobel prize for economics and a National Medal of Science in 1987 for his theories on public regulation of industry. (Lucille, however, returned to Seattle to continue her education at a local college.)

This incident did not directly impact the Walgreens chain—sales seemed to be unaffected by the headlines—but it had everything in it that Charles brought to the company: passion, conviction, and boldness tempered by fairness, forgiveness, and, ultimately, generosity.

"The investigation," concluded Robert Coven, in his 1992 article in *Chicago History*, "ironically created a bond of trust and friendship between Walgreen and Hutchins."[55] Hutchins would honor that friendship dearly at Walgreen's funeral.

From Challange to turning around for opportunity

charles's demise

Although Charles Sr. seemed robust on entering his sixties, he knew he would one day have to step down, so he starting grooming Chuck to lead the company.[56]

In hindsight it was fortunate that Charles Sr. started the succession process relatively early. In early 1939, when he was 66—"just getting into the prime of life, when you can really enjoy yourself," said the 97-year-old Chuck—and his son was just 33, Charles began to suffer from an uncharacteristic listlessness. Charles's annual physical showed nothing of concern, so he urged Myrtle to go on a trip to Hawaii with her friends. In her long-distance conversations with her husband, however, she sensed that something wasn't right and came home early.

A more thorough round of tests gave the family the very news it dreaded: Charles Walgreen Sr. had cancer. Although the doctors and family did not tell Charles—a common practice at the time—he seemed to understand what was happening.

On August 10, 1939, Charles Sr. announced he'd be resigning the presidency. "He asked me what I thought of being president, and I said, I didn't think I was qualified," Chuck said. "But knowing all the key people, I had full confidence that we'd be moving right along."[57]

The board elected Chuck as president. Because the family had not owned majority stock in the company for years—the *Fortune* article reported that the family possessed only 178,000 of the 809,000 no-par common stock, less than a quarter of it[58]—the board's decision represented a strong vote of confidence in the young man and, by proxy, his father.

"It was just like a family business," Chuck said, despite the fact that it was owned by the shareholders. "They all respected and thought the world of my Dad and did anything he thought was the proper thing to do in the company."[59]

As the winter closed in and his condition had not improved, Charles decided to try Christian Science; and although it didn't provide him a cure, it allowed him to sleep without drugs or pain. On December 8, 1939, a cablegram arrived from his friend Rear Admiral Byrd, then on his third Antarctic expedition, saying he and his men were sailing among the South Sea Islands and wished Charles was with them.

On December 9, 1939, Charles Sr. told Myrtle how much he had always loved her. The next day he fell into a coma and died a day later.

FAMILY BUSINESS
DIED

At his funeral, his former nemesis turned loyal friend, University of Chicago president Robert Maynard Hutchins, stood up and walked to the podium to eulogize Charles, with touchingly simple affection:

> Mr. Walgreen was the best friend I had. I suppose he was the best friend anyone in this room had.
>
> There was no bunk about Mr. Walgreen, no front, no pretense. He was himself always. Simple, honest, and direct. So much so that he even leaned over backwards and lied about it, to make you think he wasn't as good as he seemed from the outside, and to convince you that he didn't have any ability at all and that everything that happened was luck. He was very anxious not to have anyone feel that he had an exaggerated notion of his own importance.
>
> He really loved his friends. He didn't just like them. He didn't ever form acquaintances because he thought he could get something out of them. Mr. Walgreen never let anyone down who had any cause to rely upon him. He spent hours thinking about business problems, personal problems, domestic problems, the political future of any one of his friends without any thought of reward.
>
> If you take a simple, honest and direct man—a man who was always himself, in whom there is no false show or pretense, a man who loved his friends—you have a man who must be the best friend of all.
>
> He was our best friend. We shall not look upon his like again.[60]

Walgreen vindicated Hutchins's praise posthumously, too, when the estate attorneys discovered that in addition to his substantial gifts to his family, the University of Chicago, and six churches, he had bequeathed 2,500 shares of Walgreen stock (worth over $50,000, or almost $650,000 in today's dollars) to the Walgreen Benefit Fund. This, he had written, was intended for "needy and deserving . . . employees without regard to whether they are currently employed by the company or its subsidiaries." The Walgreen Benefit Fund surpassed a million dollars in 1950, and now has many times that, to help Walgreens employees—even those who worked there only a few months years earlier—in times of need, including terminal sickness. The executors of the estate had also discovered Charles had earmarked his $500,000 life insurance policy to start an employee retirement fund, now called the Walgreen Profit Sharing Plan, one of the very first of its kind, called "a landmark in American industrial relations."[61]

Not long after Charles was put to rest, Chuck received a package from Rear Admiral Richard Byrd. Chuck opened it carefully and slowly pulled out its contents: a map of Antarctica. "Dear Chuck," the Admiral wrote, in graceful penmanship. "Here is the coastline I named after that great American, your father, and my dear friend, Charles Walgreen. With it goes my affectionate regards to all the Walgreens. Dick Byrd."[62] If you look on a map of Antarctica today, you can still see the Walgreen Coast, running a thousand miles along the Amundsen Sea. MAGNIFICENT

Charles Walgreen's greatest legacy, however, is not a glowing eulogy or the foundations, or a seacoast, but the 4,000-plus stores that bear his name and the 150,000 people who work them. The little shop with the big ideas that he and Myrtle started a century ago has grown into something special.

That Walgreen's simple but powerful ideas of service, convenience, and caring could outlive him by six decades and counting is legacy enough for any man.

defusing a palace coup

When Chuck became the executive assistant to his father in 1935, he soon discovered that not everyone was fit to work at Walgreens and that it was now his job to ferret some of them out.

Shortly after Chuck moved into the office next door, Charles gave him a case to investigate that he would never forget. It seemed that one of the Walgreens tobacco buyers had a chauffeur dressed in lavender to drive his matching Cadillac to the Bowen Avenue headquarters each morning. The chauffeur waited there for the buyer the entire day, until it came time to drive him home that night. Chuck knew the buyer was paid well—even during the Depression, Walgreens could place an order for 6 million cigars without blinking—but he didn't think the buyer was paid well enough to afford such extravagance.

Suspicious, Chuck called a friend of his from the Rotary Club, who also happened to run the local office of the Burns Detective Agency. This gumshoe looked into the cigar buyer's background and discovered his résumé had been fabricated from whole cloth, starting with his claim of being a fire commissioner in an Ohio city. Far worse, the detective found that the buyer was skilled at soliciting kickbacks from tobacco companies and also had convinced a prophylactics manufacturer to pay him a 5 percent commission—even though he didn't purchase the products for Walgreens.

The last charge particularly irked Chuck because he had once been the company's purchaser of prophylactics, and he knew the suspect had no role in the purchase. The young vice president passed his findings on to his father, who pulled the buyer into his office for a brief conference. The buyer confessed his sins, gave back the money, and left the company without charges being brought.[63] The incident served as an eye-opener for Chuck and prepared him for harder battles ahead.

Just before World War II erupted, a much smaller war broke out at Walgreen headquarters on Bowen Avenue. One of the combatants, Charles Walgreen Jr., was as reluctant as Switzerland to fight; but the other party, Justin Dart, forced his hand. It was the kind of power struggle that is de rigueur at most corporations but almost unheard of in the placid hallways—New Yorkers would say "dull"—of Walgreens' executive offices.

Justin Dart was the kind of dashing young man who could have played himself in the movie version of Walgreens' history. Dart attended Northwestern University in Evanston, Illinois, where he met Charles Sr.'s daughter, Ruth. The two married in 1929, the same year Dart started his Walgreens career as a stock boy.

Marrying the boss's daughter didn't hurt Dart's prospects, of course, but Dart's quick climb to director of Walgreens' store operations in just three years had more to do with his native talent and unabashed ambition than it did with nepotism. (This theory held up after Dart and Ruth were divorced in 1938; a year later, the board promoted Dart to general manager.) He played an important role in developing the Super Stores that Walgreens rolled out around the country in the mid-1930s, but Dart's ravenous ego compelled him to exaggerate his part whenever he related the story to others, inside or outside the company.

Worse, Dart's oft-repeated claim that he pulled in a quick $400,000 for the company immediately after Congress repealed Prohibition in December 1933 by selling off Walgreens' stock of whiskey, which was only available by prescription under the Eighteenth Amendment, was completely fatuous. Walgreens didn't have nearly enough whiskey in stock to meet the coming demand. Walgreen Sr. knew it; so, as mentioned earlier, he had sent his buyers to Europe to ensure that Walgreens was ready when the amendment was repealed. Just weeks after the repeal, 60 percent of Walgreens stores were selling spirits, enough to account for about 10 percent of sales in most stores—all without any help from Mr. Dart.

Dart also didn't conform to the long-standing company custom of maintaining a low profile. In contrast to his colleagues, Dart was a shameless self-promoter. After learning to fly in 1936, Dart captained the company's state-of-the-art Lockheed Skydart—the first corporate plane in the country, a six-passenger machine whose two engines could zoom along at 240 miles per hour, a stunning speed for the time—to drop in on store openings and events all over the country. He once shared the controls with Rear Admiral Richard E. Byrd, Charles Sr.'s good friend, on a short sojourn from the Walgreen estate in Dixon to Chicago. After Dart radioed the control tower at Chicago's Midway Airport that Rear Admiral Byrd was his copilot, an angered airport official brought a police officer along to meet the plane when it pulled in, ready to arrest Dart for playing a prank. "Unfortunately," the *Pepper Pod* reported, "the record is blank about what the official had to say when he saw the explorer, resplendent in service stripes and decorations, stepping out of the NC17311."[64]

Dart's publicity stunts usually benefited the company, but that didn't seem to be his primary concern. He often took expensive, frivolous jaunts designed to serve only his own pleasure or ego. Before long, it became clear to his peers that the dashing Dart's first priority was himself.

Dart's personality naturally carried over to the office, too, where his mood could swing from charming to disturbing in an afternoon. At his best, he could soothe a nervous employee, console a co-worker, or beguile a job candidate. He was famous for his engaging personality, his generosity toward his subordinates (to whom he would often lend hundreds of dollars in a pinch), and his ability to inspire loyalty in his charges. But at his worst, he was boorish, self-absorbed, and terribly temperamental, once intimidating an overbearing newspaper ad man by grabbing a nearby pitching wedge and ripping into a box of talcum powder, dusting the entire room and both occupants with the stuff. He also liked to relieve stress—or possibly just show off—by firing a handgun into a stack of telephone books against the far wall of his office.

"Such prankish behavior," the Kogans wrote, "could be tolerated so long as Dart was making his contributions to the company's welfare; but within a few years his uninhibited ways and brashness would make him persona non grata to the firm's board of directors."[65]

When Dart's ego and ambition began to eclipse "the better angels of his nature," conflicts and tension grew. The company's conflicts with Dart became more pronounced after Charles became terminally ill in 1939.

As a concession to his failing health, Walgreen announced on August 10, four months before his death, that he was stepping down as president, though he would serve the company as chairman of the board of directors. As mentioned earlier, the board appointed Chuck to succeed his father as president and also appointed the talented Mr. Dart as Walgreens' general manager.

The board celebrated the promotions in the *Pepper Pod*, stating its collective belief that the duo would work well together and would "be as hard-working, as hard-hitting, and as able as any company could hope to secure."[66]

But Charles sensed the potential for trouble. Knowing the end was near,

Charles Walgreen Sr. asked his top executives to put aside their own ambitions to help his 33-year-old son manage a very difficult transition to president, and not sabotage Chuck's efforts through a palace coup. Everyone—including such heavy hitters as Roland Schmitt, Harry Goldstine, Jim Ward, and Robert Knight, who had built the company from the ground floor up—honored their mentor's final request without hesitation . . . everyone, that is, except Dart, who openly criticized Chuck's conservative approach to business decisions and made no secret of his conviction that he would have made a better president.

Dart behaved capriciously toward his store managers, rewarding and punishing them according to his whims, not their performance—creating a culture of fearful yes-men, too timid to give their boss honest opinions. Although Dart was responsible for keeping the board members fully informed, he usually kept them in the dark. Given his predilection for claiming full credit to the exclusion of all others, board members started a running joke that Dart was "a one-man team."[67]

"He was married to my sister, and he was considered a boy wonder at the time, a brilliant young man," Chuck says today. "But the unfortunate part is, after my dad died, we couldn't quite see eye to eye, and it seemed like we wouldn't be able to work together as a team."[68]

By July 1941, two years into Chuck's reign as Walgreens' president, it had become clear that the corporate marriage was failing. Board members presented a resolution asking for Dart's resignation, but Dart was not going to go peacefully into that dark night. "This place will go to the dogs without me!" he said, banging his fist on the table—unwittingly erasing any doubts the board might have had. The resolution passed unanimously.

The company spared Dart the humiliation of a public announcement, however, and granted his request to use the company plane to find his next job. The *Chicago Tribune* ran a front-page story months later, with no juicy details and no blame attributed for the transition. Dart joined United Drugs' management team—which oversaw 528 Liggett and Owl stores and 12,500 Rexall franchises—and became its president just two years later. Dart became very wealthy and powerful, ultimately gaining control over a large chunk of the original corporation under the umbrella of Dart Industries.

Though necessary, Dart's departure left Chuck Walgreen to lead the family business through the nation's most difficult economic times without his most talented—if also his most troublesome—executive. "I probably would have been scared to death if I hadn't been so close to all the key people in the company and realized their capabilities," Chuck said. "But knowing that, I had full confidence that we would move right along."[69]

In some ways, you could argue Dart might have been ahead of his time. His brash, egotistical style would have made him a magazine cover boy among the celebrity CEO set in the 1990s—but not at Walgreens, then or now. And this is the point: Although only a handful of Walgreens' most senior employees can place Dart's name today, he's the kind of person who would have been able to take over almost any other company and reshape it in his image, all the while gutting the very foundation on which it was built. Values, tradition, team spirit—these things meant little to Dart and even less when they got in the way of his own interests.

That a palace coup didn't work at Walgreens some 60 years ago—and has never come close to resurfacing since—has everything to do with why Walgreens is such a solid company today. In future years, Walgreens' leaders would be modeled on Chuck's warm, humble demeanor, not on Dart's bombastic style—and that has made all the difference.

The battle for the company's soul was fought and won in 1941.

there's a war on

In October 1940, American men between the ages of 20 and 36 registered for the draft: 16 million would enlist in the military, including some 2,500 Walgreens employees, about a fifth of the company's workforce at the time; and 291,557 Americans would make the ultimate sacrifice,[70] with 48 Walgreens workers among them.[71]

Needless to say, during the war years, business matters took a back seat to bigger issues, but business still had to be conducted. In addition to a shortage of workers, Walgreens also had to work through shortages of tires and gasoline for its delivery trucks; building materials for its stores; and tobacco, film, and canned goods for its customers. "Even maintenance was difficult," Chuck recalled.[72] Cleansers, brooms, mops—and the people to use them—were also in short supply.

Nonetheless, Chuck Walgreen—as patriotic as his father—asked his employees to deduct 10 percent from each paycheck to purchase war bonds, and they came through to the tune of $5.6 million. The stores also encouraged their customers to buy bonds, with one booth in each restaurant turned over to a bond sales agent. The effort produced another $41 million for the cause, or the equivalent of the chain's annual gross revenue just a few years earlier. (In characteristic Walgreen fashion, Chuck gave generously but quietly, just as he has given millions of dollars to the University of Michigan.)

Walgreens took its support a step farther in May 1943, when the new Pentagon opened bidding for a drugstore to fill a 6,000-square-foot space, 50 percent larger than Walgreens' biggest Super Stores. By the standards of the Pentagon, however, the store would be a boutique. Even before Pearl Harbor, the need for the Pentagon building was real enough. As the late David Brinkley wrote in his 1988 best seller, *Washington Goes to War*, "the army alone had grown from 7,000 civilian employees to 41,000" and occupied some two dozen buildings scattered throughout the Washington, D.C., area.[73] The building that Secretary of War Henry Stimson proposed would house 35,000 employees; it would have three times more floor space than the Empire State Building; it would run a mile in circumference; and it would be the world's biggest building the day it was completed. It would be far too big to fit inside Washington, D.C., proper; so the government searched for a tract of land in Virginia, settling on one that was partially occupied by a public dump.

The Army asked Congress to allocate a then-staggering $35 million for the building—solemnly promising not to go over the budget by a penny— but the massive figure predictably drew protests anyway. "We may not need all that space when the war comes to an end," objected Everett Dirksen of Illinois. "What will we do with the extra space?"[74] The honorable Mr. Dirksen needn't have worried.

In September 1941, while President Roosevelt dithered over where the building should go, the army engineers started digging without him. The rush job never relented, resulting in an accident rate 400 percent higher than the era's average for such large public projects. Three hundred architects worked their slide rules, completed their calculations, and pushed their pencils; but they still couldn't keep up with the construction workers. When one architect asked fellow architect Alan Dickey, "How big should I make that beam across the third floor?" Dickey replied, "I don't know. They installed it yesterday."[75]

By early 1943, the world's biggest building had been finished in little more than a year. But it cost $87 million—two and a half times the promised budget—and "on the day it was finished," Brinkley wrote, "it was already too small." Whereas the building had been designed to house 35,000 employees, 40,000 set up shop there in the first year alone.

Stories of the confusion that the colossal structure created among its visitors became running jokes. "One woman," Brinkley wrote, "was said to have told a guard she was in labor and needed help in getting to a maternity hospital. The guard said, 'Madam, you should not have come in here in that condition.' 'When I came in here,' she answered, 'I wasn't.'"[76]

Of the various drugstore chains that submitted bids to become the Pentagon's official pharmacist, only Walgreens proposed to funnel all profits from the store back to the Pentagon Post Restaurant Council, which supervised the building's food service. Perhaps trying to make a dent in the $48 million construction budget overrun, the Pentagon wisely accepted.

The War Department weekly, *The War Times*, stated two years later that Walgreens' "attitude was so patriotically generous that no competitor could possibly better it. Mr. Walgreen felt that since the people at the Pentagon are War Department workers, he would prefer to operate his store on the concourse entirely without profit to his company."[77]

The Pentagon store was Walgreens' only opening in 1943, but it is hard to imagine a Walgreens outlet making a bigger impact than that franchise, which operated successfully well into the 1980s.[78]

Like the rest of the country, Walgreens didn't flourish during the war years, but it survived—and emerged stronger than before. Chuck Walgreen identified many of the reasons for the chain's durability in the company's 1942 annual report: "We are fortunate in the wide diversity of the goods we stock, in the probable availability of most of them, and in that our sales effort can be effectively varied by advertising and display, all of which adds up to a high degree of flexibility and, hence, stability."[79]

When the war ended, Walgreens was alive and well. Just as other companies felt fortunate to emerge from the Depression still standing, they were content—even lucky—to survive the war. Not Walgreens. From 1941 to 1945, net profit remained stable while the chain's sales jumped from $83.7 million to $119.2 million, then soared to $141.4 million in 1946—a leap of 72 percent in five very difficult years.

When the war ended, Walgreens was ready.

where everyone meets

At a time when people often found themselves in strange cities and towns across the country—for military training, on scheduled leave, or to fill vacancies for badly needed help—Walgreens' familiar logo, central locations, and friendly surroundings served as meeting places a thousand times every day.

"I remember my girlfriends saying, 'When we get old enough, we'll stand on the corner in front of Walgreens on State and Randolph and pick up sailors,'" recalled Vivian Bosi, who grew up in the Chicago area before moving to Escondido, California. "The Great Lakes Naval Station was nearby. All the girls did that; they'd sashay up and down the sidewalk in front of Walgreens, select the sailor they wanted, pair up, go inside to the soda fountain, flirt, talk, and then go to the Chicago Theater. It was tradition." Said Arlene McCarty,

On July 2, 1942, I went into the store at State and Randolph in Chicago with some friends. Seated at a table nearby was a group of sailors. We struck up a conversation and learned they were survivors of the aircraft carrier *Lexington*, recently sunk in the battle of the Coral Sea. They were in Chicago to attend diesel school at Navy Pier. On Valentine's Day 1944, I married one of these sailors, and we had 53 years together until his death in 1997. Three sons and eight grandchildren added to the joy of those years. Now, each time I see a new Walgreens store opening, I feel a tug of nostalgia and recall many happy memories.[80]

Walgreens' role as America's meeting place extended right up to the conflict's final day. Everyone has seen the famous photo of the sailor dipping the nurse on Broadway for an exuberant smooch on V-E Day, 1945. There is still plenty of debate over the identity of the nurse—dozens have claimed to be the recipient of that kiss, and it seems impossible to prove who it really was—but there is no debating the backdrop for the iconic image: the Walgreens drugstore on Times Square.

The war was over, and Walgreens was still there.

the postwar era: 1945–1970

the power era

The end of World War II ushered in an era of renewed confidence, an era when previously impenetrable boundaries were being shattered every year. Chuck Yeager piloted a plane to a record speed of 1,600 miles per hour, more than twice the speed of sound; Dr. Jonas Salk found a polio vaccine; and Jackie Robinson dismantled the color barrier in sports for good in 1947. (Another baseball player, a former war hero named George Bush, played first base for Yale in the nation's first College World Series the same year; Yale lost 8 to 7 to Cal-Berkeley.)

Sparked by the GI Bill and fanned by good times, the University of Michigan's student body—mirroring others around the country—expanded from 20,000 enrollees in 1951 to 41,000 in 1968.[1] Those numbers included Cork Walgreen, who graduated from Michigan's College of Pharmacy in 1958.

Like the rest of the country, Walgreens had put most of its dreams on layaway during the Great Depression and World War II and now longed to satisfy 15 years of pent-up ambitions. Americans wanted to buy up every available refrigerator, dishwasher, and clothes dryer, while Walgreens sought to expand the chain, to improve the working conditions for pharmacists, and to try some bold new strategies, none of which was possible with the shortages of materials, workers, and time that the previous 15 years had seen.

Walgreens celebrated the country's hard-won peace and prosperity by putting on an elaborate nationwide radio show that it could never have justified during the war. But even in the war years, Walgreens' commitment to radio advertising was impressive. The company spent roughly $100,000 in 1940, doubled that by 1942, doubled it again the next year, and poured an incredible $500,000 into radio spots in 1944. Walgreens advertising executives went a step farther on June 17, 1945, when they put together a one-hour show called "A Walgreens Birthday Party," the company's forty-fourth, taped in the 2,500-seat Los Angeles Theater.

Radio critic Adele Hoskins reported in the *Chicago Daily News* that the program marked "the first time in the history of radio that a sponsor will supply a variety of talent on one show that looks like a roster of Hollywood."[2] The roster included Bing Crosby, Bud Abbott and Lou Costello, and the Andrews Sisters and raised $2.5 million for war bonds through the $1,000 admission price. (That year alone Walgreens had helped sell some $20 million in war bonds to the company, to its employees through voluntary payroll deductions, and to its customers through designated soda fountain booths in each store.[3])

Happy days were here again.

mergers and acquisitions

Because Walgreens had the money but not the materials or manpower to build new stores during the war, the company wisely salted away a portion of its earnings every year, earmarking the extra $1.5 million for expansion once the war had ended. In a postwar issue of the *Pepper Pod*, Chuck Walgreen announced a new era of optimism when he declared, "Extensive expansion is the keynote for 1946."[4]

But Walgreens did not expand the number of stores greatly under Chuck's reign—only about a 20 percent increase during his three-decade run. Instead, the company devoted its resources to refurbishing, replacing, and supersizing its existing outlets and to branching out into new areas, both physically and strategically.

Walgreens first dipped into its wartime nest egg to give its stores long overdue facelifts, from remodeling floor plans to installing fluorescent lighting.

By 1946, it was no longer possible to ignore that the company had finally outgrown its second headquarters on Bowen Avenue, despite four expansions over the previous 21 years. Chuck and company started building a brand new corporate office at 4300 W. Peterson Avenue on Chicago's northwest side. Opened in 1949, the new headquarters' 100,000 square feet of usable space was more than enough to house all 640 central employees, many of whom had been forced to work outside the old headquarters.

Like so many other U.S. companies in the postwar era for whom *diversification* was the buzz word, Walgreens dived headfirst into the brave new world of mergers and acquisitions. In the spring of 1946, Robert Knight received a call from Julio Lacaud, "a prominent investment banker," the Kogans wrote, to see if Walgreens might be interested in buying a slice of Sanborns, a popular chain of department stores in Mexico.[5]

The idea held more than a little appeal. When Walgreens bought Sanborns in 1946, the Mexican "chain" consisted of just two "links," with annual sales of $3.5 million; but one of those two stores was Mexico City's hallowed House of Tiles, a three-story landmark completed by a Spanish nobleman in the 1596. In 1903, a California pharmacist named Walter Sanborn and his brother Frank opened their first store in the ground floor of the eye-catching mansion and sold everything from handmade silver jewelry to home furnishings, Oriental rugs, and original art in the store's own gallery. Sanborns also branched out into food service and built its own manufacturing center to produce store-brand goods—enterprises Walgreens knew a little something about.[6]

Despite the obvious risks of investing in a foreign company, Walgreens decided it was a move worth making and put up $613,000 to claim a 27 percent stake in the company. When the bet paid off, Walgreens increased its share to 44 percent and expanded the chain into a half dozen other Mexican towns.[7]

Encouraged by the success of its first major merger, Walgreens looked south for more opportunities and found appealing ones in Puerto Rico and Houston, Texas. Though Puerto Rico is a U.S. territory, which had 2 million citizens in 1960, most of the inhabitants had never seen a big American drugstore before Walgreens opened its first outlet there in November 1960—at the same time presidential candidate John F. Kennedy announced his plan for something called the Peace Corps.

The outlet proved to be an immediate hit, offering prices 15 percent lower than local rates and the kind of selection previously available only on the mainland. Chuck Walgreen promoted Puerto Rico native Andres F. Ramirez, who had graduated from the University of Mississippi and worked for Walgreens since 1951, to run the store, continuing Walgreens' tradition of hiring local people whenever possible at its far-off stores to maintain a common touch.[8]

It worked. Walgreens built up its Puerto Rico operation to seven stores by 1971 and now operates over 50 stores on the island, the most successful and rewarding expansion under Charles Walgreen Jr.'s leadership.[9]

Batting two for two, Walgreens was all ears when Houston's Globe discount department store company came looking for a buyer after it had suffered a disastrous mishap in 1961. Stanley Danburg, the 32-year-old son of the founder of the Danburg Department stores, had built two huge Globe stores of over 100,000 square feet each and was building a third when a fire burned through over $5 million of store inventory. In spite of the setback, Danburg went through with the planned opening of the third store but quickly found himself buried in debt.

Though the entire Globe "chain" consisted of only three stores, Chuck Walgreen took the chance because all three stores were colossal boxes, with much to teach Walgreens about discounting on such a grand scale. Walgreens purchased the Globe corporation on May 17, 1962, for $3 million in Walgreens stock.

Walgreens' management team was humble enough to realize it had a lot to learn about discounting, and also about the Globe managers, so it wisely moved slowly with the new division. As vice president Cecil Campbell said, "We have to learn to walk before we can run," the very phrase the company used to describe its approach with drive-thru pharmacies and one-hour photo processing three decades later.[10]

Walgreens eased its own managers into the Globe operation, including long-time executive Roland G. Schmitt's son Robert, who ran the division, and a 26-year-old man named Charles R. Walgreen III—known by everyone as Cork (as he will be referred to here). After installing its own people at the top of the chain and getting a feel for grand-scale discounting—"Everything under the sun . . . Priced Lower!"—Walgreens picked up the pace from a walk to a run, opening a fourth store in Houston, then gigantic Globes in Baton Rouge, Louisiana; Albuquerque, New Mexico; and two in Phoenix, Arizona. By 1966, Walgreens operated 13 Globe stores, which accounted for $120 million in gross revenue.[11]

The postwar era not only expanded the roles of drugstores, it blurred the borders between virtually all retail businesses, including grocery stores, department stores, and drugstores, for starters. This helps explain why Walgreens was so ready to buy up and expand the Globe department store chain and why it eagerly jumped into the restaurant business by starting Corky's, a fast-food chain named after Charles Walgreen III, and Robin Hood's, a medieval themed restaurant, in the late 1960s.[12] But it also explains why Walgreens found itself having to fend off price wars—especially for prescription drugs—from the unlikeliest places. Walgreens only defense, then and now, was the professionalism of its pharmacists.

Though the acquisitions made big, flashy news at the time, Chuck's most important decisions were the quieter, tougher, but ultimately far more rewarding moves behind the scenes, designed to make each Walgreens store a better place to work and visit.

all power to the pharmacist

Chuck's reign might not have been as dramatic as his father's nor as dynamic as his son's; but the other two Walgreens innovated outwardly while Chuck innovated inwardly, securing the gains made by his father and setting the stage for his son's building boom in the last quarter of the twentieth century. Instead of pushing expansion, Chuck focused the company's efforts on doing what it was already doing—selling top-quality products and drugs at a fair price in a clean, welcoming environment . . . but doing all of it better.

Chuck's first priority was to improve the working conditions and status of the pharmacists who still worked in every Walgreens store. By shortening pharmacists' hours, enhancing their section of the store, and elevating their status in a number of ways, Chuck's changes cost the company real money. But he believed so deeply in his dad's conviction that the pharmacy was the backbone, even the soul, of the company—and that without it, Walgreens would be just another glorified Five and Dime—that he was willing to do whatever it took to keep Walgreens at the forefront of the field. Chuck believed that his vision of a first-rate pharmacy department run by respected specialists was essential to Walgreens' culture and to its future.

And he was right. Chuck was far ahead of his time, and he would be vindicated many times over in the decades ahead.

Chuck's first job was to cut back on the pharmacists' ungodly hours, a concern of his since he was a boy waiting for his father to come home, exhausted, after another 12-hour day. Things hadn't gotten any better for pharmacists since his father's day—and in some ways, they were substantially worse. Pharmacists still worked an average of 11 hours per day, six days a week, with only Sundays off. The work load predictably put tremendous stress on the pharmacists' health and family life, but long hours were only part of the problem. With the growth of each store's floor plan and product list, the pharmacist's duties grew, too.

"The pharmacist did not have a self-contained department," Chuck recalled. So, "he was also a salesclerk, stockman, and troubleshooter, on call for every 'emergency.' That might be the cigar girl needing change for her register or a customer needing help to insert film into a new box camera. I could see why the son or daughter of a pharmacist wouldn't see a future in the profession."[13]

Walgreens wanted to make the job manageable, starting with a sane schedule. Chuck sought to give his pharmacists a standard 40-hour work week, thereby reducing their scheduled hours by 39 percent. "Our company became the pioneer in working out a definite program of lowering hours," he said. "We couldn't do it overnight, of course, or we'd fold up. . . . We had to make all kinds of studies, see what hours were not too productive in the stores."[14]

The company brought the pharmacists' hours down step by step. Aided by the return of 1 million soldiers, the growing number of people attending pharmacy schools on the GI Bill, and the renewed interest in the profession due to Walgreens' reforms, Walgreens finally achieved the 40-hour work week by the mid-1950s. The competition was stunned, Walgreen recalled, "because they didn't see how we could operate on shorter hours. We were not too popular [with the competition] because we had all the applicants we could handle." [15]

partners in health

At the same time that Chuck Walgreen was reducing his druggists' hours, he was working to enhance their status, both in the stores and in the medical community.

In 1943, Walgreens filled a record 2.4 million subscriptions, but that number started falling the next year and the year after that. There were many possible explanations, of course, including the thousands of American men going overseas; but one possible factor struck Chuck Walgreen as particularly worrisome: Doctors were said to be increasingly reluctant to recommend Walgreens to their patients.

At the outset of the twentieth century, Marilyn Abbey explained in *Walgreens: Celebrating 100 Years*, pharmacists routinely diagnosed their customers ailments and offered recommendations for treatment. The practice was called "counter-servicing," and doctors predictably objected to it, especially as it grew more prevalent during World War II due to the nationwide shortage of physicians.[16]

Nonetheless, Walgreens couldn't afford to alienate the medical community nor to expose itself to the kind of liability that misdiagnosed conditions could create. Serendipity and smart politics conjoined at a cocktail party in 1944, when Chuck found himself chatting with his good friend Dr. Morris Fishbein, the esteemed executive secretary of the American Medical Association (AMA) and editor of the organization's opinion-leading journal, the *Journal of the American Medical Association (JAMA)*. Chuck raised the issue himself: "I'm very unhappy with how things are going," he told the good doctor, "and I'd like to do something to improve relationships. What can we do?"[17]

Fishbein was equally direct. "Don't counter-service any longer. Your stores, above all, shouldn't be doing it."[18]

Walgreen pledged that his pharmacists would desist the practice immediately—over the objections of the company's operations division—and then proposed to take this new agreement one step farther by running full-page ads in *JAMA* and *Hygeia*, the AMA's health magazine, announcing Walgreens' strict policy against counter-servicing.

Walgreens ran similar ads in 210 cities, referring to doctors and pharmacists as "partners in health," adding, "Your Walgreens pharmacist does his part by following your doctor's instructions and compounding your prescriptions with painstaking care." Walgreens' ads were so flattering that a modern reader might be tempted to believe the drugstore chain was asking the AMA for a date to the senior prom. A particularly fine example expressed "a country's thankfulness to a man who has stood by a tough job—and done it well. Mr. and Mrs. American acknowledge with pride and praise the splendid service of the family doctor." The chain also offered 13,000 doctors and dentists Walgreens "courtesy cards," which provided discounts on all Walgreens merchandise.[19]

The ads were fawning, perhaps, but undeniably effective, with both physicians and patients. Just three years after the problem had been identified, the rift between Walgreens and the AMA had been healed.

In the 1947 annual report, Chuck said, "No matter how our stores develop in size or broaden in character, the prescription department still remains the heart of our business. . . . Our relations with the medical profession have never been more mutually satisfying."[20] By keeping the two trades and their responsibilities distinct—an issue that went back to the beginning of both professions—Walgreens pharmacists earned more respect from physicians and elevated their status in the bargain.

Walgreen didn't stop there. He realized if the profession was going to appeal to the best and brightest graduates flooding out of the nation's universities after the war, it would have to provide druggists with a chance to become managers and share in the store's profits. This required incoming pharmacists to have at least a rudimentary background in the business of running a drugstore, something schools of pharmacy were certainly not prepared to teach.

This concerned Chuck so much that he decided that if the universities weren't going to teach business basics to pharmacists, Walgreens would. So in 1953, Chuck introduced the Walgreens Pharmacy Administration Seminar, inviting a dozen college of pharmacy faculty members to attend a six-week training course, "covering everything from employee relations to public relations, store planning and maintenance to merchandise handling, legal problems to bookkeeping."[21]

Walgreens eventually boiled the course down to a two-week seminar but continued sponsoring them well into the 1960s. Walgreens finally discontinued its workshops because pharmacy schools had begun to offer business courses themselves. Chuck's vision had once again been realized. (Walgreens still hosts seminars for pharmacy deans, and Walgreens now awards millions of dollars in scholarships to pharmacy students annually.)

At a time when the status of pharmacists was in limbo, both inside and outside the field, Chuck Walgreen's sweeping reforms secured the professionalism, credibility, and respect of pharmacists right up to the present day. Gallup polls consistently rank pharmacists among the most trusted professionals in the country—from 1989 to 1990 they ranked first among all professions. Although Chuck did not add substantially to the number of Walgreens stores, those 400-some outlets increased the number of prescriptions filled each year from 7.5 million in 1962 to 30 million by 1975. While the percentage of annual sales rarely rose higher than a meager 4 percent for the company's first half century, it was a robust 62 percent in 2003.

A side effect of Chuck's initiatives, and not a small one, is the generation of dedicated pharmacists attracted to the field by Walgreens' reforms, a generation that has produced almost every member of the Walgreen executive team—including former chief executive officer (CEO) Daniel Jorndt and current CEO David Bernauer—that has led Walgreens to heights its predecessors could only dream of.

Bob McKillop was just one of many talented young people whose potential Walgreens identified and developed into lifelong assets. In 1954, McKillop was a boy who spent every afternoon playing baseball with his buddies in Springfield, Massachusetts—just like Charles Sr. and his pals did years earlier on the fields of Dixon, Illinois.[22]

As the Horatio Alger story requires, one day, one of the players hit the ball through the big window of the neighborhood Walgreens, sending store manager Joe Beck flying out the door and into the street to catch the perpetrators; but he could only nab McKillop. The store manager gave the sandlot player a choice: McKillop could work off the replacement cost by stocking shelves after school, or Beck could call his parents and have them pay for it. Just about anyone who's been in a similar predicament can guess McKillop's quick answer: He promised Mr. Beck he would work it off, instead of incurring the additional wrath of his parents, which he considered "the ultimate threat."

Every day after school, McKillop would walk down to Beck's store and stock shelves without complaint. In fact, he did such a good job that when he had fulfilled his end of the bargain, Beck offered him a paid position.

"I was ecstatic," McKillop recalled. "As I left that night, he handed me an envelope with my mother's name on it. Inside was $138, the wages I would have earned during those weeks [when he was paying off the window], and a note explaining the whole situation.

"Joe Beck changed my life," McKillop said. "I worked for him all through high school. Then he helped me get a Walgreen scholarship for pharmacy school."[23] Beck might have given McKillop his break; but it was Chuck Walgreen's push to provide more opportunity, better training, and enhanced status to future pharmacists that turned McKillop's after-school job into a career—a career that culminated in McKillop's retirement in 2000 as one of Walgreens' regional vice presidents of store operations.

battling the bargain stores

Having won the battle for personnel, Walgreens then had to win the battle over price. Discounters, department stores, and even mail-order catalog companies had entered the fray. In the May 1960 *Pepper Pod*, Chuck had sounded the clarion call to his employees:

> In a growing number of markets, so-called discount drug firms are a "new" adversary. Actually, it's the same old competition under a new name. We have met them before. Pine boards [from the 1930s]. Cut-Rates [from the 1940s]. And the answers are the same: Be number one in giving top value for customer's money, be number one in treating the customer right. And don't wait to give new competitors a start. Begin with round one. Remember that customer loyalty is no security; it must be earned daily, renewed daily.[24]

Even Walgreen, however, was taken aback by Spiegel's 1960 fall/winter catalog, in which the Chicago-based company offered its credit card customers wholesale prices on prescriptions. Though it didn't spell out exactly what those prices would be, its chairman, Modie J. Spiegel, promised to save customers "25 to 40 percent from what they would pay elsewhere." Chuck Walgreen's response? "Preposterous!"[25]

But no matter how far-fetched Chuck thought Spiegel's claims, he felt the need to compete, and he did, cutting the prices on all prescription drugs, even though they were already the lowest in the field. Walgreen felt it wasn't merely customers, prices, or market share at stake, but the future of the pharmacies themselves—a battle similar to the one many brick-and-mortar retailers are waging today against Internet companies. The Spiegel approach, Walgreen said, would fail because it was "impersonal and incomplete."

Walgreen used the May 1961 issue of the *Pepper Pod* to assure his people: "There is no need to push the panic button. . . . Fact is, we thrive on competition. Always have."[26]

Three months later, Walgreen, rising to the challenge, issued a public statement.

> Of utmost importance is the within-minutes availability to doctors and patients of the thousands of drugs that help defend the health of America. No physician, no patient should be made to wait through precious days of healing to obtain medicines by mail. . . . And the public must not lose the vital physician-pharmacist-patient relationship that traditionally safeguards the patient's health. . . . We at Walgreens intend to hold fast to our role as pharmacists. Our answer is prescription prices as low or lower than any outside source—right in our neighborhood drug stores. . . . Doctors are only human. And they make mistakes sometimes—in dosages, strength of medicine, or compatibility of drugs. A knowledgeable pharmacist is able to look at a prescription and spot potential trouble. He has the ability to call the doctor for consultation; the chance, perhaps, to save a life.

Not only did Walgreen's counteroffensive—an early rendition of the arguments currently delivered against Internet druggists—stop the Spiegel strategy in its tracks, but it had the additional effect of curbing drug sales at discount houses, grocery stores, and variety stores. These competitors would rise again, of course; but just as his father had defeated pine boards, Chuck stared the discounters down and beat them honestly. However, proving once again that, sometimes, you're damned if you do and damned if you don't, Walgreens suffered a backlash from independent drugstores angered over the chain's new practice of advertising its low prices—but this was a by-product Chuck was prepared to bear.

After the dust settled, Walgreens experienced an unexpected boom in prescription sales. In May 1964, Walgreens filled 21.7 percent more prescriptions than it had the previous year; and the number of prescriptions would soon exceed one million a month. "In the late 1950s," said Sol Raab, the former vice president of store operations, "we began a much heavier concentration on our prescription business."[27]

While the overall profits from the pharmacy department were relatively small compared to today's figures, Walgreens' unwavering commitment to its pharmacies was already paying off in the 1960s and would provide the foundation for an exponential increase in sales in the years to come. During this time, long before prescription drug sales became the company's biggest profit center, Walgreens sounded its motto every chance it had: "Your prescription is our most important responsibility."

the self-service revolution

All organizations must negotiate a handful of crucial conflicts and crossroads in order to ensure their survival—and that's especially true for family companies thriving for over a century.

For Walgreens, the portentous crossroads have included Charles Sr.'s decisions to devote himself fully to the pharmacy business, to offer customers food service and milk shakes, and to risk it all to expand the business beyond all previous expectations in the 1920s—a list long enough for any man. Chuck's reign might not have been as spectacular as his father's, but he made a few decisions no less vital to the ongoing success of the company, including raising the professional standards of pharmacists and, especially, introducing self-service to the industry, which launched nothing less than a retail revolution.

Of course, the last sentence might make modern readers furrow their brows. Self-service drugstores? What's the alternative?

It's as difficult for us to fathom what preceded self-service drugstores as it is for contemporary teenagers to imagine a world in which men delivered milk and eggs to our homes, picked up our dirty laundry, and washed our windshields. But before the idea captured Chuck Walgreen's imagination more than half a century ago, no one could conceive of what a "self-service drugstore chain" would look like, either—because none existed.

The self-service idea had actually been around for decades when Walgreens had the inspiration to apply it to drugstores in the 1950s. Way back in 1916, Clarence Saunders founded the United States' first true self-service grocery story in Memphis, Tennessee. Before Saunders changed the rules, grocery store customers would give their orders to clerks, by hand or by phone (as they did at Walgreens, too, which set up the famed Two Minute Drill). The clerk would then dash about the aisles, gathering the customers' products, and then meet the customer at the cash register, wrap the goods in paper or put them in a nice bag or basket, and send them on their way.

The practice certainly seemed customer friendly, but Saunders saw the flaws in this system before anyone else did, especially its inefficient use of time and labor. So Saunders, a man whom even the chain's official history describes as "flamboyant" and who had the wild eyes and shock of gray hair of a mad scientist, decided to try something outrageous: He would design a store where customers could shop for themselves.

Saunders took it a step farther when he named his new store "Piggly Wiggly." He never explained why he gave his stores that silly moniker. When someone asked him, he'd simply reply, "So people will ask that very question." If he wanted a name that would be easily remembered, he'd found it.[28]

Given the store's crazy name and crazier concepts—wooden shopping baskets, open shelves, over 600 products (three times more than conventional stores), and replacing aisle clerks—the smart money said Saunders's shop would flop. But Saunders's very first Piggly Wiggly attracted a huge crowd of curiosity seekers for its opening day. When he opened the doors, the customers flooded through the turnstiles and ran through the aisles, thrilled to be free to do their own shopping. "This," one impressed observer said, "is the future."[29]

The anonymous visitor was right. The Piggly Wiggly stores, which were the first to provide checkout stands, first to mark a price on every item in the store, and first to use employee uniforms for safer food handling, quickly caught on. Within seven years, the chain had 1,200 stores, turning Saunders's $23,000 investment into $100 million.

Sadly, however, Saunders lost control of Piggly Wiggly's stock in the early 1920s, and he died in 1953, too soon to see his revolutionary self-service idea spread nationwide. As Piggly Wiggly's corporate history says, "Saunders's creative genius was decades ahead of his time." A&P, Krogers, and other national chains adopted the simple but powerful idea decades after Saunders first conceived it.

Of course, it's one thing to set up a self-service system in a grocery store, because most customers don't need expert advice to buy beer, bananas, or boxed cereal. But because pharmaceutical products are so critical to the customer's health, so difficult to understand, and so quick to change, experts assumed customers would never feel comfortable buying such products on their own, without assistance.

After World War II, pharmaceuticals introduced some 400 drugs each year, an explosion of antibiotics and vitamins, diet tablets, and geriatric treatments—all new to the field—a boom that was paralleled by one in toiletries, cosmetics, and other over-the-counter products. This avalanche of new goods often created confusion among customers.

Ron Stuart, a retired Walgreen worker, recalled a couple of memorable exchanges at the State and Division streets store in Chicago: "A gentleman put a Po-Do Shave Bomb on the counter and said he wanted his money back because it wasn't any good. He said 'I was set to shave, held it up to my face, pressed the button, and had a mess all over my head and the bathroom.' Another time, a woman put down a bottle of foil-wrapped suppositories and said, 'These are just too hard to swallow.' At that point, I was too timid to make any recommendations." Stuart simply refunded her money, without comment.[30]

For these reasons and more, Walgreens stood firmly with the majority of drugstore chains that believed customers would never take to self-service stores. And in the postwar years, with so much to do already, the last thing Chuck was looking for was another major initiative, and certainly not anything as ambitious and unknown as self-service. But like his father (and later, his son), Chuck was always open to a good idea when he found it.

Walgreens has a knack for bumping into the right idea at the right time, often by accident—witness the Two Minute Drill, the birth of the milk shake, and the introduction of the potato salad sandwich. As George Nuyttens, a retired corporate employee, recalled, "My brother Jack was setting type for menus in the duplicating department in 1952. He mistakenly set type for a potato salad sandwich, and the menu went out that way. We got a call from a fountain manager: 'Who came up with the potato salad sandwich? It's going over great!'"[31]

Likewise, the company stumbled upon the idea of self-service rather by accident. In 1949 Piggly Wiggly was still a regional chain, largely unknown outside the southeastern United States; and few other major retailers had even attempted to imitate them. At the time, Walgreens had dipped its toe into self-service sensibly enough by experimenting with three of Walgreens' 410 stores, but without a very deep understanding of the principles that make it work. "We had been doing it in a seat-of-the-pants fashion," Chuck said years later. "Frankly, we didn't know anything about self-service. All we really did at those three stores was to change the cashiering over to checkout counters."[32]

That same year, 1949, Chuck and six Walgreens executives flew out to

California to finalize the purchase of a 200-store chain called Thrifty, which, like Walgreens, was based on clerk service. But while they were in the Golden State, a tiny five-store chain, Sav-On, caught their attention. Sav-On had dared to try self-service and had been rewarded with greater sales because it could stock more merchandise and sell it at lower prices.

Chuck was smart enough to realize that Sav-On's success was not just a passing fad, but a great way to lower prices, increase sales volume, and reduce overhead. He also realized that instituting self-service would require more than simply installing a checkout counter near the doors. It would require "remodeling, restocking, restaffing, and, most of all, rethinking" the entire store operation.[33]

Chuck then made one of the boldest decisions in company history—if not *the* boldest—when he suddenly decided to drop the solid deal with the safe and sizable Thrifty chain to take up the risky concept practiced by the fledgling five-store chain down the street and to reengineer his entire 500-store chain to follow the Sav-On model.

When they returned to Chicago, the executives took a closer look at the three Walgreens stores already experimenting with self-service—a small store in Kalamazoo, Michigan; a middle-sized store in Springfield, Missouri; and a larger branch in Akron, Ohio—and decided they really weren't practicing the techniques that made self-service work at Sav-On.

When Walgreens has an important job to do, they give it to a busy person. Decades before business gurus urged executives to put a "champion" in charge of special projects, with an elaborate hierarchy of Masters and Minions supporting him, Walgreens figured out that the best pioneers are men on a mission, people like Pop Coulson making milk shakes and Robert Knight presenting Charles Walgreen Sr. with his proposed accounting reforms—then implementing them.

So it was no surprise that when Chuck returned from California, chomping at the bit to get going on self-service, the first thing he did was appoint an up-and-coming district manager named James P. Herring to become the first director of the "Self-Service Store Development Program." Herring's Walgreens credentials went back to 1937, when he worked as a stock boy during college. Herring went on to work for Walgreens in Phoenix, Miami, and, of course, Chicago and served as a store manager in Akron and Wichita Falls, Texas, before becoming the Houston district manager for two years—thereby hitting a good number of company hot spots—when Chuck came calling.

After giving the energetic young Herring his new job and title, Walgreen gave him his first directive: "Find out as much as you can as fast as you can." Herring did, visiting every kind of self-service store he could find across the country to unearth the secrets of success in this brave new world of retail. There was method to Chuck Walgreen's madness, because he knew that the self-service strategy was risky and that many executives needed convincing—including himself. In the May 1950 *Pepper Pod*, Chuck wrote, "As leaders in the retail drugstore field, it behooves us to investigate the possibilities of this mass retailing as a service to our customers as well as a benefit to our company." Interested, yes—but far from committed.

Herring got right to it, converting four stores scattered around the country to self-service and launching two brand-new self-service stores in Cincinnati, Ohio, and Muncie, Indiana. These "practical laboratories," as Chuck Walgreen called them, demonstrated the advantages of even rudimentary self-service over clerk service. Just one year into the experiment, Chuck wrote, "Self-service counters in conventional stores have boosted sales substantially."[34]

Walgreens learned more than that. Chuck spelled out the principal advantages of self-service in his May 19, 1952, newsletter, namely: (1) Consumers spent more at self-service stores; (2) they will travel farther to shop at one, so the stores don't have to be located in prime rent districts; and (3) the self-service stores could process more merchandise at a lower cost and sold a higher volume of goods per payroll dollar.[35]

Thus encouraged, Walgreens naturally sought to expand its self-service operations, opening eight more self-service stores in the program's second year. But as Herring's baby grew, Walgreens also discovered less-obvious lessons along the way. For example, the initial building costs for a self-service store were higher than for a conventional store because the store layout was more important—it had to be designed not for trained clerks but for unfamiliar customers who had to make their way through the store easily and effectively. The store could only pay for itself with greater floor space and more products than in a conventional store because the self-service profit margins were smaller. Self-service required a greater emphasis on displays and packaging. As the Kogans wrote, without clerks, "the package became the salesman."[36] Walgreens, a leader at marketing since Charles Sr.'s day, quickly adjusted, giving their company brands of rubbing alcohol, Dolph Insect Bombs, and Tidy Deodorant new, eye-catching labels.[37]

The change also required Walgreens to reeducate its customers on how to shop in its stores. A happy by-product of self-service was the elevation of the pharmacist from glorified clerk and stock boy to specialized professional who only handled prescriptions. "Back in those days, the clerks were often pharmacists," Chuck said in an interview at age 97. "We had to move it gradually from clerk service to self-service, because the customers were confused about what they should take off the shelves and what we should."[38]

Once up and running, however, Walgreens learned customers preferred the wider selection, lower prices, and, possibly, the additional privacy such stores offered. Walgreens' executives also figured out that when they followed the basic principles practiced by Piggly Wiggly and Sav-On, self-service delivered what it promised. What they soon surmised, however, was that it was much easier to launch new self-service stores from scratch than to convert long-running clerk-service stores to self-service—which was as tricky as retrofitting an airplane in midflight.

"That was a horrible experience, to go from a clerk-service store to a self-service store," Chuck said, with characteristic candor. "When you start with self-service, it's not too bad, like Osco [drug stores] did; but when you start with clerk service, it's harder. But I felt we had self-service licked once we got a few stores up and running. Frank redesigned the stores; and because I liked architecture [Chuck's original major at Michigan], I watched that very carefully. And we always experimented first. That paid off, too—and reduced costs, as well."[39]

In addition to the complications of converting a single clerk-service store to self-service, Walgreens' executive team ran into unforeseen snags whenever it started one self-service store in a district dominated by its traditional clerk-service stores.

"In order to make self-service pay," Chuck explained, "you had to advertise your low prices. But in clerk-served stores, with your higher cost of doing business, prices had to be higher to show a profit."[40]

This created a conflict between Walgreens stores, one with no simple solution. If the executives allowed the self-service stores to advertise their low prices, the clerk-service stores in the same cities would look bad selling the same goods at higher prices. But if the executives allowed the clerk-service stores to sell their goods at the self-service prices, they lost money. Finally, if the self-service stores had to sell their merchandise at clerk-service prices, they wouldn't attract enough customers. "[When] we swung over to self-service, that was a real challenge," Chuck said. "In cities where we had one store, that was relatively easy. But in cities where we had multiple stores, it was very difficult and costly."[41]

Walgreens tried to strike a balance between the competing needs of the two store systems, but it was never perfect. However, as CEOs from Chuck Walgreen to David Bernauer will tell you, the key then is the key now: Those who put their own interests ahead of the company's don't last very long at Walgreens.

Walgreens put this spirit of compromise—and the self-service concept itself—to the test in June 1952, when it opened a new store at 87th Street and Cottage Grove Avenue in Chicago. Though the company had originally planned to build a conventional, clerk-service store in the small spot, Chuck and his colleagues decided it was time to throw the dice when an adjacent property became available, expanding the store's space to a workable 13,000 square feet. Although it would not be the company's first self-service store, it would be the first in the Chicago area, one situated very close to the company's conventional stores. Therefore, Chuck knew, how the new store fared would have a great influence on the debate among the still-uncertain executives watching close by, likely tipping the scales either for or against the self-service strategy.

As he so often did in such pressure situations, Walgreen picked a young upstart for the honor, a 30-year-old man named Robert Schmitt, son of long-time executive Roland Schmitt. Walgreen tried to ensure that the young man was not being set up for failure by sending letters to other South Side store managers, urging them "to minimize any confusion or complications in the thinking or operation of our regular Walgreens stores" and to cooperate fully with the new self-service store.

With the company watching, the young Mr. Schmitt hit a home run. During the store's first four months, it "more than doubled the company's most optimistic estimates."[42]

(Soon thereafter, Roland invented the now-familiar automatic entrance gates, which he named the "In-a-matic," the predecessor to the automatic doors almost all major stores have today.[43]

Self-service was a hit and was here to stay. (And so was Robert Schmitt, who would become a company vice president.)

the shopping center is born

In the process of surveying other stores around the country, Walgreens found another interesting idea in Texas and California: the *shopping center*, a collection of several stores in one facility with a large parking lot, all located outside major cities—as groundbreaking then as the shopping mall would be in the 1970s. The innovation fit perfectly into the growing car culture, a way of life that introduced the interstate highway system and popularized drive-up motels, drive-in movies, and drive-in restaurants. Holiday Inn, McDonald's, and Levittown (the pioneering Long Island suburb) all came of age during the 1950s.

In the early 1950s, Chuck Walgreen and family still lived on the South Side of Chicago. So each day on his way north to the Walgreens' headquarters on Peterson Avenue, he would drive past a 21-acre vacant lot at the corner of 95th and Western in a suburb called Evergreen Park. When Walgreens decided to build its first shopping center, Chuck Walgreen decided, "This is the place," and Chicagoland real estate king Arthur Rubloff would be the agent.[44]

But, Walgreen recalled, shopping centers were still so new in the early 1950s that when they approached Rubloff with the idea, he replied, "What's a shopping center?" In fairness to Rubloff, Evergreen Plaza would be the first such development east of the Mississippi.

Rubloff bought into the project, but he had a hard time attracting other tenants because they complained the concept was "too new, too chancy, [and] too competitive with their existing locations."[45] But eventually the Fair Store—a venerable downtown Chicago department outlet—joined up, followed by Lytton's clothing store, Jewel Tea, and a Kroger grocery store.[46]

The centerpiece, however, was a massive Walgreens with 40 departments selling everything from parakeets to party supplies to auto parts to an actual ton of ice cream kept chilly behind glass freezer doors—all on the self-service model, so you could simply reach out and pick up what you wanted.

Evergreen Plaza opened in 1952, proving the naysayers wrong from day one. It was a huge hit, one big enough to change the direction of commerce in the city forever. "It was then and there," Chuck said, "that we decided we would never again open a conventional store." But, he said, "The conversion took a full ten years because we're talking about changing over 500 stores, and it wasn't just a question of changing the checkouts."[47]

Nonetheless, by 1953, just three years into the Great Experiment, Walgreens had already become the country's largest self-service business of any sort—including grocery stores like Piggly Wiggly.

The rest of the nation started taking notice. In the March 7, 1953, issue of *Business Week*, a reporter judged that, "It is already possible to see that self-service is eventually going to have a major impact on drug retailing. Some signs even point to a revolution."[48]

The prediction proved prescient, of course. Just five years later, Walgreens had either opened or converted 141 of its 410 stores in 37 states as self-service outlets. That same year, 1958, *Barron's* picked up the scent. In a story titled "Flourishing Walgreens Has Found the Right Prescription for a Retail Drug Chain," the publication said,

> Along with the drive to open self-service units in advantageous lo-cations, the company is also overhauling its older stores. The effect of this streamlining is evident in the improved operating results. Although profit margins [for self-service stores] are ordinarily lower, expense ratios compare very favorably with those of the older units. Once these new stores begin to ring up a certain volume, their prof-itability is greater than that of traditional outlets."[49]

Five years after that assessment and eleven years after Walgreens opened its Evergreen Plaza, *Value Line*, a respected Wall Street invest-ment-analysis publication, concluded that Walgreens' stock performance "should bring joy to the heart of every shareholder," a statement Wall Street analysts would be happy to repeat today.[50]

the four-way test

Under Charles, Chuck, or Cork Walgreen or Dan Jorndt or Dave Bernauer, Walgreens seems to work its hardest to reconnect with its core values when it's flying its highest—in the 1920s, the 1950s, and the 1990s. Thus, it was probably no accident that in 1955, shortly after the company's initial success with self-service, Chuck distributed to every Walgreens store and office something he described as a "prescription for living, a new version of the Golden Rule," to reinforce the basic values on which his fa-ther had built the company.

Called "The Four-Way Test of the things we think, say, or do," it consists of four simple questions:[51]

1. Is it the TRUTH?
2. Is it FAIR to all concerned?
3. Will it build GOODWILL and BETTER FRIENDSHIP?
4. Will it be BENEFICIAL to all concerned?

If these words sound familiar, it's probably because Chuck's friend Herbert J. Taylor, who composed the piece in 1932 after it came to him while meditating on how to save his failing company (it worked), gave it to Rotary International in 1946, a service club both men belonged to, which distributed it around the world.

Nine years later, in the midst of the self-service boom, Chuck had the Four-Way Test stamped on hundreds of plaques to be displayed in every Walgreens store and office. In the company newsletter issued at the same time, Chuck explained, "These four guiding principals apply to all our dealings—not only with customers but with each other. It's the one way to achieve company success—and individual success—and to earn everyone's respect along the way."[52]

"If you use a test like that for the things you say or do," Chuck said late in his life, "you won't be making mistakes."[53]

Tom Brewer has never forgotten the kindness of two strangers he met behind the counter of his neighborhood Walgreens in Fort Collins, Colorado.

It was the day before Christmas, 1959, and I still hadn't found a present for my mother. I shopped all the big department stores and as a last resort I went to the new Walgreens in the shopping center. They had it—the perfect gift for Mom from a 15-year-old boy. Imagine my disappointment when the cashier told me the total, and it was more money than I had. She must have read the look on my face, because she said, "Don't worry, honey. We'll help you out." She fished around in her uniform pocket for change, and then called for the cigar clerk to come over. The two of them helped with my purchase, and then said, "This is our Christmas gift to you."

I don't remember what the perfect gift was, but I'll never forget those two Walgreens clerks, Annabelle and Helen. In fact, when I turned 16 the next year, Walgreens was the only store I applied to, and I had the pleasure of working with them through my high school and college years and for a few years as a pharmacist.

Annabelle and Helen are the reason I started with Walgreens in 1960, and the many Walgreens employees like them are the reason I'm still with the company in 2000.[54]

chuck's legacy

Assessing Chuck Walgreen's legacy is not a simple matter, due partly to the sheer span of his tenure. He rose to CEO in 1939 and didn't step down until 1971, a 32-year run that included the end of the Depression, World War II, and the counterrevolution. His entire Walgreens career is much longer, of course, because he started when he was in grade school, delivering soups and sandwiches for his mom, and didn't end until he stepped down as a board member in 1976, after two World Wars, Korea, Vietnam, and even Granada. It is highly unlikely that anyone will ever have a longer leadership association with the company. Just trying to judge his performance in the context of his times is no small trick, as he captained the ship through every kind of water, each of which required a different tack.

Chuck became the company's second chairman—taking the reins from the founder, who also happened to be his father—at the tender age of 33. Considering the sad history of founder's sons—who rarely are even given the opportunity to run their father's companies, and if they do usually become fast failures like Edsel Ford and William (Bill) Hewlett—Chuck Walgreen's career has to be considered an unqualified success. He was happy, healthy, and easy to work for throughout his career, and his company was successful throughout.

Nonetheless, since he followed his father, comparisons are inevitable. The easiest thing to measure is the expansion rates. Charles Sr. not only founded the company but grew it to 493 stores. After Charles "Chuck" Walgreen Jr. took over, the number of stores always hovered in the 400s, closing 1963, the year Chuck stepped down as president, at 477—a net loss of 16 stores. Given that it was an era of unprecedented economic growth, Walgreens' apparent inertia is surprising.

In fairness, however, the statistics are somewhat misleading. "After the war, we started closing two little [stores] and replacing them with one Super Store," Chuck explained in an interview late in his life. "So the number of stores doesn't tell the growth story for that period. Square footage, employees, and investment were all going up, even though the number of stores was going down a little."

He also guided the increase in the number of agency stores to 1,800 nationwide. Further, sales in Walgreens stores more than tripled, from $119 million in 1945 to $367 million in 1963.

But there is little question that Senior and Junior brought different styles to the job. As one veteran Walgreens executive, who asked to remain anonymous, said, "Charles Walgreen Sr. was a hard-charger. Chuck was not the same kind of hard-charger. He was ethical, honest, pure as the driven snow, steady as she goes, and he brought self-service to our company. But you have to remember: In the fifties, [the business environment] was *not* competitive. He had his old territory, the guys out East had their territory, they all went golfing together, everyone was happy. I mean it wasn't dog-eat-dog, the way it is today."

And, yet, Chuck was a man who had the courage to convert the entire chain to self-service when most of the industry—and his executives—did not think the idea was going to fly. Said Dan Jorndt:

I never saw this myself, but it's come down in company history. Charles Walgreen Jr. was involved in lots of decisions. During board meetings, someone would be pouring his heart out and he'd listen, listen, and then just kind of lean back and put his hands behind his head. At that point, the meeting was over. You could talk for another two hours, but his mind was made up. So people learned, when he'd lean back, to wrap up quickly, and say, "All right, now: Can we do it?" It would either be "yes" or "no," never "maybe." The Walgreens are stubborn people. I mean that very much as a positive; they're certain of what they want."[55]

Another example of Chuck's decisiveness: By the mid-1960s, 50 percent of the 300-plus products Walgreens manufactured had been developed within the preceding five years, including Smoker's Toothpaste, Anefrin cold capsules, and a contact lens solution.[56]

In the final analysis, however, Chuck will likely be remembered more for the mistakes he *didn't* make—errors of excess and ignorance that plague almost all companies that last longer than a generation—and the goodwill he generated, inside and outside the company.

Chuck says his role was simply "trying to follow through the way Dad started: Treat the customer like a guest in your home and your business will do well. . . . I enjoyed my job. I was very happy. I did smile quite a bit; I do now. . . . If you're in a job you don't like, you aren't going to do well. But if you enjoy your work, time doesn't mean anything because it's not a job, it's just something you're doing."[57]

It is often said that a team's personality eventually mirrors that of its coach. It's fair to say that the same holds true for most companies. Chuck's happy, friendly approach to his work spread.

In 1964, *Chain Store Weekly* asked Chuck's old college roommate, "Beno" Borg, how the company had managed to keep all but 19 of its 479 store managers with the company that year. (Most of the 19 stepped down due to retirement or illness.) "We have a recognition," he said, "that people are more important than things."[58]

Perhaps a greater legacy than the introduction of self-service or the elevation of the pharmacist's status will be the recruitment and promotion years ago of the current generation of Walgreens' leaders. And that's where Chuck's friendly, egoless approach was so important. Recalled Dan Jorndt:

> When Mr. Walgreen Jr. was around most of us regular employees, he was very shy. If you were hired as a Chicago pharmacist—I think maybe for all of Chicago they were hiring 10 or 12 a year in the early '60s—you got to meet him. You'd go to Peterson Avenue, and they'd line you all up. You'd have on your coat and tie, and they'd walk you down the hall to his office. Whoever had brought you would say, "This is Charles Walgreen, the chairman of the board." He'd look up and say, "Hi, boys"—it was all boys then—and you'd say, "Hi, Mr. Walgreen." He'd say, "Well, good luck to all of you." And that was it, and you'd leave. But it was like an audience with the Pope.[59]

This helps explain why, in 1963, *Chain Store Weekly* described Walgreens' management team as "untainted with the power politics which afflicts the executive suites of many large companies. Its members work harmoniously toward fulfillment of a policy of building on the future on the solid base of the past."[60]

Chuck might not have been the "hard-charger" that his dad was, but you could leave worse legacies than that.

reinventing the corporation: 1970–1990

When Charles Walgreen III—better known as "Cork"—assumed the office of president in 1969, he was a mere pup of 33; but that was the same age his dad was when Chuck had become president in 1939.

When Chuck took over, the company faced all the obstacles that came with the Great Depression and World War II and proved more than strong enough to surmount them. But by the time Cork rose to the office of president, the company's external problems—inflation, recession, and a general malaise in the U.S. business community—were no match for the long-overlooked internal problems Walgreens labored under. As current chief executive officer (CEO) David Bernauer says, the great empires of

Rome, Spain, and England crumbled not because of external attacks, but because of internal breakdowns. So it is with most business dynasties. It was Cork's mission to make sure that didn't happen to Walgreens.

state of the company

Like almost every other successful U.S. corporation after World War II, Walgreens diversified its holdings far beyond its flagship business. Walgreens bought the Sanborns department stores in Mexico and the Globe chain in Texas and spent a great amount of time, energy, and money expanding both, not to mention the resources required to start Corky's, Robin Hood's, and Wag's restaurants and coffee shops.

The Walgreens stores themselves had grown just as diverse, selling all manner of merchandise in a wide variety of store designs—including those of the Agency system—which often resulted in sloppy displays, cluttered aisles, and inefficient inventories. The consistency that had been a hallmark of the chain was breaking down due to a lack of focus on the company's primary mission: operating great drugstores.

Cork's salary as president was a paltry $80,000 and it didn't go up very much when he became CEO. "But the company wasn't making any money," he said, justifying his low pay. "Gosh, in '71 or '72, we only made $8 million on $800 million in sales."[1] (Compare those figures to the current totals of $1 billion in profits on $35 billion in sales, and you see Cork's point.) "Cash was a problem, too," Marilyn Abbey wrote. "There wasn't any."[2]

Cork knew he would have to face all these issues the day his father retired at age 65. The transition process, at least, was a simple one. As Cork recalled, his father brought him into his office, said, "There's my desk, son. See ya!" and left that day for his boat, *Dixonia II*, harbored on Lake Michigan. "And that was it," Cork said. "He really let me go on my own, pretty much."[3]

Not everyone expressed such carefree confidence in the young man. "When I became president," Cork confessed, "a lot of old-timers sold their stock. 'Oooh! Not him!'"[4] (In fact, it was a costly mistake for those who did sell their stock.)

It has always been easy to underestimate Cork Walgreen—an unassuming man who does not rely on the kind of charm or intimidation that characterize the modern U.S. CEO to make things happen. And underestimating him has always been a mistake. But when he first rose to company president, even Cork had his doubts. "My first thought," he admits today, "when I saw that desk, was how little I knew."[5]

In the 2001 best seller *Good to Great*, author Jim Collins and his research team studied 11 companies that had performed an average of seven times better than the stock market over the past 15 years. The short list included such well-known U.S. corporations as Gillette, Pitney Bowes, Wells Fargo, and the far less known Walgreens. Walgreens qualified by performing a staggering 16 times better than the market from 1975 to 2000—and five times better than the much-lauded General Electric.

Collins sought to determine the unique set of characteristics that propelled these 11 companies from average to excellent, teasing out eight common denominators that even Collins didn't expect to find. Take his description of the first tenet: leadership. "We were surprised, shocked really, to discover the type of leadership required for turning a good company into a great one," Collins wrote. "Compared to high-profile leaders with big personalities who make headlines and become celebrities, the good-to-great leaders seem to have come from Mars. Self-effacing, quiet, reserved, even shy—these leaders are a paradoxical blend of personal humility and professional will. They are more like Lincoln and Socrates than Patton or Caesar."[6] Collins's "profile in courage" could double as Cork Walgreen's thumbnail profile.

Like his father, Cork did not grow up planning to work for the family business. "Back in high school, I was going to be a veterinarian," Cork said, with his trademark chuckle. "But then I started to love fishing, so my dad took us sport fishing one day near Miami." After hopping on the impressive boat, breathing the salty air, and heading out to the open seas, Cork decided that he would eschew his plans for a career in veterinary medicine to become a charter boat captain. "So my father said, 'Why don't you work real hard, and then you can be a boat *owner* and hire your *own* captain?' I said, 'Oh, you're right! That sounds like a better idea!'"[7]

But, like Chuck's father Charles, Chuck never pressured his son to become a pharmacist. "When Cork was in high school," Chuck said at his son's retirement in 1998 as CEO, "I found out from his chemistry teacher at parents' night that my son was planning to attend pharmacy school at the University of Michigan. I was both surprised and delighted."[8]

While still in high school, Cork began his Walgreens career at the Evanston, Illinois, store as a stock boy. Cork's first day, the manager treated him like any other employee, handing him a broomstick to search under the shelves for long-lost products for 75 cents an hour. Instead of being offended, Cork was pleased. "That wasn't bad money then," he said. "I saved up enough money from that job to buy my first car in 1950, a sort of used 1936 Ford four-door, for $110. I still remember it. The car was beautiful, sort of a dark green, with a gear shift on the floor and a shade in the back window you could pull down. Sort of neat for the drive-ins."[9]

Though hard-working, Cork also possessed a mischievous streak. Of his days at the University of Michigan in the late 1950s, he said:

> I could have gone either way in the pharmacy school. The story's still going around. Our pharmacy class took a tour at Abbott's lab here in Chicago. We stayed at the Pick Congress, a great hotel, and we had a big party. And I set off a cherry bomb in the toilet. Boy, it was a huge mess. Broke the porcelain and the wooden seat. Had to buy 'em a whole new toilet. It was not too bad, about $50 bucks—but still not worth it.
>
> So, I took a "sabbatical," to work in one of the stores back here and fill prescriptions for a year. The [University of Michigan Pharmacy] dean, Tom Rowe, was kind enough to let me back in. And when I graduated, I had already gotten rid of my apprenticeship, so I didn't have to do it later, which really helped me with the Illinois State Pharmacy Board.[10]

Chuck Walgreen might have been largely "hands-off" with his son's decision making over the years, "but he really arranged my [Walgreens] training to a 'T,'" Cork said. "He knew that operations was the basis for our success, so that's where I spent 80 to 90 percent of my time, plus a couple years in real estate and a week or two in just about everything else." Thus, though Cork was only 33 when he assumed the Walgreens' presidency, he had already seen and done far more than most Walgreens' employees twice his age. Nonetheless, when Cork became president, "I used to drive myself *crazy*, because I thought I had to know everything," he said. "So what do you do? You delegate. So that's what I did."[11]

looking for a few good men

Before you can delegate duties to your top people, you *need* top people. After a gradual exodus of executives retired in the early 1970s, Cork had some hiring to do. Of all the tough decisions Cork faced during his reign, promoting the right people for these appointments was probably the most important.

When it comes to Cork's selections, Jim Collins and his research team maintain Walgreen took the path less traveled, and that truly made all the difference. "We expected that good-to-great leaders would begin by setting a new vision and strategy," Collins wrote. "We found instead that they *first* got the right people on the bus, the wrong people off the bus, and the right people in the right seats—and *then* they figured out where to drive it. The old adage 'People are your most important asset' turns out to be wrong. People are not your most important asset. The *right* people are."[12]

Thanks to his training, even at Cork's young age, he already had a good sense of the breadth of the company's infrastructure, and he knew the people in the field who were doing the best work.

Instead of falling for the flash-and-dash hiring practices of other large corporations—which consists of pulling in as many big names as you can, no matter their price or their technical backgrounds—Cork

Walgreen followed key principles when he hired his top lieutenants. First, he tapped people with pharmacy degrees already working for Walgreens, usually in operations. Second, he gave them enough accountability to keep them honest and enough latitude to run the show.

"Whenever we can we hire from within, we'd much rather do it that way," Cork said. "If you have to hire your top people from outside your company, it just doesn't say too much for the people you've got. I was not nervous about giving them the rope they needed, because I read the reports, I talked to the people who were in charge. I knew what was going on."[13]

Cork took his hiring practices a step farther by creating an executive planning committee composed of his top advisors, long before most companies caught on to the idea. "We just wanted to put everybody's ideas in the pot," he said, "and then come up with a goal. That way everybody would be behind it, and everybody would know where we were going."[14]

"Cork would let you get about 20 to 30 percent outside what he thinks the ballpark oughta be," said former CEO Dan Jorndt, "because he thinks you deserve that. But if you get too far out of line, he'd call you in, and he might only call you in once every two years, so that's something you really wanted to avoid."[15]

Jorndt believes Cork Walgreen also deserves credit for ignoring the dazzle of mergers and acquisitions for the more humble—but more important, to a retail drugstore chain—field of operations, which covers the day-to-day business of getting things to run correctly in a complicated corporation. "Cork got them involved in planning our long-term strategy," Jorndt said. "That was very important, because running stores is our business."[16]

A little anecdote neatly demonstrates the difference between Walgreens' approach to personnel and almost everyone else's. Several years ago, Walgreens endowed a chair at the University of Chicago (U-C) School of Business in honor of John Jeuck, a former U-C professor who had just retired from the Walgreens board. Bill Shank, a former Walgreens vice president in charge of the legal department who served under Cork, recalled,

After the presentation, two people from Towers Perrin, a consulting firm, came up to me and asked, 'Do you get all of your management personnel from University of Chicago B[usiness] school?' I can see where they might think so, given our proximity and our long relationship with the university; but I said, 'As a matter of fact, the CEO, the president, both executive vice presidents, and our operations vice president are all pharmacists.' And they were stunned by that. And I think that's really the secret of the whole thing, that's very significant, because people like that are going to know the business from the floor up. A lot of MBAs think it's not the business, it's the management. But that's not true. You have to know the thing you're doing."[17]

Of course, even after Cork made the crucial decision to hire people already working for Walgreens who had degrees in pharmacy and strong backgrounds in operations, there was still the matter of plucking a handful of talented individuals out of the thousands upon thousands of candidates who satisfied those criteria. Long before Collins or any other business gurus were opining about the best ways to identify and manage good leaders, Cork Walgreen was doing it instinctively. Characteristically, however, Cork deflected any suggestion that he was ahead of the curve: "I think it's just a lot of luck!" he said, and he sounded like he meant it. "You just look at a guy and figure out that he's pretty darn smart, that he communicates well, and that other people look up to him."[18]

If so, Cork Walgreen has to go down as one of the luckiest corporate leaders of all time. Just a few years into his presidency, he had assembled one of the most productive management teams of any U.S. corporation of any era, a team that would lead Walgreens from good to great over two decades. Like the leadership team his grandfather had assembled in the company's first decades, Cork's crew featured a few stars who seemed to keep everything humming.

Chuck Hunter left Arthur Andersen in 1967 to become Walgreens' assistant controller; but his Walgreens career didn't take off until Cork recognized his talent and appointed him vice president of administration and chief financial officer in 1972. Hunter transformed the company's accounting system, but he is best remembered as the Father of Intercom. While other companies were installing stand-alone computers in each store, seeing only the productivity gains they could realize and missing the patient service and marketing opportunities of a connected system, Hunter recognized the power of a centrally based computer system that tied all stores together, a system later named Intercom.

In 1978, Cork made three more crucial appointments. He tapped Vern Brunner to head the marketing department, a move that eventually earned Brunner a place in the National Sales & Marketing Hall of Fame. Cork then named Glenn Kraiss, who had joined Walgreens as a soda fountain jerk while in high school in 1949, to run store operations, a job he performed with unequaled success until he retired in 1999. And finally, Cork hired John Brown from Uniroyal in 1974 and promoted him to vice president of distribution four years later. Brown revolutionized Walgreens' distribution system, building six major distribution centers during his tenure. All four appointees worked well into the 1990s, leaving the company in infinitely better shape than they'd found it.

But even among leaders of equal stature, some were more equal than others. All agree that Cork's key promotion was Fred Canning. "Putting Fred Canning in as president [in 1978] made a sea change in this company," Jorndt said. "Cork was the strategist, and now he has this guy Fred Canning, with *so* much energy, to carry it out."[19]

walgreen's wingman

Fred Canning, a native of Chicago, started his 44-year Walgreens career humbly enough in 1946 as an apprentice pharmacist. Canning was a hard-charging young man who looked and acted even then like a grizzled football coach. It seemed preordained that he would quickly rise through the local ranks, and he did, becoming the store manager in 1955. That's when

Cork, working as an administrative assistant in operations, first met Canning and was immediately impressed. It would have been hard not to be, watching this eager young manager take over a store that was filling only seven prescriptions a day and turn it into the best store pharmacy in the entire chain—an accomplishment the former company president considers his greatest achievement to this day.

In 1962 the company transferred Canning to St. Louis as a district manager; but that district had become so famously dysfunctional that corporate headquarters advised Canning not to buy a house, on the assumption that the district's days were numbered. "The [St. Louis] stores were old and run down," Cork recalled. "It was nip and tuck whether we were even going to stay there."[20]

Canning turned the district around, however, the same way he would help turn the entire company around decades later: by hiring good people, attending to every detail, setting up efficient systems, and—mostly—putting in lots of hard work.

Recalled Dick Servant Jr., who was a store manager in the district at the time:

> The St. Louis district seldom left town to go to a managers' meeting, but one year when Canning was our district manager, we all met at Northland Shopping center at 4 A.M. and left in two cars. We stopped for doughnuts on our way to headquarters at 4300 Peterson, Chicago. There, we toured the office and had lunch in the cafeteria. Toured the sign shop, where the Christmas displays were made. Made two stores before we left for Springfield, Illinois, where we ate at the Black Angus Steak House. After dining, we traveled back to our starting point, arriving at 3 A.M., 23 hours after we left, [feeling] jump-started and inspired with the Christmas season soon to come.[21]

Such hours and inspiration were the rule, not the exception, of Canning's style.

"Business wasn't great at the Normandy Shopping center store [in St. Louis]," Canning recalled, "and Dick Servant Jr. and I were always trying to improve it. Traditionally, the store closed on holidays, but one time we decided to keep it open and see what happened. Servant manned the pharmacy, and I stayed up front. We had one other employee working with us. Before we knew it, the place was mobbed, and we were frantically calling in more employees."[22]

By the 1980s, the Normandy store had become Walgreens' top store for sales and profit in the St. Louis district and even served as a test market for Hallmark. In fact, instead of leaving the St. Louis district, as many had predicted the company would before Canning took it over, by 1982 Walgreens operated 33 stores there and sales were "sensational," according to Glenn Kraiss, then the senior store operations vice president. At the end of the century, the St. Louis district had over a hundred stores and ranked second only to Chicago for self-service sales.[23]

Canning's miraculous St. Louis turnaround drew the attention of company executives. In 1965, they tapped him to become the district manager for its Mountain district, headquartered in Denver. It turned out that the man the company had recently annointed to be the new regional manager there just happened to be a guy named Cork Walgreen.

"We had a tiny office with one big desk in the middle of it," Cork remembered. "[Canning] sat on one side of the desk and I sat on the other, facing each other, because the space was so limited. But we were never there at the same time, so it wasn't a problem. He was at his district stores, I was on the road, visiting stores all the way from California and down to El Paso and up to Salt Lake City, all over the West."[24]

Despite their peripatetic schedules, the young businessmen got to know each other well. "Fred was a disciplinarian, very strict, and a good speaker, good on his feet," Cork attested. "He was just a good guy, and we were very close friends, at work and at home. When I lived in Denver, he lived just a block or two away, with his wife and eight kids. We spent a lot of time together."[25]

Thus, when Cork Walgreen was called back to Chicago in 1968 and became president the next year, he remembered his colleague in the mountains and called for him in 1972 to become director of marketing. Once reunited in Chicago, the dynamic duo went to work.

the turnaround team

"What a combination Cork and Canning were!" Dan Jorndt exclaimed.

> Cork was the quiet, shy, unassuming leader. He was not a hands-on guy, but he had a highly developed killer instinct. He's a killer, an absolute killer. He wanted this company to be good, and he had the wisdom to bring lots of talented operations people in to [run it]. He knew what was going on, and he could react. He had a clear vision, and he wasn't afraid to make hard decisions.
>
> Cork brought Fred Canning in to implement his vision. He couldn't have done it without Fred. Fred was the brigadier general, the kind of guy who'd bail out of the airplane with a parachute, take Normandy beach, take the hill! Fred Canning got the green light and ran—and he was tough. Tough! Fred was very aggressive, very much a disciplinarian. People respected him. He knew the business and came up through the stores. His instincts were tremendous.[26]

The pair made a powerful one-two punch—and had to. When they joined forces at the forefront of the company in the early 1970s, Walgreens' to-do list was long, indeed—from cleaning up the aisles to clearing out the subsidiaries to clearing the bottom line of red ink.

The first step was discipline. "Fred was very insistent on people being here on time," stated Bill Shank, in a considerable understatement. Canning could put the fear of God even into executives. "During a bad snowstorm, John Rubino, who was the vice president for human resources, was stuck out on the expressway, at five to eight, with traffic stopped. He was so desperate to avoid Fred's wrath that he pulled his car over into the snow, climbed over the fence, and came into the meeting all covered in snow. He was so determined to make that meeting—and he did."[27]

Before they were plucked to lead the company, Walgreen and Canning already had developed strong opinions about some of the company's woes—and how to solve them—during their time together in the Denver office.

"There were all these things in the aisles," Cork Walgreen told Marilyn Abbey. "You couldn't even walk without bumping into something. We thought we could sell everything and anything."[28]

"In those days out west," Walgreen said in a recent interview, "Sav-On was the premier store—neat, clean, streamlined—and we were sort of messy and cluttered, so we wanted to be at least as good as they were. But it was convincing the rest of the people in Chicago that was the hard part. They thought if we put it on the floor, it'd sell better; but instead the customers just tripped over it and sued us!"[29]

After Cork was installed in the front office, he recalled, "we conducted customer interviews, and they told us that the stores were crowded and messy—which I already knew. So that was the starting point of a big clean-up for us."[30]

Clean up they did. Editors don't stop the presses to send photographers and reporters out to watch workers mop floors, dust shelves, and clear clutter out of the aisles, and business gurus don't write best sellers about the discipline, determination, and elbow grease such a drive requires. But customers notice, and customers care—and that was enough motivation for Cork and Canning to keep going. In some respects, the duo's first initiative—clean it up!—best reflected the basic values on which the entire turnaround was founded: short on sizzle, but lots of steak.

Anyone familiar with Ray Kroc's compulsive neatness—he was famous for determining a particular McDonald's commitment to cleanliness simply by checking under the ridge of a toilet with a cosmetic mirror—will be appalled at just how far the famed fast-food franchise has fallen. While McDonald's has been failing to fulfill simple customer needs like clean tabletops, clean floors, and clean bathrooms—not to mention fast, friendly service—a seemingly endless parade of McDonald's managers spent the 1990s introducing product after product, gimmick after gimmick, while their stock, market share, and customer satisfaction have all fallen dramatically. (McDonald's recently tapped Jim Cantalupo, a former McDonald's executive from the glory days, to save the troubled franchise. He has responded by announcing a back-to-basics movement to fix the underlying problem of basic customer service—the very drive Walgreens initiated three decades ago.)

Walgreens' efforts to clear the aisles continues to this day, surpassing its original standards, taking the principle to extremes they couldn't have imagined 30 years ago, as the following story from Dan Jorndt indicates: By the mid-1980s, Walgreens had succeeded in making its stores much cleaner and easier to navigate than they had been just a decade earlier. They had learned that 70 percent of Walgreens' shoppers were women; and women had made it clear that they wanted the aisles in every store to be not only clean and clear but even free of promotional displays. "Nothing in the aisles!" recalled Jorndt, who was the regional director for Chicago stores at the time.

"No mess, no clutter. All our surveys said our stores were cluttered. So we took all the stuff hanging down from the ceiling, took all the signs off the windows. But the surveys still came back saying we're cluttered because although we'd demanded nothing in the aisles, ever, no displays, we always had an asterisk: 'Except baskets of Walgreens products'—these ugly baskets we had up and down the aisle selling our house brands.

"So I get a call one day from a district manager, Mike Arnoult.

'[Dan,] can you drop into the store in Wheeler?' [a Chicago suburb just five minutes from the corporate headquarters in Deerfield].

'Mike, it's not open yet,' I replied. 'It opens next week.'

'I know,' he said, 'but I want you to see something.'

'Well, just tell me what it is,' I said.

'No, Dan, you gotta come out here and see it.'

'Mike, I don't have any time for this,' I protested. But Arnoult insisted. So I finally acquiesced, arriving at the store that morning. And what he's done is taken down all the Walgreens baskets and banners. So all the aisles are perfectly clear in this brand new store. It looked tremendous.

And Mike said, 'Whatya think?'

And I said, 'Mike, this looks *fantastic*.'

'So Dan,' he asked, 'can I open the store this way? Can I do this?'

'Of course!'

'But you know the marketing guys will flip when they come in here and see all those Walgreens baskets down,' Arnoult said, 'because that's mandatory.'

'I'll handle them,' I assured him, so that's how Arnoult opened the store. Well, it wasn't 24 hours before I got a call from Fred Canning, who got a call from marketing, asking us to put the baskets back up immediately.

'Mr. Canning, I will put them back up,' I said, not wanting to come off as disrespectful. 'But I want you to go look at them first.'

'All right,' Canning said. 'I'll go look at them. But they're going back up.'

"And this is where Providence comes in," Jorndt says today. "The town of Wheeling is just down the street. Now, dumb luck, Canning runs into Cork on the way, and they decide to go out to the store together.

"Well, they walk in the front door, Cork and Canning and Vern Brunner—the best marketing guy this company has ever had. We're all waiting to hear what they're going to say—and this is where Cork was a visionary. He said, 'I think it's *great*.' And you've got to give

Cork credit: He had cajones. He said, 'This is the reason why we haven't been able to get our aisles clear. We've always had the asterisk that the Walgreens displays in the aisles are okay. I want this in every store!'

"That tells you something about Cork Walgreen. He had steel. Real steel. For a guy who wasn't in the store 24 hours a day, he really got it! It's just like every profession: There are people who get it, and there are people who never get it. And Cork Walgreen got it!

"And remember, Fred's the brigadier general, Omar Bradley, and President Roosevelt just said, "This is it." And you know what Fred said? 'Yes, sir!' You've got to give him credit, too. Not many strong leaders—and Fred was a *strong* leader!—can do that.

"That little event changed the way our stores look, markedly," Jorndt concluded. "A lot of things happen that work out well [that] you really don't think about ahead of time. You figure it out looking back. But that one decision made our stores so much better—with a cleaner, brighter, more organized look—that it helped drive our pharmacy business, because no one wants to come into a pharmacy and trip over all this stuff just to get to the back of the store. Eew! They figure, 'These guys can't be good at pharmacy! Their stores are dirty and messy!'"[31]

Walgreens moved on to bigger refurbishing projects. Just a few years after customer surveys concluded that Walgreens stores were "junky, disorganized, hard to shop, with merchandise clogging the aisles"—even Cork confessed many of the old stores looked "beat up"—between 1975 and 1980, Walgreens remodeled 20 percent of the old stores. By 1979, Walgreens had 688 stores—the result of the company's first major expansion since the 1920s—with 45 percent having opened in the late 1970s.

In the words of former Michigan football coach Bo Schembechler, a friend of the Walgreens, "You must remember that you are coaching attitude as much as skill. I work on a guy's attitude from the minute he gets here. Encouragement. Criticism. Screaming. Winking. Kicking. Yelling. Nodding. Ignoring. It's all part of coaching attitude, because attitude equals motivation. If I coach the right attitude, we can win, we can beat anybody."[32]

Cork, Canning, and their lieutenants gave Walgreens a new look and a new approach, but what they really gave the corporation and its employees was a new attitude—an attitude of discipline, pride, and perfection. That attitude, more than anything else, would launch the company to heights never before imagined.

killing off their little darlings

After Walgreens' new leaders cleaned up the stores and removed all clutter from the aisles, they turned their attention to cleaning up the company's portfolio and selling off all extraneous businesses and ventures. Early in his tenure, Cork came to the conclusion that Walgreens was spread too thin as a corporation—by being involved in too many things that weren't drugstores—and spread too thin as a drugstore, too—by trying to be too many things to too many customers.

The problem Cork and company faced was one of the corporation's own doing. Like most successful U.S. businesses after World War II, Walgreens loaded up on mergers and acquisitions—though not as voraciously as other corporations, nor as nonsensibly.

In addition to purchasing Mexico's Sanborns department store chain in 1946 and Houston's Globe chain in 1962, Walgreens opened three restaurants: Corky's in 1967; Robin Hood's in 1968; and Wag's, a coffee shop named for Walgreens' symbol on the New York Stock Exchange, in 1976. They were all retail, all service, but not drugstores—what Walgreens does best.

Walgreens didn't stop there. It went on to forge a partnership with St. Louis's 50-store Schnucks grocery store chain in 1976, to open 10 optical centers in its Walgreens stores in 1977, and to attempt to revitalize its sagging network of agency stores in the 1970s under John Rubino, who later served as vice president of human resources.

In each case, Walgreens enjoyed an initial surge of excitement followed by a long, dull stretch of operating a company or division it only partly understood—a cycle experienced by virtually every other corporation that caught the acquisition bug, though many had it much worse than Walgreens. Most of these mergers and start-ups were rewarding in the short run but ultimately proved out of step with the direction of the parent company and more distracting than they were worth. *challenges*

As Lew Young, former editor in chief of *Business Week*, wrote years ago,

> Back in the sixties when conglomerates were the rage, Jimmy Ling was down in Washington appearing before an anti-trust committee describing why conglomerates were not in restraint of trade. He put up a chart that said, "How many people in LTV [then Ling-Temcon-Vought] know the steel business?" He had just bought Jones and Laughlin. The answer? A big red zero was the next chart in his presentation. I bet today Jimmy Ling wishes the answer to that hadn't been zero, because when Jones and Laughlin went down, Ling lost control of LTV.[33]

Tom Peters and Robert Waterman wrote in their groundbreaking 1982 best seller, *In Search of Excellence*,

> It is a simple fact that most acquisitions go awry. Not only are the synergies to which so many executives pay lip service seldom realized; more often than not the result is catastrophic. . . . [A]cquisitions, even little ones, suck up an inordinate amount of top management's time, time taken away from the main-line business. . . . [W]ith merger mania as prevalent as it is, it seems worthwhile to illustrate rather exhaustively the almost total absence of *any* rigorous support for very diversified business communications. . . . Virtually

all the growth in the excellent companies has been internally generated and home-grown.[34]

Walgreens got religion years before *In Search of Excellence* came out, but
it took the company almost two decades to finish the job. Cork and company started cleaning house by closing the Corky's line in 1977, just 10
years into the venture, and then let the Globe chain go in 1978, when they
discovered the division was creating unwanted competition for Walgreens
stores in the area. The directors ended the partnership with the Schnucks
chain in 1981, the same year they closed the Walgreens optical centers,
and dropped Sanborns in 1984 after the dollar fell so dramatically relative
to the peso that doing business in Mexico no longer made sound business
sense. Finally, Walgreens got out of the food business for good in 1988,
when it closed both Robin Hood's and Wag's, selling the latter's remaining
87 posts to the Marriott Corporation. Bottom line, in a mere 11 years,
Walgreens had divested itself of seven substantial divisions.[35]

Walgreens wasn't afraid to sell off franchises that cut closer to the
bone—and the heart. When superpremium ice creams like Häagen-Dazs
and Ben & Jerry's came out in the 1970s, Walgreens realized its store-
brand ice cream was no longer a cutting-edge, luxury product and closed
its eight ice cream manufacturing plants and, with them, the coffee
brand, too, because the roasting operation operated out of one of the ice
cream plants. The fact that Walgreens' ice cream had been introduced by
Cork Walgreen's grandfather in 1916 and scooped into a glass of chocolate malt by Pop Coulson in 1922 to invent the milk shake didn't deter
the grandson for a second. For him, the decision was surprisingly easy, utterly bereft of sentiment: Making ice cream and processing coffee no
longer added up.

The executive committee just as coolly decided that the Agency system, despite efforts to build it up to its original robustness, had to go as
well. Even John Rubino, the man responsible for its brief renaissance in
the 1970s, described it as a "difficult but inevitable decision," a victim of
its own success. "Agency growth was placing more demands on corporate

warehousing and delivery at the same time the company's own growth rate was beginning its meteoric rise."[36]

"At one time, we had 2,000 Agency stores," Cork said. "We just kept shrinking the number down. And the company couldn't grow because the Agencies were in the markets we wanted to enter; but they were old, small, slow, high-priced, dirty in some cases. So we just shut down the whole division."[37]

What's noteworthy about this tidal wave of divestments is that many of these divisions were actually making money when Walgreens closed or sold them. Perhaps most remarkable, however, was Cork's determination to put aside family feelings to do what was best for the company's future. An author once observed that when it comes time to edit a piece of literature, all writers have difficulty cutting their favorite lines, even if the limitations of space and scope require it. But, she advised, if you want the piece to work, "You have to kill off your little darlings."

Of course, that's easier said than done, especially when it involves components for which employees and customers alike harbor strong affection and when cutting them would require releasing or retraining hundreds or thousands of employees. This is why most companies hang on to divisions and products and policies long after their usefulness has worn out, in much the same way we hang on to favorite shirts and old hats long after they've become embarrassing to everyone but us.

Not so Walgreens. When it came time to make tough decisions on the fate of the food service division, Cork and company were courageously objective in making their assessment—even though the food service division brought in a third of company profits for most of the twentieth century and still accounted for $100 million a year in gross revenue well into the 1970s; even though Cork's grandmother started Walgreens' food service back in 1910, when she made sandwiches and soups and pies for her son Chuck to deliver to Charles's first store on Cottage Grove; and even though Walgreens counters and booths and tables gave the chain an indelible identity as America's meeting place for generations of families, couples, kids, and even veterans during the war years.

Despite all that, Cork, Canning, and company compared the stores they had to the stores of the future and decided that food service had to go. As Jim Collins wrote in the *Harvard Business Review* in 2001, a

good example of iron-willed leadership comes from Charles R. "Cork" Walgreen III, who transformed dowdy Walgreens into a company that outperformed the stock market 16:1 from its transition in 1975 to 2000. After years of dialogue and debate with his executive team about what to do with Walgreens food-service operations, this CEO sensed the team had finally reached a watershed: the company's brightest future lay in convenient drug stores, not in food service.

Dan Jorndt, who succeeded Walgreen in 1998 as CEO, describes what happened next. "Cork said at one of our planning committee meetings, 'Okay, now I am going to draw a line in the sand. We are going to be out of the restaurant business completely in five years.' At the time, we had more than 500 restaurants. You could have heard a pin drop. He said, 'I want to let everybody know the clock is ticking.'

"Six months later," Jorndt continued, "we were at our next planning committee meeting and someone mentioned just in passing that we had only five years to be out of the restaurant business. Cork was not a real vociferous fellow. He sort of tapped on the table and said, 'Listen . . . I said you had five years six months ago. Now you've got four and a half years.'

"Well, the next day things really clicked into gear for winding down our restaurant business. Cork never wavered. He never doubted. He never second-guessed."[38]

When asked about the story, Cork recalled his cabinet's response, with a chuckle. "They were, 'Whoa! Wake up call.'"[39]

Cork can laugh now, but his people weren't laughing then. They were rushing back to their offices, getting on the phone, and making it happen. They did; when Cork's five-year deadline was reached, Walgreens was officially out of the food business.

What's striking, however, was Cork's utter lack of reservation. When asked if he had any hesitation about the decision, he replied, "No, not really." Nor did he talk with his father before cutting loose the beloved food division. "I never consulted with my dad on any decisions—not a one—because I was afraid he'd disagree with me!"[40]

"Cork is a shy man, smart, with a photographic memory and a laser-sharp instinct for excellence," Jorndt said. "His standards were very high, and everybody wanted to rise to those standards. Cork was not a hands-on CEO, but he made it a point to know everything that was going on in the company. He made the decision to get out of all our peripheral business, and he was single-minded about it. It took us 15 years, but it was a steady march."[41]

the systems behind the smiles

Disciplined employees, clean stores, and a focused strategy comprised the foundation for Walgreens' turnaround; but if the management team stopped there, no one would be writing books about the company's amazing rise to the top of U.S. businesses.

In his acclaimed 1990 book, *Customers for Life*, Carl Sewell, the nation's top luxury-car dealer, explained how he built a quarter-billion dollar business by following a few straightforward principles. In Chapter Five, for example, titled "Systems, Not Smiles," Sewell said that the warm, fuzzy sides of customer service—saying please and thank you, for starters—are nice and important but only the icing on the cake, not the cake itself. Customer service requires doing the job right the first time, and having a plan in place to fix things fast when you don't. "Having systems that allow you to do both those things," he wrote, "are more important than all the warm and fuzzy feelings in the world. . . . What's needed in restaurants, car dealerships, department stores, and every place else is systems—not just smiles—that guarantee good service."[42]

In Walgreens' case, "good systems" includes modern accounting methods, efficient distribution designs, and cutting-edge computer networks to ensure that the products that customers want are there when they want them.

Shortly after Cork took over Walgreens, he assessed the company's health and determined they had a strong need to improve cash flow, especially during an inflationary period. Company chief financial officer (CFO) Chuck Hunter had the answer: Switch from FIFO accounting to LIFO accounting—or from "First In, First Out" to "Last In, First Out." In a nutshell, it's the difference between an escalator and an elevator. On an escalator, the first people to step on are the first people to step off. That's "First In, First Out." As people pile into an elevator, however, the last ones who squeeze in are the first ones to get out (assuming all are going to the same floor, of course). That's "Last In, First Out."

Changing the company's accounting system from FIFO to LIFO would minimize reported earnings because they would be selling the most recent—and therefore highest priced—inventory first, thus keeping profits down, and taxes down with them. That, in turn, increased cash flow, which decreased loan liabilities and interest expenses.

Because no other drug chain had considered using LIFO accounting, Cork's executive team checked out every angle with everyone who might be affected—including creditors, auditors, and tax advisors—before finally making the move. The company's calculated gamble paid off, with the stock price rising from $10 to $13 in late 1975.

Cork Walgreen gives all the credit to Chuck Hunter, "really a very forward thinking guy," Cork said. "He was the only one [on the executive board] who was there when I came in. The rest of the guys were my guys. But he was terrific. LIFO was really his decision."[43] Hunter did for Walgreens' accounting what Robert Knight had done a half century earlier: He brought the company's financial systems into the modern era and forced everyone else to follow.

After Walgreens successfully instituted the LIFO system, it decided to fix its distribution system. When it examined the setup carefully, the executive committee didn't like what it saw. "Our physical distribution was terrible and old fashioned," Cork says today. "It sometimes took *two weeks* to get an item you'd ordered, which is death in this business. So we hired a guy from Uniroyal, John Brown, who did a great job and got us going. We rebuilt the entire system. So now we are probably on the leading edge in that area, too."[44]

"Retail is very Darwinian, I always say," Jorndt remarked. "It's always survival of the fittest, and the fittest are the ones that serve the customers best. The distribution system we started to build in the [1980s] and continue to expand helps us do just that."[45]

walgreens goes high-tech

Perhaps nothing demonstrates Walgreens' determination to evolve from a dowdy midcentury drugstore chain to a high-tech retailer better than its commitment to cutting-edge computer technology.

At the dawn of the Cork Era, "Computers weren't used much," he said. "Even for payroll, for instance, we used to have to take the cash out of the drawers in each store, count it out, and put it in envelopes for each individual employee and hand them out. I think our people were generally very honest, but there were probably some temptations—'One for me, two for me!'—and this was in the 1960s!"[46]

After getting computers installed in every store, which numbered about 400 or so when Cork's tenure began, Chuck Hunter, the CFO behind the FIFO-LIFO switch, and John Brown tried to create something spectacular: Walgreens' Intercom system, which, if it worked, would prove as important to the company as self-service.

Hunter, Jorndt said, "had the vision of an online pharmacy, which became Intercom. He could see there would be mountains of paperwork to manage third-party prescriptions [thanks to the growing number of HMOs and the like], and we needed a system to handle that."

Although intended to process insurance paperwork more efficiently, "Ultimately," Jorndt said, "Intercom's biggest advantage was as a customer service tool." Just as FedEx was founded to handle the Federal Reserve's overnight delivery needs (thus the name FedEx) but ended up serving a far broader function for millions of people sending in bills, college applications, and office documents at the last minute, Intercom proved to be even more beneficial in serving everyday customers than health care providers.[47]

Hunter's vision was ambitious but elegant. He imagined a system that would link all Walgreens pharmacies to a central data bank, and also to each other, through computer servers and satellites—a pharmaceutical Internet, essentially, before the term "Internet" even existed—thereby allowing pharmacists to pull up the histories of Walgreens customers anywhere in the country, even if the customers had just moved, were on vacation, or simply found themselves across town from their usual store.

Like a lot of good ideas, however, this one ran into trouble right out of the gate. In 1976, Walgreens piloted two versions of the program in St. Louis and Des Moines, Iowa. The first version was based on the United Airlines system of tracking passengers on its flights, substituting Walgreens' stores for United's planes and Walgreens' customers and their prescriptions for the passengers. The other version simply didn't work.

"It just didn't have the turnaround we needed," Cork said. "They were going to stop it, and I said, 'No, you can't do that.' I didn't want to pull it out after we'd educated our customers to use it. And so we had two different systems going on at once. We really bet the whole company on it. We put millions into it, and we were not making that much then."[48]

So if Intercom failed? "Then we'd be in big trouble!" he said with a laugh. "I don't know if it would have sunk the company, but it would've sent millions down the drain, and the future of Walgreens would have been a lot different. There's no way we could grow like we are today. But we knew if this thing worked it would be fantastic." Following Intercom's "false start," Walgreens committed millions more to the project; and after years of tedious debugging, they tried it again, "as we held our collective breath," Cork said.[49]

It worked. By the early 1980s, every store in the chain was hooked up to the Intercom system, connecting every store's pharmacy records to the central system and the central system to every store.

"Intercom is clearly one of the biggest things we've done," Jorndt said. "With Intercom, we've got one central record of everyone's information, and I believe we're still the only retailer who has that. You can walk into any Walgreens anywhere, and if you can remember your name, we can get your records. Only the U.S. government sends more data through satellites than we do. That was a great thing that we did for our customers."[50]

"It was miles ahead of the other drug stores," said Bill Shank. "That gave us a great advantage, and still does."[51]

Walgreens pressed its advantage when it launched Intercom's $150 million successor, Intercom Plus, in 1998, which expanded Intercom's original capability by organizing each store's workflow, allowing the pharmacist to focus less on his or her inventory and more on consulting with clients.

Once again, Walgreens' high-stakes gamble paid off.

vindication

The most important work Walgreens' management did during the Cork Era—including instilling discipline, cleaning up the stores, eliminating extraneous businesses, and creating the Intercom system—was done quietly with little publicity. You would be hard-pressed to find Walgreens' name in business books until the 1990s. But the groundwork laid in the 1970s started drawing attention in the 1980s.

Walgreens started knocking off milestone after milestone: its 500 millionth prescription in 1980; the first drugstore chain to top $2 billion in 1981; ranking first in sales, earnings, and market penetration among drugstores in 1983; opening Walgreens' 1,000th store in 1984 (with Illinois Governor Jim Thompson and Cary Grant doing the honors); and breaking $3 billion in sales in 1985—just four years after topping $2 billion. By the middle 1980s, word had gotten out on the Walgreens secret. In 1985, *Dun's Business Month* named Walgreens one of the nation's five best-managed companies, and the *Wall Street Transcript* crowned Walgreen and Canning the country's best retail drug chain executives, the first of seven times they'd receive it that decade.[52]

"They worked so well together," Bill Shank said, "and the results reflect the fact that both of them know the drugstore business inside and out."[53]

"Watching those two work together was like watching FDR and Patton," Jorndt added. "They put together an outstanding management team, the equal of any team in retailing, and supported them for an amazing 20-year run."[54]

poised to pounce: 1990–future

"this is dan jorndt, how may i help you?"

W algreens hit the last decade of the twentieth century—its tenth decade—at full speed. It could boast 1,564 stores, 48,500 employees, 100 million prescriptions, $6.05 billion in gross revenue, and $175 million in profits. Instead of becoming complacent, however, Walgreens set its course for the best decade of its now 103-year history.

That it occurred on the heels of Fred Canning's departure makes it all the more impressive. When Canning stepped down in 1990 after a 12-year run as president, few thought such a dynamic, demanding, and ambitious leader could be replaced; and they may well have been right. It would be hard to overstate Canning's importance to Walgreens' rise in the 1970s, 1980s, and even the 1990s, after he had left the company set up for continued success.

When you look back over Walgreens' long history, it's easy to see that there have always been very talented people in the front offices, but it's the combination of soft and hard skills at the very top that have sparked the company's greatest eras. Charles Sr. seemed to embody both sides himself—his engaging, warm personality coupled with his iron will and unequaled ambition. Chuck and Justin Dart seem to have the combination covered between them; but when Dart's ego became too much to deal with, Chuck lost a vital element of intensity in the front office.

Cork reestablished the formula when he promoted Fred Canning, and the combination might have been the most successful in Walgreens' history. Fred Canning had all the energy, talent, and charisma of Justin Dart, but without the overwhelming personal ambition that negated many of Dart's virtues. Dart would have been happy to see Chuck and the family pushed aside for his own benefit, while Canning was the most loyal soldier Cork could have ever wished for. The man Cork picked to replace Canning was just as talented, and just as loyal.

But the challenges facing Canning's successor in 1990 were very different from the ones Canning confronted when he became president in 1978.

The next Walgreens president would not have to bring discipline, order, and confidence to a sagging company. Cork, Canning, and crew had already seen to all that. The turnaround had been completed. No, the seventh Walgreens president would have to bring determination, to avoid the pitfalls of self-satisfaction; imagination, to take advantage of Walgreens' new place in the world; and a killer instinct, to make tough decisions with a single-minded focus.

The Walgreens board, led by Cork, decided Dan Jorndt was that man. This one decision alone, wrote Jim Collins, in his best seller, *Good to*

Great—in which he described how the 11 best Fortune 500 stock performers over the past 25 years did it—has separated Walgreens from such competitors as the Eckerd Company (acquired by JC Penney in 1997). "The contrast between Jack Eckerd and Cork Walgreen is striking," Collins wrote. "Whereas Jack Eckerd had a genius for picking the right stores to buy, Cork Walgreen had a genius for picking the right people to hire," a comment that covers leaders from Fred Canning to Dave Bernauer. "Whereas Jack Eckerd failed utterly at the single most important decision facing any executive—the selection of a successor—Cork Walgreen developed multiple outstanding candidates and selected a superstar successor," that successor being, of course, Dan Jorndt, who followed Cork as president in 1990 and as chief executive officer (CEO) in 1998.[1]

In a tradition dating back to Charles Sr., in choosing Jorndt, the board had promoted a Walgreens lifer who worked his way up from the stores to the front office. "I can tell ya," Jorndt said, "I knew I wanted to work for Walgreens from the time I was 18 years old."[2]

He took a few turns to get there, however, and a few more to become the company president. Jorndt worked for his neighborhood drugstore— an independent outfit named Losby's Drug—on the north side of Chicago—as a delivery boy and, thanks to his mother, who worked the overtime shift at the hospital down the street, got a second job in the pharmacy there. That hospital store just happened to be run by a retired Walgreens man, "who told Walgreens stories night and day," Jorndt said. "So I had little bugs about Walgreens in my head."

In 1959, Jorndt enrolled in pharmacology at Drake University in Des Moines, Iowa. (You might have noticed that a Harvard degree does not impress many in the halls of headquarters; they're more concerned with what you've done than where you went.) He intended to return to take over the hospital pharmacy after graduation. "The deal was set when I was a freshman in college," he said. "I'd get an apartment back in Chicago and three meals a day in the cafeteria. That was going to be my job, my life."

Recalled Dan Jorndt, in the middle of my freshman year,

They loaded a bunch of us on a bus and took us on a field trip to go see a Walgreens store in Des Moines. It was run by this guy named Wayne Wait, who wore white short-sleeved shirts and a bow-tie—so clean cut, he squeaked.

He took us over to the grill of this big Walgreens. He talked to us about what a good company this was—how you can get ahead at Walgreens, how you can have a nice life at Walgreens, raise a family, have the profit sharing. And when he got done, it was like I was hit with lightning. I *knew* I wanted to work for Walgreens. I went home and told the guy back at the hospital, "I'm going to work here through college, but then I'm going to work for Walgreens."[3]

Jorndt worked briefly for another chain in California before starting his Walgreens career in 1963. The young pharmacist quickly advanced from assistant manager to store manager to district manager to regional vice president—a rapid climb that required leading his family on a whiplash-inducing journey from Chicago's North Side to Milwaukee, back to Chicago's west suburbs, out to Albuquerque, and back to Chicago yet again, for the last time, in 1975. The most interesting stop, Jorndt said, was the one in the middle of it all: Albuquerque.

"When they asked if I wanted to go to New Mexico, I said, 'Are you crazy?' Well, they said, we're losing money, and we need some help. So we moved to Albuquerque. I had a nice four-bedroom ranch for just $190 a month. We loved it! We were there almost five years, and it became a very good district." So good, in fact, that when Jorndt's district rose from one of the worst to first in the company in both sales and profit, the company asked him to return to headquarters to give a little speech on how they did it. "That's to remind you," he said, "that performance gets recognized at Walgreens."

Likewise, when Jorndt was promoted to Chicago regional vice president, the flagship region ranked last and was still falling fast. Yet seven years later, Jorndt had pushed it to the top in sales and profit.

Walgreens recognized Jorndt's outstanding performance many times on his journey—the Walgreens "report card" system guarantees that everyone short of the "cabinet level" receives a detailed, quantified evaluation every year—until finally Cork Walgreen made him an offer he literally couldn't refuse. As Jorndt remembered it, in 1989,

Cork called me and said "I've seen your work, I've seen your résumé. You should be the treasurer." I said, "Mr. Walgreen, I'm flattered, but I'll never take a job that doesn't have a report card." And that job didn't. So he said, "All right. I'll talk to you later."

Then he calls me in his office the following Monday, and that was a very big deal. It was like seeing God. He asked me, "Have you thought of my offer?" I said, "I have, but if it's all the same to you, sir, I'll be content to run the Chicago region."

Then he says, "Okay, now listen to me. You are going to be the treasurer." And I said, "Yes, sir!"[4]

After an eight-year stint as treasurer, in 1990, Walgreens named Jorndt president of the company—ushering in the company's most exciting era.

plain and proud of it: the anti-enron

When Jorndt settled into the same position Cork Walgreen had first occupied 22 years earlier, Jorndt looked out on a company that was dramatically different from the one that Cork had seen when he first sat there.

"I'd say Cork and Fred [Canning] did four major things for Walgreens," Jorndt said. "They cleaned up the company, they started the big consolidation—getting rid of everything we didn't need—they got our balance sheet straightened out, and they made us very profitable again. They set the stage so that in the nineties we could really grow! And we've built on that."[5]

Walgreens has enjoyed some wonderful runs in its century-long history, but arguably one of its best eras was the Jorndt Epoch (1990–2002). That success seems to have depended as much on the bold decisions the company made as on the dumb mistakes it didn't—mistakes that virtually every other U.S. company, it seems, was only too willing to entertain.

"We have an expression," Jorndt explained, holding his index finger up in the manner of a Greek orator. "'We're not looking for the silver bullet, the answer to all our prayers.' The best three examples: diversification, acquisition, and dot-coms." He elaborated: "We didn't get caught up in the diversification frenzy this time around. When everyone was diversifying in the 1980s and 1990s, we were consolidating. And then came the acquisition frenzy, when all the drugstores were buying up other drugstores. Rite Aid was buying up everybody, CVS was buying up everybody, Eckerd was buying up everybody."[6]

After dabbling in the dual practices of diversification and acquisitions for decades, Walgreens cured itself once and for all in the 1980s. Some observers might say that the last straw was the lukewarm results the company experienced after it gobbled up other stores, including Rennebohm's 65-year-old chain in Wisconsin, Kroger's 21 SuperX's in Houston, and MediMart's 66 outlets in New England, which had been previously uncharted waters for Walgreens.

Of this trio, MediMart makes the best case study. Purchased in 1986, when Walgreens had some 1,000 stores, one analyst said, "It appears to be a perfect fit."

Recalled Cork Walgreen, "It worked out fine, but it was rough going in the beginning. "We got a lot of inventory we didn't need, we initiated an immediate and massive remodeling plan, and we lost quite a few MediMart people. Our stores were run differently from what [the former MediMart employees] were used to, and it was difficult [for them] to learn all our systems and management philosophy." Cork then provided a convenient example. "Before the acquisition, MediMart top management would call their store managers and say, 'I'm coming today.' So the managers would be set, with coffee and doughnuts waiting. But we Walgreens people would just show up, unannounced, because that's how you get the real condition of the store. I used to call my visits 'parachute drops.'"[7]

(Cork's approach harkens back to his grandfather's technique of making surprise visits, admonishing clerks who greeted him loudly by name during unscheduled visits to please keep his identity a secret, or else the entire purpose of the trip would be defeated. What worked then still works today.)

Walgreens finally concluded that it no longer made any sense to buy someone else's stores and spend all the time, money, and managerial talent to contort the building and its inhabitants to fit the Walgreens mold. They ultimately decided it was far better—and faster and cheaper, in the long run—to start from scratch.

"We said, 'We're not buying anybody,'" Jorndt stated. "Why would we buy old real estate? Why would we buy 20- and 30-year-old strip-center locations? We march to our own drummer now."[8]

The third mistake Walgreens didn't make, Jorndt added,

Was getting "caught up in the whole dot-com craze. Boy, in this very boardroom, we have some very powerful directors, and they said, "You guys are going to miss the boat!" But one thing our people are good at is getting out a pencil. Remember the deep discount drug stores—Phar-More, Drug Emporium, others—that all got into the dot-com craze? Well, our people would pencil it out, and they'd get down to the bottom line, and they said, "These guys are losing money!" And all our folks who hadn't penciled it out said, "They can't be! They're opening stores, they're expanding!" But the numbers guys said, "Trust us: It doesn't pencil out."[9]

The pencil people were vindicated when the pure dot-com converts suffered losses while Walgreens sailed on by, setting company record after company record each year.

According to Collins, that Walgreens stoic confidence precluded falling for such fads is typical of the good-to-great companies.

They weren't driven by fear of what they didn't understand. They weren't driven by fear of looking like a chump. They weren't driven by fear of watching others hit it big while they didn't. They weren't driven by the fear of being hammered by the competition.

No, [they] are motivated by a deep *creative* urge and *inner* compulsion for sheer unadulterated excellence *for its own sake*.

Never was there a better example of this difference than during the technology bubble of the late 1990s, which happened to take place right smack in the middle of the research on *Good to Great*. It served as an almost perfect stage to watch the difference between great and good play itself out, as the great ones responded like Walgreens— with calm equanimity and quiet deliberate steps forward—while the mediocre ones lurched about in fearful, frantic reaction.[10]

Jorndt summed it all up by saying:

Well, acquisitions didn't pencil out for us, diversification didn't pencil out for us, and the dot-coms didn't pencil out for us, either. We had competitors who spent $30 [million] to $50 million to buy dot-com companies; and, you watch, they're going to have to write it off as a big loss sooner or later, because they're not getting any return on that. We said, You know what? We'll develop our own. If we go and spend even $15 million on a dot-com, there are a lot of other things we can't do. It's just not worth it.[11]

Walgreens also avoided the more garish temptations that other corporations succumbed to during the excessive 1990s, including preening (and ultimately pratfalling) for the press, indulging CEOs beyond all reason, and creating artificial corporate cultures to mask woeful deficiencies in truly fundamental values.

"I started going to Wall Street in 1982," Jorndt said, "and it just seemed to me, the more the company is trying to tout itself, over the long term, the more the words ring hollow. If you're doing the job, it'll sell itself. You don't need to talk about it. We don't ever spend any time trying to sell ourselves. We don't tout it. Just do your job, and they'll know." When asked if the Walgreens way would work if the company were based amid the flashy, celebrity CEO culture of Manhattan, Jorndt replied, "I don't think it would. We're not highfliers, we're lowfliers. The expression I use is, 'We're plain, and we're proud of it'—because we *are* plain, and we *are* proud of it!"[12]

Walgreens' low-flying ways contrasted mightily with all the buzz created by the 1990s' countless highfliers, many of whom ultimately fell down to earth, often quite hard. The examples of gluttony are far too numerous to cover here, but a brief crash course of the decade's worst elements is instructive for contrast. From 1990 to 2000, average CEO pay rose 571 percent, while the average worker pay rose 37 percent during the same decade.[13] The CEOs of 23 large corporations under investigation by the Securities and Exchange Commission (SEC), the Department of Justice, and other agencies for accounting irregularities earned 70 percent more than the average CEO, for a total of $1.4 billion between just 1999 and 2001. Meanwhile, the stock of those 23 companies lost over $500 billion—representing a 73 percent drop—as they laid off over 160,000 employees, which equals the entire Walgreens workforce.[14]

During a decade that gave us Tyco's Dennis Kozlowski's purchase of seven mansions, worth between $2.3 million and $18 million;[15] ImClone's Sam Waksal's shameless courting of celebrities like Mariel Hemingway, Harvey Weinstein, and Mick Jagger;[16] and Kmart CEO Charles Conway's $23 million salary for two years while his company filed for bankruptcy, sending 22,000 employees home (all while the Kmart board was busy forgiving a $5 million "loan" to Conway);[17] Walgreens gave the press virtually nothing to chew on. No celebrity CEOs, but no scandals, either.

Jorndt still lives in the same modest home in Northbrook, Illinois, that he bought when he moved back to run the Chicago region in 1975. He still has the same friends—mostly current and former Walgreens store managers—and he made, at his peak in 2002, less than $2 million in base salary and bonuses.

The stunning lack of egos in the Deerfield headquarters also precludes the company from having to fall for such traps. When considering the culture of compensation excess just past, Jorndt is characteristically direct: "It just makes you sick. In plain English, you want to throw up."[18]

> Over time, very rich companies that make lots of money tend to *build* thicker carpets, more airplanes, more perks, and fancy apartments into their budget, because they have so much, they don't know where to spend it!
>
> We've never had that problem, [Jorndt said with a chuckle]. We've always *needed more* money to grow our company, and certainly that includes the last 20 or 30 years.
>
> We've kept it pretty low-key here. But you've got to be moderately competitive [with salaries], because you don't want good people leaving. But the bottom line is, the last vice president we lost was in 1984, and he left for a bigger and better job. Well, it turned out it wasn't bigger, or better. But we haven't lost anyone at the officer level in 18 years.
>
> There's *so* much growth and opportunity in this company today. It's the old saw: If you're working real hard and achieving and being recognized for it, why would you go somewhere else? I can tell you, we've had people offered two and three times what they're making here, but they almost never go. The head hunters get tired of calling after a while, and they stop. Starting with our district managers on up, they get calls all the time—here's a bigger job, here's a better job, here's more money—but they stay!
>
> So it tells me, you need enough money to be able to look in the mirror and say, "I get compensated fairly for what I do." But when you start getting the apartments in New York and the corporate jets . . . well, if those things are real important to you, you probably won't make it here, because those things are not very important to anybody else here. Bass tend to swim with bass, trout tend to swim with trout. The right kind of people seem to be attracted to us.[19]

That would certainly include Cork, Canning, and Jorndt, three highly talented executives who could have made a big splash at another company but chose lower pay and much lower profiles to stay at Walgreens. They might not have too much in common with other corporate leaders around the country, but they do with the leaders of the other 10 "good-to-great" companies described in Jim Collins's book, *Good to Great*. The leaders of the 11 good-to-great companies, Collins wrote, "are some of the most remarkable CEOs of the century, given that only 11 companies from the Fortune 500 met the exacting standards for entry into this study. Yet, despite their remarkable results, almost no one ever remarked about them!"[20]

Collins research team discovered that these 11 good-to-great companies received roughly half as much press coverage as did their less impressive competitors. "Furthermore," he wrote, "we rarely found articles that focused on the good-to-great CEOs."[21] In fact, there is a paucity of information on the company outside of trade publications. The national media pays Walgreens almost no heed—which Walgreens much prefers—and even the Chicago media (including academic journals and historical books) rarely mention the company or its leaders.

This, in an era where you can't visit a newsstand and not see former GE CEO Jack Welch's face, for this success or that scandal. "In over two-thirds of the comparison cases," added Collins, the first national researcher to investigate the company thoroughly, "we noted the presence of a gargantuan personal ego that contributed to the demise or continued mediocrity of the company."[22]

Jorndt believes Walgreens is fortunate to be in the retail business, which he feels is more likely to attract hard-working, energetic, and largely ego-free workers than other industries can. "If you want to get rich quick, you're probably not going to go into retailing in the first place," Jorndt said. "You either like retailing or you don't. People who've been at it all day can tell you, it's very tiring, very enervating. We're always on it. There's no rest in retailing. People who are in it and like it, *stay* in it and do well in it. This company sort of weeds out people early on, and the people who stay, they catch the fever."[23]

Another trend that grates Jorndt is the tendency of nascent, high-tech companies to contemplate their navels over their "corporate culture."

"Every dot-com starts out by saying, 'What's our corporate culture?' Well, you don't have one! You can't just adopt one, or manufacture one. This culture here is real, and it goes back a long long way. It's something solid, something tangible."[24]

In Jorndt's view, the depth of a company's culture depends not only on the longevity of the business itself, but also on the people who work there. Jorndt observed:

> Once you get to the store manager level, [Jorndt said,] we have virtually no turnover. People stay. It really helps that the top 30 people all grew up in the company and have been around a while. They know the culture. They've lived it, they've soaked it up. So it's pretty easy for them to pass it on.
>
> The word *family* is bandied about too often when people talk about companies, but I think it really applies here. Everybody doesn't like everybody here, but *almost* everybody likes *almost* everyone. It's okay to disagree, and we disagree plenty, but everyone respects everyone. . . .
>
> If you work hard, and perform, you'll get recognized. Everyone's got a report card, and you have to treat people right. In the old days, maybe we could say, "Well, John may be an S.O.B., but look at his numbers!" Not anymore. In the old days, you could manage that way—do it or regret it—all by fiat. But as the world changed, we changed, too. Now, you've got to do two simple things: Be a high performer and be nice to people.[25]

It's worth noting that Jorndt rose to the highest post by doing just that: performing well and being nice. Bill Shank, former head of Walgreens' legal department, explained Jorndt's appeal with one simple example: "When you call Dan Jorndt," Shank said, "he says, 'This is Dan Jorndt. How may I help you?' That's how he's lived his life."[26]

Jorndt is equally impressed by the people who work for Walgreens. "I always say, all people can be spread out on a bell-shaped curve, in every company, but I think our people are just a click or two to the right. The goodwill that people have for this company is not unique, but it's rare. So many businesses don't have the goodwill of the majority of their employees, and this company does. And I think it starts with the Walgreens family, and this caring attitude that, 'Hey, We all work for this company, so let's all work to make it better.'"[27]

Jorndt tells a story first printed in the company newsletter about two pharmacy technicians in Indiana, named Silvia and Helen. Silvia worked in the Merrillville, Indiana, Walgreens store, and Helen worked in the Griffith store, about five minutes apart. They first met over the telephone, having the kind of conversations Walgreens workers have, about transferring refills, about loaning inventory, whatever's going on. Soon enough, however, they became friends over the phone and eventually met each other once a month for a cup of coffee.

They're just workaday pals at Walgreens [Jorndt said]. But one day Silvia calls for Helen, and she's not there, she's sick. Well, what's the matter? The person who answers the phone at Helen's store tells Silvia that Helen has to go on dialysis. Her kidneys have failed. And her whole family is trying to get a kidney for her, but no one's a match.

You know what's coming [he says, nodding to his listener]. But it still gets me. Silvia goes home—she has a family of her own—and her five-year-old son says, "Mom, you and Helen are so close, you're soul mates. I'll bet you're a match." And the chances of just anyone being a match is 1 in 5,000, I've learned. So Silvia goes in and checks: She's a match! Two weeks later, she's donating a kidney to her pal that she's only known two years and only seen face-to-face maybe ten times! Oh, man. It's something. Now that's a one-in-a-million story—but it happened here![28]

A big part of the culture that Walgreens workers pass on is not about wearing a tie to work or flip-flops or working in an office, a cubicle, or a big open space, but the basic, old-fashioned combination of discipline, structure, and ambition established by previous generations.

"I've noticed something in my time here," Jorndt said. "People like rules, and if they're simple and attainable, they really like them. That's why Moses wrote up 10 rules, and not 25 rules, or 10 suggestions. They work that way. I really believe that running a big company like this is just like running a *good, strong* Walgreens store: You have to hire good people, be square with them, and treat the customer right. That's it. The same rules apply."[29]

Discipline has always been a pillar of Walgreens' "corporate culture" and its best eras—the unprecedented expansion of the 1920s, the introduction of self-service in the 1950s, and the renaissance of the 1980s and 1990s. The company's ambition—its goals—has been a pillar of the culture, too, according to Dan Jorndt.

We set high goals here, very high goals. The board even asks, "Do you really want to set it that high?" We don't have a lot of goals, just a few major ones. We set them very high, and the people will be very disappointed if we don't reach them.

You've got to believe in it, too. The boss has to be more committed than anyone else, because people can read you, better than you think. If the boss believes in it and works harder than everyone else, then everybody jumps on board. It doesn't matter if you're selling cameras behind the counter at Walgreens, or insurance, or anything else. You've got to believe in what you're saying, where you're going. If you're heart's in it, people know that. And if you're heart's not in it, they'll know that too. Just like a dog can sense it if you're afraid or not.[30]

Suffice it to say, Jorndt's heart, head, and, not least, his guts were in it during his 12 years running the company. Every Monday morning he'd send out an intranet message "of how proud we should be to be working for Walgreens, to be Americans, totally inspiring stuff," legal director Bill Shank recalled. So inspiring, in fact, that they've been compiled by the company into a compendium called "Jorndt's Jolts" and given to all the stores. "One of my favorites was this Jorndt quote: Don't be afraid to bite off more than you can chew; you'll be amazed how big your mouth can get."[31]

"I guess I'm too conservative generally, but not when it comes to goals," Jorndt said. "I recall some audible gasps when I said we would have 3,000 stores open by the year 2000."[32] In fact, most people there thought he was crazy.

They had good reason to gasp. When Jorndt said that in 1991, Walgreens only had 1,646 stores; but on May 11, 2000, Walgreens opened its 3,000th store. He had seemingly bitten off more than he could chew; but as he predicted, his mouth proved bigger than people expected.

getting the right people ready

Expanding the franchise by such exponential leaps could not be accomplished by simply buying or building more stores to hit Jorndt's lofty goals. Walgreens needed something deeper, something more substantial, to avoid the disasters that other companies—Boston Chicken, MCI, and Global Crossing, to name just a few—inflicted on themselves by expanding too far too fast and without enough forethought.

What Walgreens needed, first and foremost, was a coherent, comprehensive strategy—a unifying theory, if you will—to guide all their efforts and decisions along the way. And the North Star they settled on was simple and elegant, as all North Stars should be: Walgreens decided it would become the nation's most convenient drugstore.

In an era when thousands of Americans pay others to shop for them and millions pay others to care for their children, time, more than money or space, has become the most treasured commodity of the modern American.

Jim Collins believes this simple epiphany was crucial in separating Walgreens from the rest. In researching the incredible stock perfomance of "such an anonymous—some might even say boring—company," Collins asked Cork Walgreen for the secret.

> Finally, in exasperation, he said, "Look, it just wasn't that compli-cated! Once we understood the concept, we just moved straight ahead." What was the concept? Simply this: the best, most conven-ient drugstores, with higher profit per customer visit. That's it. That's the breakthrough strategy that Walgreens used to beat Intel, GE, Coca-Cola, and Merck. In classic hedgehog style, Walgreens took this simple concept and implemented it with fanatical consistency.[33]

Starting from the top, if you want to be the nation's best, most conven-ient drugstore, you first have to be a drugstore, which means you have to be run by druggists. Jorndt and his advisors committed themselves to being a first-class drugstore run by pharmacists, not bottom-line retailers or hired guns from other, unrelated companies, just as Charles, Chuck, and Cork had done before them. Jorndt said,

> We decided to make all managers become nationally certified phar-macy technicians to make sure our store managers were really com-fortable with pharmacy. We just roped it on our store managers. At the time, it was one of those things that very few people thought could be done—very few—and now 80 percent are certified, and you can't become a store manager without the certification.
>
> I was in Memphis in 1999, where the store manager is one of these great old-school guys. He obviously had something on his mind, so he asked to talk with me in the back of the store. The district man-ager who was there with me apparently knew what it was about and left us alone.

Once we got by ourselves, the store manager says, "I've taken that [pharmacy board] exam three times, and I just can't pass it. Will you let me off the hook?" I thought for a moment, and said, "Well, what would you do in my shoes?" He thought for a moment and said, "I wouldn't let me off the hook." I said, "You're right. But you haven't made up your mind to pass it. You're not dumb. So if you apply yourself, really apply yourself, you'll pass." Well, I just got a letter from him about six months ago saying, "I just wanted you to know: I passed the test." You want to have people have high expectations—for themselves and the company.[34]

More stores require more people, of course. To double the number of stores in a decade, Jorndt's team had to find thousands of new employees, without diluting the character of the company. To do so, Jorndt stuck to Walgreens' traditional philosophy of hiring as much as possible from the Walgreens extended family—aunts, brothers, daughters, and the like—and promoting from within the company whenever it could.

This was far easier to do at Walgreens than it would be at other companies. At Walgreens' biannual managers' meeting in 2001, almost 5,000 people gathered in Nashville. To open the meeting, Jorndt asked all those who had a relative working at Walgreens to stand up. The result?

Well, eyeballing the crowd, I'd say 60 to 70 percent of our top people have someone in their family working for the company. One guy's dad had 47 years of service. Another had 33. I just wrote a 30-year congratulation letter to Paul Bonk in Iowa. His dad was a 55-year Walgreens man. One of our brightest young men's dad just retired with 37 years at Walgreens.

I think that really says something good about Walgreens. When your dad tells you, "You should work at Walgreens," that's a good sign. Because if they didn't really believe in the place, they wouldn't want their own children working in that company.[35]

"You'll have to forgive me if I go on about Walgreens," Jorndt said, taking a momentary pause, "but I really do mean it."

Despite the preponderance of extended family members hired to work for Walgreens, the company's promoting practices don't give any dispensation for nepotism. Having a father or a sister working for Walgreens *might* help you get in the door, but it won't help you stay there or move up—even if you're the offspring of company legends.

Cork Walgreen's six sons all worked for Walgreens, but only Kevin is still with the company, working his way up to a vice president for store operations, with no guarantee that he will one day lead the business. (Demonstrating the family aversion to self-promotion, Kevin politely but steadfastly declined to be interviewed for this book, not wanting special treatment.)

A key to any good corporation, of course, especially one growing as fast as Walgreens was in the 1990s, is the ability to identify, develop, and promote talent in the field. For that, Walgreens relies on its 15 store operations vice presidents. As Jorndt said,

They're really the flag-bearers for our company. Their job is going from store to store, teaching and listening and looking for talent, because talent can get lost out there when you're so spread out. And you never know when someone is going to pop up. So these people serve as talent scouts.

The district manager might say, "Well, John's pretty good" or "Dan's pretty good." But when the vice presidents go in there with all their years of experience and all the moxie they've got, they might see a young guy with some talent and say, "I'd like you to move this individual into an even bigger operation. Let's see what he's got. Let's challenge him."

We have an expression called the Quantum Leap. We like to give people quantum leaps, which work like this: You come in, a young college graduate, a hard-charger. We give you a store after a year and a half or so, and you're just knocking the blocks off it. So we could leave you there for three or four years, or we could say, "You know what, after just one year, let's jump this person up a few stores. Let's give 'em a $15 million store, and see what happens." And you know what? We're right 70 to 90 percent of the time. So that does great things for the company. We get that productivity, but more importantly, that individual says, "You know what, I'm killing myself, but they're noticing!"[36]

If this philosophy sounds familiar, you might recall how Charles Sr. assembled his inaugural class of managers in the 1910s and how quickly they moved up—seemingly before their time—yet they were able to do the job, again and again. Once more, what worked way back then still works today. The Quantum Leap theory not only ensures a fresh supply of young talent, but it inspires everyone to get noticed.

Jorndt pointed out,

Sometimes other people see a young person moving up, and they say, "Why did that person get promoted?" Well, here it is. Everybody gets a report card. Look at the treatment of people and the work ethic. Those are the two things we look at.

We probably had 30,000 people 15 to 20 years ago, and today we have 150,000. And I think we've slipped maybe 10 percent in terms of being connected to each other, and I think [we've] slipped only that much because we've really worked on it. We're still about 90 percent of what we were, in terms of the family feeling of closeness, when we were just one-fifth the size we are now.[37]

a good corner is a good corner

After devising effective systems to expand the number of good employees, the next step was to expand the number of stores. Having soured on the idea of growth through acquisitions, under Jorndt, Walgreens launched an unprecedented building program—and a very specific one, at that. Instead of buying old buildings or leasing mall spaces and the like, Walgreens stuck to a crystal-clear plan of creating nothing but brand-new, freestanding stores with lots of free parking on busy street corners—ideally, "Main and Main."

By doing so, in less than a decade, Walgreens established the kind of immediately identifiable, almost iconic presence on thousands of street corners nationwide that only a few companies like McDonald's once enjoyed, with a clean, crisp, consistent appearance that tells you before you even pull up that you're about to enjoy a high-quality shopping experience.

A good example of Walgreens' commitment to these basic principles occurred when Walgreens bought a chunk of land in Seattle just a block from the site Charles Walgreen Sr. almost leased while on his honeymoon in 1902. A hundred years later, Walgreens opened a new store there. As Jorndt stated in *Walgreens: Celebrating 100 Years*, "A good corner, we like to say, is a good corner. . . . Every corner we build on [today], we're there because we want to be there."[38]

In other words, when it came to opening new stores, Walgreens would accept no more leftovers, no secondhand stores, and no makeshift compromises—just good, new stores on good, central corners.

Walgreens took this basic strategy to extremes that must have seemed crazy to the competition, but it worked amazingly well for Walgreens. The cognescenti would go so far as to close a profitable store in a good location—sometimes paying $1 million to get out of the lease—just to move a half block away to a busy corner. When Walgreens gets serious about an idea, they get serious.

"Store by store, block by block, city by city, region by region," Collins wrote, "Walgreens became more and more of a hedgehog with this incredibly simple idea."[39]

Walgreens took another big step for customer convenience when it opened a freestanding store in Indianapolis with a drive-thru pharmacy and a one-hour photo lab—the nation's first such store—in 1992. Today, over 70 percent of Walgreens offer those services, and the number rises every day. Truth be told, the drive-thru service and one-hour photo labs add a lot of work and complication to each store's operation, but Walgreens' philosophy trumps any complaints: If it can be shown that a new feature will increase customer convenience, they'll do it. Dan Jorndt observed,

Our company is now 103 years old, but we've opened 3,400 of our 3,800 stores in the past 10 years. Now, how can that be? Well, along with moving to freestanding stores, we relocated all our strip centers and all our downtown stores to new sites. So, just the net in the past 10 years is more like 2,000 new stores, but we've also relocated 1,400. So here's a 103-year-old company, where 80 percent of our stores are less than 10 years old. I don't think there's a retail company anywhere that can say, "Gee, we're going on 103 years, and our average store is 5 years old!" But that took a tremendous amount of discipline and a certain amount of guts to say, "We're going to do that. We're going to generate cash and put it back in the company." And we've been reinvesting about a billion [dollars] a year into new stores.

You've probably heard it a hundred times around these halls, and if you haven't you probably will: "We believe in crawl, walk, run." Crawl, figure out what's going on, and once we get it figured out, start walking, and once you get that right, you go like hell!

The best example of that is one-hour photo finishing. We started one-hour photo finishing in 1984, and we tweaked it and tested it and marketed it, and we kept fooling around with that until about 1995 or 1996. All that was crawl, crawl, crawl. We couldn't get it figured out, but we didn't give up. We knew there was something there.

Finally, in the mid 1990s, a-ha! We got it. We figured out we've gotta have the right price, we've gotta have well-trained technicians, we've gotta have the right equipment. We finally got the whole ball of wax right. And then, conservative me, we had a meeting, and we say, "All right, we've got this thing figured out: We're going right from crawl to run. Because we've been studying this for 10 years!" We laid out a plan that was going to cost us $50 million and take four years to train 20,000 people, remodel—at the time—about 1,600 stores, and get all this new equipment. I mean, it was like the Normandy invasion, and I thought that was a high goal.

Then I went out to visit the stores for a month or so. When I got back, Glenn Kraiss, who was our head guy in the stores then, but is now retired, said, "Dan, I don't want you to be mad at me, but while you were gone, I had a little meeting with that group to start planning this rollout for one-hour photo finishing." I said, "Good!" And he said, "Well, I kind of shocked them, because I opened the meeting by saying, 'Look, we're not going to have this meeting. We're going to have this meeting in a week. I want everyone to go back for a week and figure out how we can roll this out in one year instead of four.'" I said, "I'm proud of you, Glenn. How'd your next meeting go?" And he said, "We're going to do it." Well, to be honest, I thought they might be crazy, but it took us about a year and three months. He was right!

So here's an example, where this great guy, Glenn Kraiss, who was closer to the stores than I was, who says Jorndt thinks he's aggressive with four years—well, watch this! And I wasn't involved at all. He had the meeting, he challenged them, they came back in a week with everything they were going to need to do: real estate, planning, training, photo people. They said [Jorndt slaps the table], "We're on board!" And we did it. Boom! One year!

It gets back to the leader believing it can be done. I think if those people would have came back and said "It'll take a year and a half, or two years," Glenn might have bought it. But they didn't. They came back and said, "You want a year? We think we can do it."

Well, do you think any of those folks who were a part of that amazing success story were talking to head hunters for that year? [Jorndt can't help chuckling at the thought.] And when everyone's ready to check out, I think we all want to look back and say, "Did

I make a difference here? Did I raise a good family? Did I contribute to the community? Did I contribute to the country? Did I contribute to the church? Did I make just a little difference?" I think everyone would go to their maker happy if they made just a little difference. When you can look back and say, "Hey, I was part of that team that rolled out one-hour photo in one year, at Walgreens, the number-one one-hour photo retailer in the world! In a year! I was part of that!" That lifts people up, and I think it keeps their heads up![40]

Jorndt's enthusiasm was contagious and moved mountains. In 1990, Walgreens filled 100 million prescriptions, the ninth straight year of 20 percent jumps, and maintained double-digit leaps throughout the decade.

And, just two years after Jorndt stunned his audience by announcing Walgreens would have 3,000 stores open by the year 2000, "everyone got on board [and] we blew past it with a hundred stores to spare."

The new expansion, however, depended largely on entering new markets and setting up the nationwide distribution systems and infrastructure needed to make them work. In fact, Walgreens discovered that the more densely its stores covered a new city or an older established market, the cheaper it would be for them to operate them all—thus increasing profit per customer. Diving into new markets, head first—not backing off—proved to be the key to making the incredible expansion work. It was during the Cork Era that Walgreens truly had become a nationwide chain for the first time.

"Then," Jorndt said, fully pumped up, "we said we'd have 6,000 stores by 2010, and there was just a little gasp. You'll see!"[41]

passing the torch

When Cork Walgreen stepped down as CEO in 1998 and chairman in 1999, he could look back on a company that had grown from $1 billion in sales when he took over to $13 billion when he retired. "I just sort of got in there and started working," he said modestly.[42]

When asked how he felt about passing the torch, he replied not with some sentiment about the emotions involved, but with his characteristic unsentimental perspective. "Well, I sure hope the company keeps doing well," he said, "because 99 percent of what I own is Walgreen stock. I'm not very diversified, I can tell you that!"[43]

In 1998, Jorndt replaced Cork as CEO, too. Jorndt decided to retire as CEO in early 2002 and as chairman in 2003, leaving the company in the best shape of its long history. David Bernauer became president in 1999 and CEO in 2002.

When Jorndt looked back on his run, just months before he left the company, he couldn't remember any particular "low-lights," just occasional frustrations.

I was so mad one time I kicked this fire plug, and I almost broke my foot. There's always aggravation. If you're never aggravated, the chances are you really don't have your head up and you're not trying very hard. You're going to have disappointments. You don't hit every ball out of the park. You strike out some of the time.

But it's like going to the dentist: All you remember is the nice smile, you don't remember the pain. If you're in retail, a lot of nights you go home and bang your head. A lot of things can go wrong—and they do. But after 39 years, all I remember is the nice smiles.

The high points for me, really, have just been the people I've worked with. They're in my heart and in my head. It's irreplaceable what that has meant to me, these Walgreen people.[44]

Though such a successful CEO at another company would probably hang on or wait for a golden parachute, Jorndt made it a point to leave quietly, while still on top—a move he firmly believes is in the best interest of the company.

Companies need a certain amount of turnover to keep fresh blood in the higher ranks, fresh perspectives. And that's why I'm stepping down when I am. I'm still pretty young, I'm in good health, and I have lots of energy—but it's time. I said years ago this is when I was going to step down, and I am. If you stick around too long, people are afraid to come to you with bad news, with disagreements.[45]

Jorndt harbored typically strong views on who should succeed him.

When Home Depot, the number-two company in retail, has to go outside their company to get their CEO, that's a problem. When Albertson's—at number five—has to go outside, that's a problem. Something's wrong if companies that big can't find someone in their own ranks good enough to do that job.

That's never been our problem at Walgreens. Our problem is just the opposite—man, are we deep!—because everyone comes up through the company.[46]

Another company executive, who asked to be anonymous, underscored the wisdom of promoting even the company's top leaders from within. "A lot of companies' employees and executives come from outside," she said, "so they have to take the 'Our Company 101' course when they sign on. Because we have plenty of good people already here to promote, we don't have to do that here."[47]

hello, my name is dave

Because Walgreens had so many viable candidates, it wasn't hard to find one who satisfied all the criteria for the top job: a pharmacist by training, a Walgreens "lifer" who had done most of the company's jobs on the way up, and an executive more devoted to Walgreens' humble values than to Wall Street's glitz and glitter.

As Jorndt observed, retail attracts a certain kind of person; and the man they settled on, David Bernauer, not only fit all of Walgreens' criteria, but had caught the retail bug early. His father managed a JC Penney in Wadena, Minnesota, where David worked for a few summers before switching over to an independent pharmacist. He recalled,

> The drugstore did quite well, but even at that age I could already see all the inefficiencies and all the things [the pharmacist] was missing. His newspaper ads were very poorly done compared to what JC Penney was doing. He had good people; he didn't have to hire very often, but when he did, his process was inept. And there were some inventory control systems Penney had in place that he couldn't necessarily replicate in his small store but he could learn from, like bringing in more new items and being more current with his stock. Just some business basics, really. I figured I had to go someplace else to learn.[48]

In the summer of 1966, after his junior year in the college of pharmacy at North Dakota State University (NDSU), Bernauer interned at Walgreens in West Allis, Wisconsin. "My objective was to get into pharmacy; I liked retail, and I thought I wanted to own my own store," he said. "From what little research you could do in those days, Walgreens looked like the best choice of drugstore chains in the Midwest you could work for."

During a single month—June 1967—Bernauer left the bucolic, footloose lifestyle of a college student so fast he risked getting whiplash. On June 3, he graduated from NDSU with a bachelor's in pharmacy. One week later, on June 10, he married his college sweetheart, Mary. On June 19, he started his 36-year career at Walgreens as a pharmacist in Milwaukee. Then, "as near as I can figure," he said with a sheepish grin, "my son was conceived on June 23. My life was set, and I've just been filling in the details ever since."[49]

It was a busy month.

Bernauer approached his Walgreens journey as a marathon, not a sprint. He said,

> I think, like most successful people at Walgreens, I didn't have a grand scheme or a plan to get ahead. I always just focused on doing the best I could at my job, first and foremost, then getting to understand the impact I had on people who were affected by the job I was doing, starting with my customers and going to my employees, up to my managers. And then you have to figure out what are the things that impact your job. Once you understand that, you start to understand more about the entire operation of the company, in concentric circles around your job, and that allows you then to redefine the job you have and [to] expand the responsibilities you have and the impacts you have. You start doing that, and that's when people at Walgreens start to recognize you, and say, "This is someone who could do something in another job."
>
> One of the things that has made Walgreens successful is the culture that the company has established. Certainly, ethics are important, but the thing I focus on is this: At Walgreens, you have to understand pretty quickly that if you want to get ahead, it's not about protecting your interest in your particular store or division, but working toward the greater good of the company, thinking beyond the narrow scope of your job. There is a tremendous amount of cooperation with other people in the company.[50]

Bernauer's career trajectory was far from meteoric, progressing in regular steps—but that's also how it's done at Walgreens. The race to Deerfield is truly not to the swift but to the steady. "I don't know that there were any certain points when I can look back and say, 'Boy this is the point when my career took off,'" Bernauer said. "There's only one job I ever asked for in the company, and in that case, I first had to convince the top people we needed to create the position of chief information officer (CIO), because of a couple retirements that happened at once. They went for it, and I got the job."[51]

Bernauer advanced to president in 1999 and to CEO in the fall of 2002—but in characteristic Walgreens style, his manner didn't change at all.

If you arrange to meet him at Walgreens' headquarters at 9 A.M., you'll invariably find yourself standing behind a knot of sales representatives at the reception desk waiting to make their pitches to Walgreens' buyers. As you stand and stew, nervously checking your watch, don't be surprised if you suddenly feel a tap on the shoulder from a tidy, midsized man who asks if you're his scheduled appointment. "I thought so," he'll say, then reach out his hand and introduce himself. "I'm Dave," and his unassuming stick-on nametag confirms it. "Let's go to my office."[52]

When you notice that the receptionist at the front desk has not even batted an eye at the appearance of the CEO amid the swarm of sales reps, you get the sense that he's done this more than once—maybe every day. The fact that none of the sales reps seem to take notice, either, suggests that they've seen him many times themselves or that he's so low profile they don't even recognize him.

constant competition

It is the modest man from Wadena, Minnesota, who's now charged with leading the company into its second century, a century that promises to be every bit as unpredictable as the company's first.

Nonetheless, Walgreens can already identify many of the forces that will shape its strategy in the coming decades, including intensified competition.

Having outlasted once venerable chains like Shapiro, Liggett's, and Thrifty's, among others, and surpassed Eckerd, Rite Aid, and CVS, it's fair to say Walgreens has held its own and has to be considered the greatest drugstore chain over the past century.

(When longtime rival Rite Aid was posting record profits at the end of the millennium, Walgreens executives couldn't quite figure out how they were doing it—and with good reason. It turns out that at least four Rite Aid executives overstated earnings by some $1.6 billion, leading to an artificially inflated stock price, which padded the executives' incentive-laden pay packages. At the time, Rite Aid's restatement was the largest in the history of U.S. business. When prosecutors produced a tape secretly recorded by an employee, all four executives, including former CEO Martin L. Grass and former chief financial officer [CFO] Franklyn M. Bergonzi pled guilty and are now serving jail time.[53])

Even among those who play clean, however, Walgreens still faces enough competition to keep it honest. "Those guys are in our stores night and day," Jorndt said. "Why? They're focused retailers! They figure if they learn one little thing from Walgreens, it's worth it. And we're in their stores all the time doing the same thing."[54]

These days, however, the number and variety of competitors has expanded greatly and now includes "mass merchants" like Wal-Mart, which currently ranks third in prescriptions filled behind only Walgreens and CVS. Wal-Mart has had its own problems, of course, but it promises to be a formidable force for some time to come. Bernauer explained,

When you look at our industry, 80 percent of what's sold in the front end of the store comes from "big boxes" [like Wal-Mart], and that's important to understand. So in other words, when you look at our categories—you're talking paints and batteries and stationery, all those things—all that stuff we sell in the stores, 80 percent of all of it sold nationwide is [also] sold in food stores like Krogers and mass merchants like Target and Wal-Mart; 15 percent of it is sold in other drugstores; and 5 percent of it is sold in Walgreens. So, when we start talking about competition, one of the keys to remember is that our competition is much more about grocery stores and mass merchants than it is about other drugstores. So now we have to focus on that."[55]

Of course, competition is nothing new, going back to the days Charles Sr. had to battle the cheap "pine boards" during the Depression and Chuck had to stare down Spiegel's and the like. Walgreens has always found a way to separate itself from the rest.

Walgreens breaks down the current competition into two categories—big boxes and drugstores—and has created two different approaches to face them. Bernauer explained,

> How we compete against drugstores is much more of an execution issue, since we're all trying to accomplish roughly the same thing. The question is: Who can do it better? But with the big boxes, the biggest difference is that, obviously enough, they're big boxes, and we're a small box. We have a much smaller trade area than they do. But because it's a smaller trade area, it means we can offer more convenience—a quick stop compared to a long stop.[56]

Walgreens' second advantage over the Wal-Marts of the world is the target area of each store. Because a typical Wal-Mart super center draws from a 15-mile radius of customers, it attracts a much broader mix of consumers than does a Walgreens, which might draw from a 5-mile radius, allowing the store to enact more niche marketing than Wal-Mart can.

"We get a pocket of population that is unique, in some way," Bernauer said, "so that allows us to tune our store to the specific neighborhood we're serving, in terms of age, income, race, even local events. We are continually developing that and finding the tools to broaden the mix of options of what's in each store. So that gives us a real advantage."[57]

Despite all the evolutions Walgreens has undergone over the century, some things never change, and three of them are location, location, location. Bernauer observed,

> The primary thing I'm focused on right now, on a strategic basis, is site selection. Now you wouldn't think of that as a strategy, maybe more of a tactic; but because of the nature of our business and the importance of being close to the customer, locating and designing the store is a big way we can improve. We spend a lot of time on that. We

apply a lot more science to it than we ever did before, and we've enhanced that, too. Over the last 10 years, we've opened 3,000 stores and only closed two stores due to poor sales. That's not bad.[58]

walgreens' advantages

Ambitious

When asked how Walgreens has managed to keep a step ahead of its rivals for over a century, Cork Walgreen shrugged, chuckled, and said, "I don't know. We just stick to our knitting, so to speak, stay focused, and try never to be satisfied that we've made it. You always [have] to run faster than the competitors. It's like Jorndt used to say, 'Be a moving target, because they're harder to hit.'"[59]

Walgreens has never moved faster than it's moving right now. The number of prescriptions filled, the profit per customer, the years of record profit, and the number of store openings have all been growing since 1975; and they hit new heights each year—all with virtually no debt incurred along the way.

When Cork Walgreen retired in 1998, Walgreens got a letter from a Mr. and Mrs. Robert Rose, longtime Walgreens stockholders. "We have been shareholders for many years and want to thank you, Mr. Walgreen III, for all you've done for us," they wrote. "We purchased 50 shares of Walgreen stock many years ago. Today it's grown to 3,600 shares and is worth more than $100,000. Selling our shares would be like losing a family member. We just can't do it." It's hard to think of too many other U.S. companies whose stock alone can engender such loyalty.[60]

In 2003, Walgreens opened more than one new store a day, over 400 for the year—roughly equal to the total number of stores the entire chain could boast for the middle five decades of the previous century, from 1930 to 1970—including three a day for the month of August 2003, the end of Walgreens' fiscal year.

Such remarkable growth creates problems, too, of course. Said Dan Jorndt:

How do you inculcate and expand the culture to all the employees in 4,000 stores when you can't meet all the workers? It is a bigger challenge. We're going to have both Dave Bernauer and [President] Jeff Rein in the stores a lot. People love to see the leaders in the stores. We've got senior vice presidents and operations vice presidents on the road constantly.

We just keep trying and trying. We keep changing, and we keep going. Every strategy gets tested. There is no magic formula, and there's no strategy that lasts forever. Every strategy runs out of gas eventually. So you've gotta keep changing.[61]

the future is now

For all the vicissitudes of the drugstore business, the industry's future looks bright. "The prescription business has a 50-year ramp-up coming," Jorndt told Marilyn Abbey. "People are going to live to be 80 and 90. At 50, you take six prescriptions a year. At 60, it's 11 a year. At 70, it's 15."[62]

Without doing the math, you can see that Walgreens' pharmacy department—the very division that Charles and Chuck insisted on promoting and perfecting even when it brought in just 3 or 4 percent of the stores' sales volume for over a half century—will be the locus of the company's revenue in the foreseeable future.

"Over 60 percent of our sales are prescriptions, and that's going up," said Cork, who is still very much on top of the many details that make Walgreens run. "The average prescription is close to fifty bucks, today, and the average sale in the rest of the store is about seven bucks."[63] Furthermore, the average store now fills about 300 prescriptions a day, up from only 20 prescriptions a day in the 1960s.

The catch is, however, that the store's net profit margin on prescriptions has dropped to about 2 percent today, according to Cork. This speaks to the growing competition in the health care field and to the increasing pressures from HMOs and the like to keep health care costs down.

But Walgreens has seen the future, and the future is health care. To meet this growing and ever-evolving demand, the company has created a division called Walgreens Health Initiatives (WHI), which includes a Pharmacy Benefits Manager. Walgreens is also stepping into the growing field of home care services for those people who receive long-term help at home and has launched a specialty pharmacy program for patients with chronic diseases that require complicated pharmaceutical regimens. Cork also believes Walgreens will be at the forefront of new drug therapies and more affordable generic drugs.

Granted, everyone this side of Nostradamus seems to do a horrible job predicting the future, including the many "futurologists" who told us we'd be jetting around in flying cars by now and living in space colonies, yet failed to anticipate the Internet or global terrorism. Yet some things seem certain.

"With the current U.S. population, right now we can probably have 12,000 or so stores around the country," Cork said. "If we keep on opening 400, 500, 600 stores a year, we'll get there by 2015, maybe 2020 or so. We've got a ways to go yet, but there will come a time when we have to look at other businesses."[64]

Walgreens has no current plans to enter the Canadian or overseas markets. Instead, the company intends to do more of what it does so well now: provide convenience for drugstore customers.

Whatever the future holds, two bets are safe: Walgreens (1) will have the courage to anticipate the changes ahead and (2) will not lose sight of its commitment to customer service. Bernauer explained,

> We're conservative in our values, but we're not conservative in our execution or in our planning. The fact that we're quiet does not mean we don't have resolve or intensity or determination. We've made some pretty bold decisions, and we're continuing to do that. We don't have many stores left [that were] built before 1990, yet we're taking down 15 percent of them a year and replacing them.
>
> But I guess on a strategic basis, what we are focused on hasn't

changed a whole lot. There are current issues always, like Medicare and drug coverage issues. But our basic business hasn't changed: site selection, convenience, customer service. If we get those things right, we'll be in good shape.[65]

"Here's the thing in a nutshell," Jorndt said. "We preach this around here all the time: Running your core business is the hardest thing to do. It's not that exciting, it's not that new, it's very tiring! You're driving this eight-horse team down this mountain road—you better be focused! You better not be looking at the scenery or focusing on your girlfriend in Santa Fe."[66]

"I guess the press thinks we're sort of a boring company," Cork said. "We just keep plodding along, and we don't have any debt. The CEOs are still paid way below the hotshots, and should be. We may be boring, but it works." When asked what his grandfather would think if he were to spend a week meeting the current executives, studying the growth charts, and visiting the stores, Cork said, "I hope he would be proud," then mulls it over a little longer before adding, with subtle but unmistakable satisfaction. "And I think he would be."[67]

walgreens financial facts

Corporate Headquarters
Walgreen Co.
200 Wilmot Road
Deerfield, IL 60015
Phone: (847) 914-2500
www.walgreens.com

Founded in 1901 in a 50-by-20-foot neighborhood store on Cottage Grove and Bowen avenues on the South Side of Chicago.

As of August 31, 2003:

   Number of Employees: 154,000

   Number of Stores: 4,227

   Sales: $32.5 billion

   Net earnings: $1.176 billion.

   Share price: $32.57

   Earnings per share: $1.14

David W. Bernauer, Chairman and CEO

Jeffrey A. Rein, President and COO

historic highlights

1871   Charles Sr. born October 9, Rio, Illinois.

1893   Charles moves from Dixon, Illinois, to Chicago.

1901   Walgreen buys his former boss Isaac W. Blood's store at 4134 Cottage Grove and Bowen avenues for $6,000.

1909   Walgreen buys his former boss William G. Valentine's drugstore at Cottage Grove Avenue and 39th Street, Walgreen's second store. A chain is born.

1910   Myrtle starts making soups, sandwiches, cakes, and pies for Walgreen's second store, thereby starting the chain's first food service division.

1916   All Walgreens stores—then numbering nine—are consolidated as the Walgreen Co.

1921   Walgreens opens its first store inside Chicago's "Loop" at 17 E. Washington, in the Venetian Building, sending fountain manager Ivan "Pop" Coulson to work in the new store to ensure its success. One day in 1922, Coulson adds two scoops of Walgreens' famous Double Rich Ice Cream to the malt powder and milk and stirs it in the mixer, thereby inventing the milk shake. The creation fuels an unpredented expansion in Walgreens stores.

1927   Walgreens opens its first store in New York, at 1501 Broadway and 44th Street, in the Paramount Theater Building—a huge success that attained folklore status in the city for all the future actors that whiled away their afternoons there.

1934   On February 15, 1934, the 483-store Walgreens chain opens on the New York Stock Exchange, with the letters WAG.

1939   On August 10, Charles Sr. resigns as president, and the board names his son Charles Jr. ("Chuck") to replace him. On December 10, Charles Sr. dies of cancer.

1941   Due to irreconcilable differences between general manager Justin Dart and company president and CEO Chuck Walgreen, the board forces Dart to resign, and a palace coup is averted.

1943   In May, Walgreens opens a 6,000-square-foot store—its biggest, at the time—in the Pentagon, donating all profits from the store back to the Pentagon Post Restaurant Council, which supervised the building's food service.

1950   Walgreens opens its first self-service store, which proves to be so successful that Walgreens converts or builds all of its stores to be self-service.

1952   Evergreen Plaza opens in suburban Chicago, the area's first shopping center, with a colossal Walgreens as the centerpiece. "It was then and there," Chuck says, "that we decided we would never again open a conventional store."

1969   The board names Charles ("Cork") Walgreen III to replace his father Chuck as company president and soon adds the title of CEO.

1978   Fred Canning rises to company president, forming a highly effective partnership with Cork.

1976   Walgreens' innovative "Intercom" system is launched, linking all Walgreens prescription departments together, allowing Walgreens' customers to get their prescriptions at any Walgreens outlet they visit just by remembering their name.

1984   Walgreens opens its 1,000th store, marking the beginning of the first major expansion since the 1920s. Sales top $3 billion the next year.

1990   Fred Canning retires as company president after a legendary 12-year run. Dan Jorndt is named to replace him.

1992   Walgreens opens its first freestanding corner store with drive-thru pharmacy.

1994   Walgreens opens its 2,000th store.

1998   Cork Walgreen retires as CEO. Dan Jorndt takes over. Cork retires as chairman in 1999, with Dan Jorndt assuming that title, too.

2000   Walgreens opens its 3,000th store.

2002   Dan Jorndt retires as CEO, turning over the reins to David Bernauer. Jorndt retires as chairman in 2003.

2003   Walgreens opens its 4,000th store.

notes

preface

1. Marilyn R. Abbey, *Walgreens: Celebrating 100 Years* (Deerfield, IL: Walgreen Co., 2001), 7.

1   from humble beginnings

1. Herman Kogan and Rick Kogan, *Pharmacist to the Nation* (Deerfield, IL: Walgreen Co., 1989), 63.
2. Kogan and Kogan, 13.
3. Taken from Lee County Historical Society pamphlet; also available on http://www.rootsweb.com/~illee/history.htm.
4. Myrtle Walgreen, *Never a Dull Day* (Chicago: Henry Regnery, 1963), 71.

5. Author interview with Chuck Walgreen, May 23, 2003.

6. Kogan and Kogan, *Pharmacist to the Nation*, 15.

7. Walgreen, *Never a Dull Day*, 72.

8. Marilyn R. Abbey, *Walgreens: Celebrating 100 Years* (Deerfield, IL: Walgreen Co., 2001), 73.

9. Donald L. Miller, *City of the Century: The Epic of Chicago and the Making of America* (New York: Simon & Schuster, 1996), 65.

10. Ibid., 15.

11. Ibid.

12. Ibid.

13. Ibid.

14. Author interview with Bill Shank, May 22, 2003.

15. Miller, *City of the Century*, 24.

16. Ibid., 17.

17. Erik Larson, *The Devil in the White City* (New York: Crown, 2003), 16.

18. Ibid., 37–38.

19. Larson, *The Devil in the White City*, 12.

20. Ibid., 52.

21. Ibid., 14.

22. Ibid., xii.

23. Ibid.

24. Malcolm Jones, *Newsweek*, February 10, 2003.

25. Miller, *City of the Century*, 16.

26. George A. Bender, *Great Moments in Pharmacy* (Parke, Davies & Company, 1965), http://www.pharmacy.wsu.edu/History/history01.html.

27. Edward Kremers and George Urdang, *History of Pharmacy*, 4th ed., rev. Glenn Sonnedecker (Madison, WI: American Institute of the History of Pharmacy, 1976), 19.

28. Ibid., 35.

29. Ibid., 157.

30. Ibid., 161.

31. Ibid., 262.

32. Ibid., 223.

33. Ibid.

34. Mark Pendergrast, *For God, Country and Coca-Cola* (New York: Basic, 2000), 9.

35. Larson, *The Devil in the White City*, 38.

36. Ibid., 41.

37. Kremers and Urdang, *History of Pharmacy*, 205.

38. Nick Steneck and Joe Borda, *Ann Arbor Observer*, May 1995, 38–46.

39. Ibid.

40. Pendergrast, *For God, Country and Coca-Cola* , 10.

41. Larson, *The Devil in the White City*, 86.

42. Walgreen, *Never a Dull Day*, 73.

43. Kogan and Kogan, *Pharmacist to the Nation*, 18.

44. Ibid.

45. Walgreen, *Never a Dull Day*, 73.

46. Ibid.

47. Ibid.

48. Ibid., 75.

49. Paul Harvey, "The Rest of the Story," January 6, 1996.

50. Walgreen, *Never a Dull Day*, 75.

51. Kogan and Kogan, *Pharmacist to the Nation*, 28.

52. Abbey, *Walgreens: Celebrating 100 Years*, 94.

53. Walgreen, *Never a Dull Day*, 70.

54. Ibid., 3.

55. Ibid., 11.

56. Ibid., 6.

57. Ibid., 7.

58. Ibid., 16.

59. Ibid., 37.

60. Ibid., 38.

61. Ibid., 52.

62. Advertisement from the First National Bank, *Chicago Tribune*, March 30, 1890.

63. Walgreen, *Never a Dull Day*, 59.

64. Ibid., 49.

65. Ibid.

66. Ibid., 43.

67. Ibid., 65.

68. Ibid., 67.

69. Ibid., 68.

70. Ibid.

71. Ibid., 70.

72. Ibid., 79.

73. Kogan and Kogan, *Pharmacist to the Nation*, 35.

74. Ibid., 34–35.

75. Ibid., 35.

76. Abbey, *Walgreens: Celebrating 100 Years*, 14.

77. Kogan and Kogan, *Pharmacist to the Nation*, 35.

2 the start of something special: 1910–1929

1. Marilyn R. Abbey, *Walgreens: Celebrating 100 Years* (Deerfield, IL: Walgreen Co., 2001), 16.

2. Herman Kogan and Rick Kogan, *Pharmacist to the Nation* (Deerfield, IL: Walgreen Co., 1989), 44.

3. Ibid., 42.

4. Mark Pendergrast, *For God, Country and Coca-Cola* (New York: Basic, 2000), 15.

5. Kogan and Kogan, *Pharmacist to the Nation*, 44.

6. Zinger's Ice Cream Parlor and Sweets, "A Brief History of Ice Cream," http://www.zingersicecream.com/history.htm.

7. HistoryChannel.com, "The History of Household Wonders—History of the Refrigerator," http://www.historychannel.com/exhibits/modern/fridge.html.

8. The Heptune Classical Jazz and Blues Lyrics Page, "I Scream, You Scream, We All Scream for Ice Cream," http://www.heptune.com/lyrics/iscreamy.html.

9. Abbey, *Walgreens: Celebrating 100 Years*, 16.

10. Kogan and Kogan, *Pharmacist to the Nation*, 44.

11. Ibid.

12. Myrtle Walgreen, *Never a Dull Day* (Chicago: Henry Regnery, 1963), 107.

13. Videotaped interview with Chuck Walgreen, July 1994.

14. Walgreen, *Never a Dull Day*, 108.

15. Kogan and Kogan, *Pharmacist to the Nation*, 46.

16. Ibid., 47.

17. Thomas J. Peters and Robert H. Waterman Jr., *In Search of Excellence* (New York: Warner, 1982), 225.

18. Kogan and Kogan, *Pharmacist to the Nation*, 49.

19. Author interview with Dan Jorndt, October 23, 2002.

20. Charles R. Walgreen Sr., *Pepper Pod* 1, no. 1 (December 1919).

21. Ibid.

22. Kogan and Kogan, *Pharmacist to the Nation*, 57.

23. Ibid.

24. Ibid., 59.

25. Michael MacCambridge, ed., *ESPN Sportscentury* (New York: Hyperion, 1999), 96–99.

26. Kenneth C. Davis, *Don't Know Much About History* (New York: Avon, 1990), 257.

27. Ibid., 257; and Abbey, *Walgreens: Celebrating 100 Years*, 57.

28. Author interview with Charles Walgreen Jr., May 23, 2003.

29. National Film Board of Canada, *Entre Amis/Between Friends* (Toronto: McClelland and Steward Limited, 1976), 86.

30. Author interview with Charles (Cork) Walgreen III, July 10, 2003.

31. Ibid.

32. Ibid.

33. Videotaped interview with Chuck Walgreen, July 1994.

34. *Chain Store Age*, 1925.

35. Ibid.

36. Kogan and Kogan, *Pharmacist to the Nation*, 70.

37. Ibid., 70.

38. Ibid., 71.

39. Abbey, *Walgreens: Celebrating 100 Years*, 3.

40. Walgreen, *Never a Dull Day*, 139–140.

41. Author interview with Chuck Walgreen, May 23, 2003.

42. Charles R. Walgreen Sr., *Pepper Pod* 3, no. 1 (August–September 1923).

43. Abbey, *Walgreens: Celebrating 100 Years*, 2.

44. Author interview with Dan Jorndt, October 23, 2002.

45. Kogan and Kogan, *Pharmacist to the Nation*, 88–96.

46. Ibid.

47. Ibid., 89.

48. Ibid., 73.

49. Ibid., 90.

50. Ibid.

51. Ibid., 94.

52. Ibid., 95.

53. Ibid., 89.

54. Ibid., 89.

55. Ibid., 66.

56. Ibid., 89; also available on the company Web site, http://www.aptea.com.

57. Ibid., 88.

58. Ibid., 87.

59. Company brochure, Walgreens archives.

60. Kogan and Kogan, *Pharmacist to the Nation*, 97.

61. Ibid., 81.

62. Author interview with Chuck Walgreen, July 10, 2003.

63. Kogan and Kogan, *Pharmacist to the Nation*, 98.

64. Ibid., 100.

65. Ibid., 100–101.

66. *Chain Store Review*, September 1928.

67. *Chain Store Review*, June 1929.

68. *Chain Store Review*, September 1928.

69. *Chain Store Review*, August 1929.

70. Ibid.

71. Ibid.

72. *Chain Store Review*, October 1929.

73. Ibid.

74. Kogan and Kogan, *Pharmacist to the Nation*, 105–106.

75. John Nickerson and Company, *A Chronicle of Progress* (New York: author, 1929); from Walgreens archives.

76. Ibid.

77. Ibid.

3   nothing to fear: 1929–1945

1. Kenneth C. Davis, *Don't Know Much About History* (New York: Avon, 1990), 270–271.

2. Ken Burns, *Baseball* (New York: Alfred A. Knopf, 1994), 197.

3. Harold Melvin, *Chicago: Growth of a Metropolis* (Chicago: University of Chicago Press, 1973), 362.

4. Ibid.

5. Charles R. Walgreen Sr., *Pepper Pod*, January 1932.

6. *Pepper Pod*, January 1931.

7. Author interview with Dan Jorndt, October 23, 2002.

8. Charles R. Walgreen Sr., company publication, Walgreens archives.

9. Marilyn R. Abbey, *Walgreens: Celebrating 100 Years* (Deerfield, IL: Walgreen Co., 2001), 28.

10. Walgreens 1931 Annual Report.

11. Herman Kogan and Rick Kogan, *Pharmacist to the Nation* (Deerfield, IL: Walgreen Co., 1989), 119.

12. Letter from Arthur Anderson, Walgreens archives.

13. Kogan and Kogan, *Pharmacist to the Nation*, 48.

14. Ibid., 145.

15. Ibid., 126.

16. Ibid.

17. Abbey, *Walgreens: Celebrating 100 Years*, 92.

18. Ibid.

19. Kogan and Kogan, *Pharmacist to the Nation*, 121.

20. Russell Stover Company Web site—http://russellstover.com.

21. Kogan and Kogan, *Pharmacist to the Nation*, 123.

22. Abbey, *Walgreens: Celebrating 100 Years*, 21.

23. Ibid.

24. Frederick C. Klein, "As a Boy in Chicago," *Wall Street Journal*, May 22, 2000.

25. Davis, *Don't Know Much About History*, 271.

26. Kogan and Kogan, *Pharmacist to the Nation*, 119.

27. Ibid., 130.

28. Curt Smith, *The Storytellers* (New York: MacMillan, 1995), 28.

29. Ibid., 58.

30. *Pepper Pod*, December 1934.

31. Kogan and Kogan, *Pharmacist to the Nation*, 143.

32. Ibid., 96.

33. Ibid., 143.

34. Ibid.

35. "500 Corner Drugstores," *Fortune*, September 1934.
36. Anonymous, "Hazelwood: Its Masters," from the archives of the Chicago Historical Society.
37. Myrtle Walgreen, *Never a Dull Day* (Chicago: Henry Regnery, 1963), 212.
38. Abbey, *Walgreens: Celebrating 100 Years*, 72.
39. Author interview with Chuck Walgreen, May 23, 2003.
40. Ibid.
41. Ibid.
42. Kogan and Kogan, *Pharmacist to the Nation*, 147–148.
43. Ibid., 148.
44. Ibid., 149.
45. Author interview with Chuck Walgreen, May 22, 2003.
46. Robert Coven, "Red Maroons," *Chicago History* (magazine) (Spring/Summer 1992), 20–37.
47. Ibid., 22–24.
48. Ibid., 20.
49. Personal letter of Charles Walgreen Sr., from the Chicago Historical Society archives.
50. Coven, "Red Maroons," 20–37.
51. Ibid., 32–34.
52. Kogan and Kogan, *Pharmacist to the Nation*, 159.
53. Ibid.
54. Ibid., 160.
55. Coven, "Red Maroons," 36.
56. Author interview with Chuck Walgreen, May 23, 2003.
57. Videotaped interview with Chuck Walgreen, July 1994.
58. "500 Corner Drugstores," *Fortune*.
59. Abbey, *Walgreens: Celebrating 100 Years*, 22.
60. Kogan and Kogan, *Pharmacist to the Nation*, 163–164.
61. *Chicago Daily News*, in Kogan and Kogan, *Pharmacist to the Nation*, 172.
62. Letter from Richard Byrd, Walgreens archives.
63. Kogan and Kogan, *Pharmacist to the Nation*, 150.
64. *Pepper Pod*, 1937.
65. Kogan and Kogan, *Pharmacist to the Nation*, 154.
66. *Pepper Pod*, 1939.

67. Kogan and Kogan, *Pharmacist to the Nation*, 174.

68. Videotaped interview with Chuck Walgreen, July 1994.

69. Ibid.

70. Peter Jennings and Todd Brewster, *The Century* (New York: Doubleday, 1998), 239.

71. Abbey, *Walgreens: Celebrating 100 Years*, 41.

72. Videotaped interview with Chuck Walgreen, July 1994.

73. David Brinkley, *Washington Goes to War* (New York: Random House, Ballantine Books, 1988), 70.

74. Ibid., 71.

75. Ibid., 73.

76. Ibid., 74.

77. U.S. War Department, *War Times*, 1943, from the Walgreens' archives.

78. Letter from Secretary of War Henry Stimson to Charles Walgreen Sr., September 12, 1945, Walgreens archives.

79. Walgreens 1942 annual report.

80. Abbey, *Walgreens: Celebrating 100 Years*, 54–55.

4 the postwar era: 1945–1970

1. John U. Bacon, *Blue Ice: The Story of Michigan Hockey* (Ann Arbor: University of Michigan Press, 2001), 135.

2. Herman Kogan and Rick Kogan, *Pharmacist to the Nation* (Deerfield, IL: Walgreen Co., 1989), 183–184.

3. Ibid., 184–185.

4. *Pepper Pod*, March 1946, Walgreens archives.

5. Kogan and Kogan, *Pharmacist to the Nation*, 188.

6. Marilyn R. Abbey, *Walgreens: Celebrating 100 Years* (Deerfield, IL: Walgreen Co., 2001), 85.

7. Kogan and Kogan, *Pharmacist to the Nation*, 188–189; and Abbey, *Walgreens: Celebrating 100 Years*, 85.

8. Kogan and Kogan, *Pharmacist to the Nation*, 221–222; and Abbey, *Walgreens: Celebrating 100 Years*, 45–46.

9. Abbey, *Walgreens: Celebrating 100 Years*, 46.

10. Kogan and Kogan, *Pharmacist to the Nation*, 226.

11. Kogan and Kogan, *Pharmacist to the Nation*, 228; and Abbey, *Walgreens: Celebrating 100 Years*, 47, 51, 67–68.

12. Kogan and Kogan, *Pharmacist to the Nation*, 227–228; and Abbey, *Walgreens: Celebrating 100 Years*, 47.

13. Videotaped interview with Chuck Walgreen, July 1994.

14. Abbey, *Walgreens: Celebrating 100 Years*, 59.

15. Videotaped interview with Chuck Walgreen, July 1994.

16. Abbey, *Walgreens: Celebrating 100 Years*, 59.

17. Kogan and Kogan, *Pharmacist to the Nation*, 181; and author interview with Chuck Walgreen, May 22, 2003.

18. Kogan and Kogan, *Pharmacist to the Nation*, 181.

19. Ibid., 183.

20. Walgreens 1947 annual report.

21. Abbey, *Walgreens: Celebrating 100 Years*, 74.

22. Ibid.

23. Ibid., 73.

24. *Pepper Pod*, May 1960.

25. Kogan and Kogan, *Pharmacist to the Nation*, 224–225.

26. *Pepper Pod*, May 1961.

27. Kogan and Kogan, *Pharmacist to the Nation*, 225.

28. Company Web site, www.PigglyWiggly.com. See "About Us," All in a Name.

29. Kogan and Kogan, *Pharmacist to the Nation*, 197.

30. Abbey, *Walgreens: Celebrating 100 Years*, 93.

31. Ibid., 72.

32. Kogan and Kogan, *Pharmacist to the Nation*, 199.

33. Abbey, *Walgreens: Celebrating 100 Years*, 64.

34. Kogan and Kogan, *Pharmacist to the Nation*, 200–201.

35. *Pepper Pod*, May, 19, 1952.

36. Kogan and Kogan, *Pharmacist to the Nation*, 210.

37. Abbey, *Walgreens: Celebrating 100 Years*, 64.

38. Author interview with Chuck Walgreen, May 22, 2003.

39. Ibid.

40. Abbey, *Walgreens: Celebrating 100 Years*, 64.

41. Ibid.

42. Kogan and Kogan, *Pharmacist to the Nation*, 204–205.

43. Ibid., 210.

44. Kogan and Kogan, *Pharmacist to the Nation*, 201.

45. Abbey, *Walgreens: Celebrating 100 Years*, 67.

46. Kogan and Kogan, *Pharmacist to the Nation*, 202.

47. Abbey, *Walgreens: Celebrating 100 Years*, 67.

48. *Business Week*, March 7, 1953.

49. *Barron's*, April 1958.

50. *Value Line*, 1963, Walgreens archives.

51. Kogan and Kogan, *Pharmacist to the Nation*, 209.

52. *Pepper Pod*, December 19, 1955.

53. Abbey, *Walgreens: Celebrating 100 Years*, 45.

54. Ibid., 54.

55. Abbey, *Walgreens: Celebrating 100 Years*, 11.

56. Ibid., 46.

57. Ibid., 7–8.

58. *Chain Store Weekly*, 1964, 231.

59. Abbey, *Walgreens: Celebrating 100 Years*, 54.

60. *Chain Store Weekly*, 1963, 230.

5 reinventing the corporation: 1970–1990

1. Author interview with Cork Walgreen, July 10, 2003.

2. Marilyn R. Abbey, *Walgreens: Celebrating 100 Years* (Deerfield, IL: Walgreen Co., 2001), 9.

3. Author interview with Cork Walgreen, July 10, 2003.

4. Ibid.

5. Ibid.

6. Jim Collins, *Good to Great* (New York: HarperCollins, 2001), 12–13.

7. Author interview with Cork Walgreen, July 10, 2003.

8. Chuck Walgreen's speech, from Walgreen Co.'s videotape of the tribute to Cork Walgreen III on his retirement, 1998.

9. Author interview with Cork Walgreen, July 10, 2003.

10. Ibid.

11. Ibid.

12. Collins, *Good to Great*, 12.
13. Author interview with Cork Walgreen, July 10, 2003.
14. Abbey, *Walgreens: Celebrating 100 Years*, 9.
15. Author interview with Dan Jorndt, October 23, 2002.
16. Ibid.
17. Author interview with Bill Shank, May 22, 2003.
18. Author interview with Cork Walgreen, July 10, 2003.
19. Author interview with Dan Jorndt, October 23, 2002.
20. Abbey, *Walgreens: Celebrating 100 Years*, 79.
21. Ibid.
22. Ibid.
23. Ibid.
24. Author interview with Cork Walgreen, July 10, 2003.
25. Ibid.
26. Author interview with Dan Jorndt, October 23., 2002.
27. Author interview with Bill Shank, May 22, 2003.
28. Abbey, *Walgreens: Celebrating 100 Years*, 9.
29. Author interview with Cork Walgreen, July 10, 2003.
30. Ibid.
31. Author interview with Dan Jorndt, October 23, 2002.
32. Bo Schembechler and Mitch Albom, *Bo* (New York: Warner, 1989), 153.
33. Lew Young, *Views on Management*, in Thomas J. Peters and Robert H. Waterman Jr., *In Search of Excellence* (New York: Warner, 1982), 292.
34. Peters and Waterman, *In Search of Excellence*, 293, 296, 300.
35. Abbey, *Walgreens: Celebrating 100 Years*, 51–52.
36. Ibid., 82.
37. Author interview with Cork Walgreen, July 10, 2003.
38. Collins, *Good to Great*, 32–33.
39. Author interview with Cork Walgreen, July 10, 2003.
40. Ibid.
41. Abbey, *Walgreens: Celebrating 100 Years*, 95.
42. Carl Sewell, *Customers for Life* (New York: Pocket Books, Simon & Schuster, 1990), 23.
43. Author interview with Cork Walgreen, July 10, 2003.
44. Ibid.
45. Author interview with Dan Jorndt, October 23, 2002.

46. Author interview with Cork Walgreen, July 10, 2003.

47. Abbey, *Walgreens: Celebrating 100 Years*, 71.

48. Author interview with Cork Walgreen, July 10, 2003.

49. Ibid.

50. Author interview with Dan Jorndt, October 23, 2002.

51. Author interview with Bill Shank, May 22, 2003.

52. *Wall Street Transcript*, in Abbey, *Walgreens: Celebrating 100 Years*, 51.

53. Ibid.

54. Author interview with Dan Jorndt, October 23, 2002.

6   poised to pounce: 1990–future

1. Jim Collins, *Good to Great* (New York: HarperCollins, 2001), 46.

2. Author interview with Dan Jorndt, October 23, 2002.

3. Ibid.

4. Ibid.

5. Ibid.

6. Ibid.

7. Marilyn R. Abbey, *Walgreens: Celebrating 100 Years* (Deerfield, IL: Walgreen Co., 2001), 78.

8. Author interview with Dan Jorndt, October 23, 2002.

9. Ibid.

10. Collins, *Good to Great*, 160–161.

11. Author interview with Dan Jorndt, October 23, 2002.

12. Ibid.

13. Arianna Huffington, *Pigs at the Trough* (New York: Crown, 2003), 14.

14. Ibid., 12.

15. Ibid., 36.

16. Ibid., 37.

17. Ibid., 12.

18. Author interview with Dan Jorndt, October 23, 2002.

19. Ibid.

20. Collins, *Good to Great*, 28.

21. Ibid.

22. Ibid., 29.

23. Author interview with Dan Jorndt, October 23, 2002.

24. Ibid.

25. Ibid.

26. Author interview with Bill Shank, May 22, 2003.

27. Author interview with Dan Jorndt, October 23, 2002.

28. Ibid.

29. Ibid.

30. Ibid.

31. Author interview with Bill Shank, May 22, 2003.

32. Author interview with Dan Jorndt, October 23, 2002.

33. Collins, *Good to Great*, 92.

34. Author interview with Dan Jorndt, October 23, 2002.

35. Ibid.

36. Ibid.

37. Ibid.

38. Abbey, *Walgreens: Celebrating 100 Years*, 94.

39. Collins, *Good to Great*, 93.

40. Author interview with Dan Jorndt, October 23, 2002.

41. Ibid.

42. Abbey, *Walgreens: Celebrating 100 Years*, 9.

43. Author interview with Cork Walgreen, July 10, 2003.

44. Author interview with Dan Jorndt, October 23, 2002.

45. Ibid.

46. Ibid.

47. Author interview, 2003 (date withheld for anonymity).

48. Author interview with David Bernauer, June 19, 2003.

49. Ibid.

50. Ibid.

51. Ibid.

52. Ibid.

53. Huffington, *Pigs at the Trough*, 174.

54. Author interview with Dan Jorndt, October 23, 2002.

55. Author interview David Bernauer, June 19, 2003.

56. Ibid.

57. Ibid.

58. Ibid.
59. Author interview with Cork Walgreen, July 10, 2003.
60. From Walgreen Co.'s videotape of the tribute to Cork Walgreen III on his retirement, 1998.
61. Author interview with Dan Jorndt, October 23, 2002.
62. Abbey, *Walgreens: Celebrating 100 Years*, 60.
63. Author interview with Cork Walgreen, July 10, 2003.
64. Ibid.
65. Author interview with David Bernauer, June 19, 2003.
66. Author interview with Dan Jorndt, October 23, 2002.
67. Author interview with Cork Walgreen, July 10, 2003.

index